Getting Funded

Getting Funded

Proof-of-Concept, Due Diligence, Risk and Reward

Chandra S. Mishra

palgrave
macmillan

GETTING FUNDED

First published in 2015 by
PALGRAVE MACMILLAN®
in the United States—a division of St. Martin's Press LLC,
175 Fifth Avenue, New York, NY 10010.

Where this book is distributed in the UK, Europe and the rest of the world, this is by Palgrave Macmillan, a division of Macmillan Publishers Limited, registered in England, company number 785998, of Houndmills, Basingstoke, Hampshire RG21 6XS.

Palgrave Macmillan is the global academic imprint of the above companies and has companies and representatives throughout the world.

ISBN: 978–1–137–38449–2

Library of Congress Cataloging-in-Publication Data

Mishra, Chandra S., 1962–
Getting funded : proof-of-concept, due diligence, risk and reward / by Chandra Mishra.
pages cm
Includes bibliographical references and index.
ISBN 978–1–137–38449–2 (hardback : alk. paper)
1. New business enterprise—Finance. 2. New business enterprise—Management. I. Title.

HG4027.6.M57 2015
658.15′224—dc23 2015009271

A catalogue record of the book is available from the British Library.

Design by Newgen Knowledge Works (P) Ltd., Chennai, India.

First edition: September 2015

10 9 8 7 6 5 4 3 2 1

To my parents,
Swami Dharmaprakashananda Saraswati and Satyabhama

CONTENTS

Part IV Is the Reward Worth the Risk and Effort?

FIGURES

FOREWORD

Convergence of Entrepreneurs and Investors

Both entrepreneurs and investors must recognize the importance of understanding and implementing entrepreneurial processes for their mutual benefit. In reality, both the entrepreneur and the investor ***live*** the entrepreneurial process, for better or worse. Indeed, this practice book is an outgrowth of *The Theory of Entrepreneurship: Creating and Sustaining Entrepreneurial Value* by Mishra and Zachary, which presents a unified two-stage entrepreneurial process; namely, Entrepreneurial Value Creation Theory. With its core of value creation, Entrepreneurial Value Creation Theory delineates and links the stages and processes of the first venture formulation stage and followed by the venture monetization stage.

When an entrepreneur begins to ponder creating a venture, they must consider the opportunities that they have discovered or could create, as well as examine their intentions. In this first stage of the venture formulation processes, the main elements are entrepreneurial intention and opportunity relative to the available resources. The entrepreneur will likely reexamine the three elements of intention, opportunity, and resources many times during the venture formulation stage as they build their competence or ability to attract investors.

Venture formulation can begin with either external stimuli of entrepreneurial intention or opportunity. And within this sub-process of formulation, the entrepreneur compares both intention and opportunity with available resources. The development of the critical element of entrepreneurial ability is vital in convincing external investors to invest. The entrepreneur may engage in multiple iterations of these venture formulation processes, including the regeneration of a continuing firm as it builds new ventures or competences from within.

When an entrepreneur discovers or creates an opportunity, they must compare or coordinate the chosen entrepreneurial opportunity with available resources and their intentions. The entrepreneur must ask the question, "Do I have sufficient entrepreneurial abilities or competence for this venture?" When the entrepreneur is limited in resources, adjustments must occur and, possibly, other opportunities might arise as a better match. It is the challenge of the entrepreneur to move ahead through the stages of thinking and action in relation to all possible venture opportunities that may have been recognized. Said another way, the entrepreneur might ask themselves, "How can I adapt my intention and resources to enable an identified opportunity?"

It should be noted that Entrepreneurial Value Creation Theory is a two-stage theory. The venture formulation stage utilizes the process of trial and error as a critical segment toward building experience and capabilities to continue toward finding investors. Through a sequence of iterations and feedbacks, beginning with matching a given opportunity and their cognition with the available resources, intention, and adaptability, resulting in an adjustment of the resources enabling further trial and error processes, entrepreneurs may build competence toward the creation of a totally new venture or a regeneration of a continuing firm including a family firm, as it builds new ventures or competences from within.

In sum, the entrepreneur derives their abilities to create a venture from examining their intentions and the opportunities as the two main elements of venture formulation in comparison to the available resources for the chosen venture. The entrepreneur must build competence to sufficient propel into the critical second stage of monetization and attracting external investors. Only a few entrepreneurs survive this stage and others take years to achieve their competence sufficient to move forward to venture monetization. Both entrepreneurs and investors need to understand these formulation processes and efforts to be able to identify entrepreneurial competence, which is critical to investment decisions that facilitate and create the actual venture.

Next, the core of monetization is risk mitigation for both the entrepreneur and the investor. If the entrepreneur transitions too soon or without sufficient entrepreneurial competence, investors will not want to invest. This second stage of monetization transforms the entrepreneurial competence to generate entrepreneurial reward and sustainable value. This reconfiguration is achieved by using a business model design that embeds value appropriation mechanisms and dynamic capabilities.

Simultaneously, during monetization, investors face an adverse selection when the entrepreneur's ability is uncertain and the venture quality is difficult to assess. Entrepreneurs can offer the investor incentive signals to invest, such as their entrepreneurial competence and the amount of personal financial investment. To approach an investor too early, before the entrepreneurial competence is sufficiently developed, may signal to the investor that the entrepreneurial ability or the venture quality is low. Venture delta estimates the implied risk of loss and the Venture Capital Asset Pricing Model (VCAPM) yields the expected rate of return.

Getting Funded: Proof-of-Concept, Due Diligence, Risk and Reward represents an in-depth view of how to garner external investment funds for a new venture. Mishra offers a venture capital investment model that focuses on the entrepreneur and investor relationship that desires to merge opportunity with management while achieving the core task of risk mitigation. The tools of risk mitigation are customer value concept, deal structure alignment, and business model design. Mishra identifies potential investor involvement in a venture that might lead to increased value.

Getting Funded then asks and answers the fundamental questions in the decision-making processes of an investor and for which the entrepreneur must provide answers; that is:

(1) Is the market opportunity real and large enough?
(2) Is the business model efficient and sustainable?
(3) Is the reward worth the risk and effort?

To evaluate customer value opportunities, Mishra offers opportunity scores to rank potential customer-value opportunities as well as how to analyze the strengths and weaknesses of competitors. He further examines the market size and growth via the market factor method and the market buildup method as well as industry life cycle analyses. Given these two areas for evaluation by all entrepreneurship creating new ventures, Mishra also provides a framework, and the tools to assess the customer value concept, as warranted.

Identifying an efficient and sustainable business model is essential to attracting and retaining investors, when needed. The entrepreneur and the investors need to know how to efficiently scale the new venture and, in particular, how to configure the value chain and the supply chain to meet customer demand efficiently and effectively. Revenue models are crucial for monetization. Overtime the startup time, a series of funding rounds will be needed. *Getting Funded* suggests rules of bootstrapping, hiring, and resources mobilization during the monetization stage of the venture. Again, adjustments to the business model design are needed in order to increase the competitive advantage as well as the return on investment.

Finally, entrepreneurial rewards cannot materialize without risk and effort. Mishra offers a framework to develop a risk profile of a venture as well as an efficient risk mitigation plan. These tools can assist both the entrepreneur and the investor to estimate the likelihood of investment loss and the size of maximum investment loss. It is equally important for the entrepreneur and the investor to know the venture valuation to determine the likelihood of exit and the expected timing. Mishra offers a framework to develop an investor exit plan as well as select potential strategic acquirers based on an investment thesis and venture strategy. Finally, the incentive mechanisms are examined relative to motivating the entrepreneur and the investor.

In *Getting Funded*, Mishra offers a straightforward rendition of an array of challenges facing the entrepreneur and the investor as well as specific tools to address these challenges. This book is a must read for all entrepreneurs and investors who wish minimize their differential risks and work effectively together toward their desired respective rewards. The knowledge gleaned from this book will greatly enhance the odds of entrepreneurs and investors striking deals that work for their mutual benefit and success.

RAMONA KAY ZACHARY
The City University of New York
Baruch College

ACKNOWLEDGMENTS

I am indebted to several individuals, especially to my former students, and the entrepreneurs and investors, with whom I have worked, who have inspired me to write this book. To date, the art of investing in a new venture has been limited to the intuition and experience of a few successful investors. This book presents a systematic framework that investors and entrepreneurs can use to analyze the investment risks of a new venture in order to refine the customer value concept and business model design, and realign the management incentives, such that the investment loss can be minimized and the likelihood of venture success can be maximized. The framework and tools can help the entrepreneurs to improve the investor-readiness of their venture and increase the likelihood of their getting funded.

I am especially grateful to Professor Ramona K. Zachary, a colleague at Baruch College and my co-author of the book, *The Theory of Entrepreneurship*, for her support and encouragement during the preparation of this manuscript. I am grateful to Charlotte Mariona, a former editor at Palgrave Macmillan, who liked the concept of the book and encouraged me to develop it further. I am grateful to Sarah Lawrence, Editorial Assistant at Palgrave Macmillan, who has been very supportive during the preparation of the manuscript. I also thank the editorial staffs at Palgrave Macmillan, who have been supportive during the preparation of this book. I am also grateful to Kathleen Marusak for her help with copyediting and Keegan Dunn for help with the index.

I am indebted to several entrepreneurs and investors who have shared their ideas with me during last several years. Many of these ideas, which are critical to a startup's success, helped me to shape the venture investment model developed in this book. I am also grateful to several authors who have developed tools to guide investors and entrepreneurs in helping them build successful ventures. Some of those ideas are incorporated in developing the venture capital investment model in this book. I am grateful to David Gobeli for some of the early ideas we had shared several years ago when I was planning to write the book.

Finally, I am indebted to my family members for their love, encouragement, and support during the preparation of the book. I am grateful to my wife, Sharada, for her love, patience, and encouragement. I am also indebted to my son, Sachit, who contributed significantly to the ideas developed in this book, and whose brilliance always amazes me. I am indebted to my daughter, Mitsi, for her love and support. Without the love and support of the family, one can accomplish very little.

Chandra S. Mishra
Florida Atlantic University
Boca Raton, FL 33431

PART I

Introduction

CHAPTER ONE

Investment Model: An Overview

Risk management is at the heart of the entrepreneurial process. *Getting Funded* develops a venture capital investment model, the core of which is efficient risk mitigation. Effective risk management is a core competency of successful investors and entrepreneurs. The deal-killer risks, incentive-alignment risks, and path-dependent risks should be addressed very early, and the critical operational risks should be addressed as early as possible. The remaining operational risks should be addressed as they occur. Investors invest in high-ability entrepreneurs with high-growth, high-margin businesses. Six potential areas are explored for investors to add value in a startup. The characteristics of high-ability entrepreneurs are explained. The investor criteria are examined. Entrepreneurial ability alone is not enough for an investor to accept an investment proposal, although it can be the main reason for an investor to reject a proposal. Common flaws with business plans and entrepreneur presentations can be easily fixed by the entrepreneur to improve the odds of "getting funded." An entrepreneur should not approach the investor for funding until the startup is investor ready.

Getting Funded provides the tools and framework critical for a startup to improve the odds of its success, including developing an investment thesis, formulating the customer value concept, refining the business model and strategy, preparing a risk mitigation plan and investor exit plan, determining the venture valuation and a risk-adjusted equity share for the investor, structuring the investment terms and conditions, aligning management incentives with investor objectives, and evaluating the venture's risk profile and investment potential. If the framework and tools are employed by the entrepreneurs before or after they write a business plan, it will improve the odds of their getting funded. Even without the need for external funding, the analysis of a venture's investment potential will improve the odds of the venture's success. For an investor, the framework and tools provided here will limit their investment loss and improve their return on investment.

Investors receive thousands of business plans and only a few receive funding. Most are rejected. In this book, we delve into the investor's mindset, the tools, and the foundations that are important to investors and to entrepreneurs. Note that the entrepreneur, possibly including their friends and family, is the very first investor in their startup, investing their human capital and scarce financial resources. We examine and develop a framework on which to base the business concept, to conduct due diligence research and analysis, to refine the business model and reformulate the business strategy, and to develop a risk and reward structure that protects investment money and incentivizes the entrepreneur to successfully manage the opportunity to create and share value.

Entrepreneurship is a process of creating and sharing value, the management of a business opportunity. Customer value drives opportunity. A business model is formulated with the goal of creating, delivering, and monetizing the customer value efficiently. That business model requires several refinements before it acquires funding. The business model should be efficient and sustainable. A compelling customer value proposition, an addressable market size big enough to achieve scale economies, and a superior relative advantage in a particular industry are what will help to prove the customer value concept. A well-defined customer value concept is the basis of a sustainable business model design.

Several assumptions are made when designing a business model and formulating a business strategy to successfully execute and sustain that business model. These assumptions must be tested and the associated risks must be mitigated. For example, the current team may need partners, or additional resources and capabilities, to execute the success factors critical to the venture's success. Risk mitigation is critical to the venture's success and a key goal for management. A successful venture needs to target specific milestones, and the critical success factors associated with those milestones should be identified. Investors prefer to work with management teams who are flexible and willing to refine their business models and strategy to ensure risk mitigation and a successful exit for the investors.

Getting Funded develops a venture capital investment model that mitigates the risk of investment loss, provides an adequate return to investors, and provides sufficient incentives to entrepreneurs to achieve the milestones necessary for a successful exit for investors. Often the funding amount requested in the business plan is not adequate, and the use of the funds as stated in the business plan may not be appropriate for the venture's current priorities. Investors in the current round would like to ensure adequate funding is available to achieve the milestones necessary to prepare the venture for the next financing round. The venture valuation is tricky, given an insufficient history of the venture's operating data. The return to the investor is determined by the investor's exit options, the anticipated exit valuation, the percentage of equity offered to the investor, and the risk profile of the venture. Investment terms and conditions are essential to protect the investment and incentivize the entrepreneur.

The value created in a venture is shared among several participants, including founders, investors, management, employees, customers, support service providers, and the community. Investors provide capital and actively aid the value creation process in a new venture. The investment potential of a startup is judged by product marketability, deliverability, and venture fundability. Individual investors, institutional investors, angel investor groups, and crowdfunding platforms receive thousands of business proposals from entrepreneurs asking for funding every year. Only a few business proposals receive funding. Several reasons are cited herein to illustrate why some entrepreneurs and business plans get funded and why others do not. Several reasons are also cited to explain why some funded ventures succeed and others do not.

Customer value drives the value creation and is the foundation of a business model. There are several ways to define a business model. We view a business model as a means to efficiently create, deliver, monetize, and sustain the customer value. The critical success factors and the competitive forces in a particular industry are strategic to the business model design and the venture success. Furthermore, investors also consider the size of the addressable market; it is difficult to scale a business if the addressable market is small.

Often the business model proposed in a new venture business plan must be refined before the investors feel comfortable in funding the venture. The information gathered from due diligence research on customers, market size, and competition is used to refine the early business model. Key assumptions and value drivers underlying the business model should be tested. Key milestones and the key resources and capabilities to achieve those milestones will be identified here. Using the critical success factors as a basis, the strengths and weaknesses of the venture's resources and capabilities can be assessed. Investors assess whether there is a need for additional resources and capabilities in order to mitigate the venture's risks and increase its odds of success.

The data gathered from a due diligence analysis helps to reformulate the business model and assess the resources and capabilities necessary to successfully execute the critical success factors and mitigate the risks, thus ensuring the venture's success. Funding is needed to finance the venture growth and mitigate risks. Investors evaluate whether the type and amount of funding is appropriate for the current priorities and adequate to achieve the proposed milestones before the venture is ready for another round of funding. Investors will fund a venture in several rounds—known as stage financing—to mitigate their investment risk. The entrepreneur is incentivized to achieve specific milestones and mitigate certain risks before the entrepreneur may return to receive another round of funding.

The milestones for investor exit are critical, as they enable the investor to exit and realize their expected return on investment. In a financing round, the investor may consider the time to bring the product to market, the time to achieve sustained positive cash flow, the total financing necessary to allow the investor to exit, the valuation of the venture, and the percentage of equity fair to both investors and entrepreneurs in order to provide an adequate return to the investor and at the same time adequately incentivize the management.

Investor criteria commonly employed when qualifying an investment opportunity are based on the underlying investment risks of the opportunity (see chapter 8). Macmillan et al. (1985) identified six categories of risks related to investing in a startup: the risk of failure to implement the business model (i.e., implementation risk), the risk of failure of the management (i.e., management risk), the risk of competition (i.e., competitive risk), the risk of failure of the entrepreneur to lead the team (i.e., leadership risk), the risk that the investor may not realize the expected return (i.e., liquidity risk), and the risk of failure to bail out the investment in adverse performance situations (i.e., bail-out risk).

Kaplan and Stromberg (2004) grouped the risks into three broad categories, namely internal risks, external risks, and execution risks. Internal risks are mainly due to unknown abilities of the entrepreneurial team and the performance of the product. External risks are external to the startup, such as market demand uncertainty, competitive threats, regulatory and legal uncertainties, investor exit uncertainty, financial market uncertainty, and so on. Execution risks are due to the failure of the business model and strategy, including the product development strategy and financing strategy. The internal risks of a venture are greatest in the early stages and gradually decline as the venture develops. The external risks and execution risks span the entire life cycle of the venture.

Investors invest in a high-risk, high-growth startup at a lower valuation when the venture valuation is more uncertain, and exit at a higher valuation when the venture valuation is more certain. The venture valuation increases as the venture matures and the venture uncertainty is reduced. Investors with their industry knowledge and company-building expertise help the entrepreneur build the business and mitigate the risks, increasing the likelihood of the venture's success. The venture failure rate is lower with the participation of external investors. Generally, the startup failure rate without the participation of an external investor is as high as 80 percent in the first four years, but with investor participation, the startup failure rate drops significantly to below 40 percent.

Investors invest in a startup when the business concept is already proven and the business is ready to grow. Thus, many unsuccessful ventures are eliminated at the concept-testing stage before the entrepreneur can approach the investor. Investors help grow the business to a stage when the venture's valuation exceeds the investor's anticipated exit valuation, at which time the investors exit. Investors, as value arbitrageurs, invest at a lower valuation multiple and exit at a higher valuation multiple, and they hedge their investment risk by actively participating in the venture. The venture valuation multiple and the basis of the valuation, such as the venture's sales or the operating cash flow, are low at the investment stage and high at the investor exit stage, thus enhancing the investor's rate of return. Investors exit in four to six years, on average, after the investment.

The venture capital investment model is summarized in figure 1.1. At the core of the venture capital investment model is risk mitigation. Successful entrepreneurs and investors are effective risk managers. Effective and efficient risk mitigation is their core competency. In figure 1.1, we show three groups of critical risks, namely the deal-killer risks, the path-dependent risks, and the incentive-alignment risks. The deal-killer risks are primarily associated with the customer value concept, which should be addressed very early, before the entrepreneur should approach the investor for funding. Deal-killer risks are less obvious at first, but they appear in hindsight after the venture has failed (Gilbert and Eyring, 2010). Deal-killer risks arise from the unexamined assumptions about the basic customer value premise of the venture. The deal-killer risks, for example, include the customer demand risk, the product performance risk, and the product unit price and unit cost risk. The customer value concept is based on the customer pain point, competitors' weaknesses, market demand factors, addressable market size, and competitive price point. These topics are addressed in chapters 2, 3, and 4.

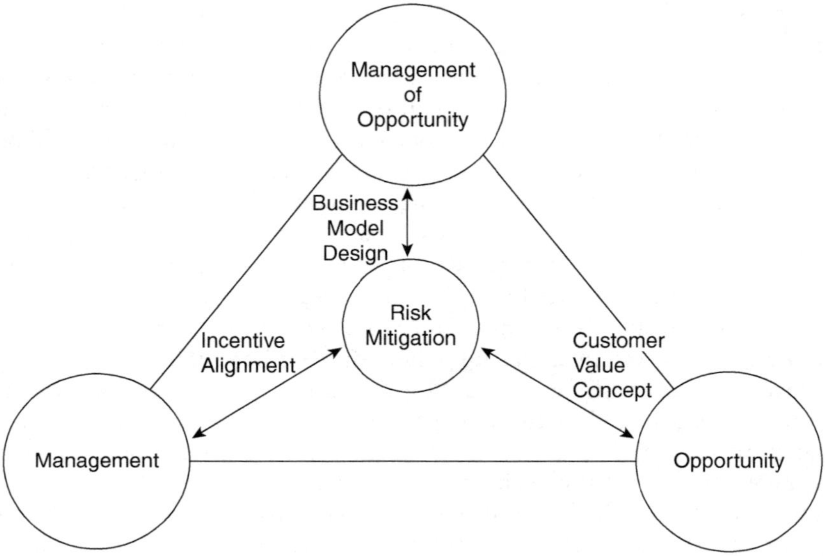

Figure 1.1 Venture capital investment model.

Path-dependent risks are strategic risks; and these risks are associated with the business model design and venture strategy. After the deal-killer risks associated with the customer value concept are addressed, the path-dependent risks should be addressed next. Because the business model and strategy are built on the customer value definition, it would be appropriate to test and address the path-dependent risks only after the deal-killer risks associated with the customer value definition are addressed. The business model design may also change after the customer value is redefined. The business model design should be efficient and sustainable. The business model design is based on the customer value concept, critical success factors particular to the industry to which the venture belongs, value chain configuration and cost structure, sales and revenue model, and resources and capabilities required to execute the operating plan and achieve the stage milestones. The business model design and financing stages are addressed in chapters 5, 6, and 7.

A venture should not lock into key partnerships and make key hires until the business model is stabilized. The incentive-alignment risks arise when the entrepreneur and management may not have sufficient ability and incentives to execute the business model and strategy, or when the interests of the entrepreneur and management are not aligned with those of the investors. The incentive-alignment risks are addressed by the investment agreement and employment contracts at the time of investment, and by monitoring the management performance over the venture development. The investment structure should align the incentives of the entrepreneur with the objectives of the investors. The investor objectives are to achieve a superior investment performance and include minimizing the risk of investment loss, enhancing their investment liquidity, and achieving a higher exit valuation. The entrepreneur and management should be provided with sufficient economic incentives consistent with these investor objectives. The risk-reward structure of an investment opportunity, the risk profile of the venture, the risk of investment loss, a risk mitigation plan, the venture valuation including the valuation of any intellectual assets the venture may own, a minimum percentage of equity for the investor, the maximum capital that may be available to a startup given its stage of development, the investor exit plan, and an investment structure aligning the incentives of the entrepreneur and management with those of the investors are addressed in chapters 8, 9, and 10.

In figure 1.1, the three critical drivers of the risk mitigation strategy are the quality of the market opportunity, the ability of the entrepreneurial team, and the efficiency and sustainability of the business model design to manage the opportunity to achieve sustained positive cash flow in the shortest time. The three drivers are linked to the entrepreneur's risk mitigation strategy and they together determine the return on investment. The investors consider whether the market opportunity is real and large enough, whether the business model is efficient and sustainable, and whether the reward is worth the investment risk and investor effort. In assessing the market opportunity, the investor determines whether the customer pain is real and widespread, whether the customer is willing to pay for the product or service, whether the product has a relative advantage that is superior to the competitors' products and the substitutes, and whether the addressable market size is large enough to realize the expected scale economies.

Customer value is central to the business model design and its success. The customer value is based on a careful selection of target customers and a set of resonate-focused value propositions that would be most valued by the target customers relative to the competition. Customer value must address the customer pain. The target customer must value and be willing to pay for the relative advantage of the product. When the customer value concept is ill defined, the business concept is then flawed, leading the venture to potentially fail early. It may take a few iterations to arrive at the appropriate customer value definition. The entrepreneur should wait to approach the investor until after the customer value concept is tested and stabilized. Mishra and Zachary (2014) developed a two-stage entrepreneurial value creation model for new ventures, where the first stage of the value creation process includes the experimentation and effectuation of the customer value concept (see the foreword).

The business model design is founded on the customer value definition. The business model design and the underlying value chain (i.e., the value-added activities) are formulated to create and deliver the customer value efficiently and profitably. In assessing the business model design, the investor determines whether the business model is cost and capital efficient, whether there are sufficient resources available and whether the management team has the ability and incentives to execute the proposed business model, and whether the business model is scalable and sustainable. A business model can provide sustainable scale economies (i.e., the operating margin increases at an increasing rate, as the business model success feeds back positively to generate additional value), when the business model has high operational efficiency, customer and supplier lock-in capabilities, differential advantage, and product market complementaries (Mishra and Zachary, 2014).

Business model efficiency includes both cost and capital efficiencies. The business model lock-in is the capability to lock in customers, suppliers, employees, and strategic partners, so that these participants will not switch to another competitor. Business model differentiation leads to a sustained positive cash flow. Furthermore, the business model complementaries are created when the business model can leverage the existing product or service in adjacent markets, or leverage the existing customer base to sell new products or services. Business model complementaries can be created when the company and its strategic partners create and deliver additional customer value. As the business model design is based on the customer value definition, a weak customer value definition can also weaken the business model design. A strong and proven customer value concept is a prerequisite to a sound business model design.

Finally, the investor, in assessing whether the reward is worth the investment risk and their time and effort, determines how the investment can be structured to mitigate the investment risk and protect the investor in adverse situations, how the investment structure can enhance the investment liquidity, and how the investment structure can provide sufficient incentives to the entrepreneur and management to build and grow the business to a stage when the investors can exit. The investor first determines the risk profile of the venture and estimates the risk of investment loss, based on which the venture's valuation and the investment structure are determined. The risk profile of the venture is in turn based on the customer value definition, the business model efficiency and sustainability, and the ability and incentives of the management to execute the business model in creating, delivering, and monetizing the customer value.

A risk mitigation plan should be prepared at the time of investment such that the venture risks of high priority can be mitigated early and efficiently with the funding provided by the investors. An early warning system consisting of key performance indicators can be designed with the operating plan such that the investor can be warned of a potential adverse event in advance. The risk mitigation plan offers possible strategies to test and alleviate the impact of adverse events on the venture's performance, thus increasing the odds of its success. The risk mitigation plan also stipulates how the investor can bail out of the investment and recoup their principal if the venture is not successful.

The entrepreneur is better off accepting money from a proactive investor who is effective in mitigating the key risks with their business building expertise and industry knowledge. Proactive investors are the right strategic partners for the entrepreneur. A proactive investor also prepares a risk mitigation plan and the investor exit plan at the time of investment. With passive investors, the venture failure rate is high and the investment return is low (see chapter 9). The entrepreneur is better off not accepting money from a passive investor. The venture valuation and a risk-efficient investment structure can be more effectively determined when the risk profile, risk mitigation options, and investor exit options are examined at the time of due diligence. The likelihood of the entrepreneur receiving funding increases when they cooperate with the investor and provide the requisite data to enable the investor to prepare the risk mitigation plan and an investor exit plan.

Proactive investors plan for risk mitigation and exit strategy at the time of investment, and actively participate in building and growing the business. In comparison, passive investors may simply serve on the investee's board. Macmillan et al. (1985) found, in a survey of venture capital investors, that 40 percent of investors evaluate all investment risks prior to investing in a venture; these investors are labeled as "purposeful risk managers." Another 25 percent of the investors are labeled as "parachutists," who plan a clear exit path prior to investing in a venture. The rest of the investors, about 35 percent, would rather impose a minimum number of restrictions and are thus labeled as "determined eclectics."

Entrepreneurs should do an evaluation of prospective investors before approaching them for money or accepting their money. Entrepreneurs now have access to many online resources to obtain investor information.

For example, TheFunded.com provides the background information and the ratings of investors and venture capital firms. The ratings are assigned by registered entrepreneurs. The ratings are based on several dimensions of the investor's behavior and investment approach, including the investor's track record, operational competence, execution assistance, deal terms, pitching efficiency, and so on. TheFunded.com manually verifies and approves every entrepreneur prior to accepting their registration in order to disqualify potential gaming by the investors and to prevent disingenuous comments by disgruntled entrepreneurs.

Zheng (2011) examined the comments posted by the entrepreneurs at TheFunded.com and found that most comments were indeed relevant to the competence of the investors and the level of their operational assistance to their investees. The comments posted by entrepreneurs are positive, negative, or neutral. The entrepreneurs also comment on the investor's attitude and ethical behavior. An entrepreneur may use TheFunded.com to evaluate the potential investors before approaching them or accepting their money. As investors care about their reputation, they also adjust their behavior to improve their image among entrepreneurs. Limited partners, whose money venture capital investors manage, also use TheFunded.com ratings to evaluate the investors when investing in new funds.

Value-Added Investors

Venture capital investors are actively involved with the venture in which they invest, unlike other financial investors who trade financial securities such as stocks, bonds, and options to make money by exploiting financial market inefficiencies. Venture capital investors are business builders. They help the entrepreneur build and grow a business in exchange for a percentage of equity in the venture. They provide their company-building expertise and industry knowledge in building and growing the business. Dotzler (2001) surveyed a group of founders of life sciences ventures to examine the value-added role of venture capital investors and the importance of these functions from the perspective of the entrepreneur. Dotzler found that the most important area where an investor may add value is in assisting the venture to obtain future financings, such as how much additional money to raise, when to raise it, and in making introductions to prospective investors. The other important value-added areas are in assisting the entrepreneur to formulate the business strategy and recruit the senior management team, and in serving as a mentor to the entrepreneur and providing feedback on the entrepreneur's performance.

Thus, the investor's company-building expertise, industry knowledge, contacts, and investor network are some of the important resources the investor uses to add value in a new venture.

Pratch (2005) studied a leading venture capital firm, Vesbridge Partners, to understand how investors help their investees build and grow their business, besides supplying financial resources. Vesbridge Partners developed a unique framework focusing on six key value-added areas (called the value levers) to mitigate risk and create value in a startup. The six value levers are the business model design, management team, customer acquisition, future financings, market positioning, and investment liquidity. Each time the investment firm finances a startup, it evaluates these six key areas for the potential to add value to the startup. Vesbridge's investment partners also use these six key areas to monitor a venture's performance and their risk mitigation strategy. Investors use their company building expertise and extensive industry knowledge and contacts to add value in these six key areas.

Venture capital investors, by taking an active role in their investees, can enhance their rate of return by five to eight times. For example, Pratch (2005) quoted the experience of Vinod Khosla, an early stage investor at Kleiner Perkins, who claimed that his rate of return was in the order of 70 percent when he had actively taken part in the business, as opposed to a mere 8 percent when he had simply served on the boards of his investees. The venture investor thus has a great incentive to be an active participant in building and growing a business, thereby earning superior returns. Passive investors who might simply serve on the board of a startup are less likely to earn superior returns. An entrepreneur should also evaluate prospective investors along the above-mentioned six key areas for the investor's potential to add value to their startup. It is instructive to ask the investors how they may add value in these six areas before accepting their money. The money alone will not help the startup when the money comes from a passive investor who may not take an active role in building and growing the business.

The first value lever that the investor may employ to add value is that of shaping the venture strategy and business model design, the means through which the entrepreneur can exploit a market opportunity. The venture strategy and its business model define the target customer and the value propositions, formulate the customer engagement model, and identify the selling channels and key partnerships. Critical success factors are also identified to monitor the success of the strategy and business model, and to ensure that adequate funding is available to execute these success factors. The business model and strategy determine what resources and capabilities may be needed and when, as well as how much funding will be needed to match the key milestones to the financing rounds. Key milestones include customer acquisition targets, revenue targets, key hires, product completion, and so on. The venture strategy produces an operating plan, a template the investor expects the management to use in executing the business model. The business strategy and the operating plan are continually updated as business and market conditions change. The objective of the investor's involvement in the strategy formulation is to reduce the management's trial-and-error risk to a minimum (Pratch, 2005).

A strong and committed management team is at the heart of the venture value creation and risk mitigation. A great operating plan is of little use if the management doesn't have the ability and incentives to execute it. Investors spend about one-third of their time in helping the company recruit a capable management team and other key talents. The investor's industry contacts and affiliations attract outside talents to join the startup. Having a strong management team in place can help secure future financing at a higher valuation. An early stage venture typically starts off with a strong technical or product development team, then adds sales and marketing talent, followed by bringing in an outside professional management team as the venture matures. It is not advisable to bring in an outside professional management team until the business concept is proven and the business model stabilized. In the meantime, the company needs flexibility in its operating plan, which is best provided by the founders. The professional team is often more wedded to a fixed operating plan.

The third value-added function of the investor is to engage in an active business development strategy on behalf of the venture. The investor introduces the entrepreneur to major customers and strategic partners. The startup by itself doesn't have the credibility or resources to attract potential strategic partners. The investor's affiliation with the startup certifies the venture's viability and provides the credibility in attracting strategic partners and important customers. The investor also provides the resources needed to acquire the capabilities to serve the major customers. A major customer who is uncertain about the company's product or technology may consider purchasing the product when the company has a relationship with a well-known investor. The greater the investor's reputation capital, the greater is the likelihood of product success and revenue growth. An investment from a reputed investor shortens the time to bring a product to market. The shorter the time to bring the product to market, the lower is the venture risk and the greater is the venture valuation offered by the prospective investors. The executives of large companies and major distributors may not take a call from the startup's management team, but they would take a call from a well-known investor.

The fourth key area where the investor may add value is in securing future financing for the venture. Several funding rounds may be needed before the venture can achieve a sustained positive cash flow. The investor's reputation and network of contacts in the venture investment community help the startup secure future financing rounds. The investor's active involvement with the venture in mitigating risks and creating value increases the likelihood of obtaining follow-on financing for the venture. Investors generally co-invest, such that they form investor syndicates either for the current round or for the future rounds to meet the current and future financing needs of the startup. Investor syndication also validates the lead investor's decision to invest in the startup, ensures that sufficient capital is available to grow the venture, brings in more company building and industry expertise for the venture, and diversifies the investment risk among the members of the syndicate.

By co-investing in several startups, an investor can diversify their risk in more investments than their own limited capital would allow. The investor, by participating in investor syndicates, develops strong contacts in the investor community that help the investor to secure future financing for their investees. The lead investor, who conducts the due diligence on a potential investee, prepares a list of targeted co-investors for joining them in the current and future financing rounds. The lead investor typically serves on the board of the investee and monitors the performance on behalf of the investor syndicate to ensure that the venture achieves certain milestones to qualify for follow-on financing in the future.

The fifth area where the investor may add value is in helping the venture to build a powerful brand in the market. The venture may have a superior product or has created a new product category. With the industry knowledge and contacts, the investor can help position the product in the industry to dominate a market segment, thus building a powerful brand. The stronger the potential brand, the greater the venture valuation, and the easier it is to receive follow-on financing. In the case of a new product category, the product acceptance would take time. However, the investor's reputation and ability to attract a network of strategic partners and major customer accounts can enhance the speed of product acceptance in the mainstream market. The investor can help create a strong brand identity for the product in the industry and explain to the public media and market research analysts why the product will dominate a market segment. The investor is an effective spokesperson on behalf of the startup and may participate in prominent industry conferences and trade shows promoting the product brand.

The sixth area for the investor to add value to a startup is in achieving venture liquidity. The investors, management team, and key employees hold the venture's stock and stock options that are mostly illiquid assets, such that they are restricted to selling to the public, or an active market does not exist where these shares can be sold at a fair valuation. Investors having an affiliation with the investment banking community can help the venture achieve liquidity. With the venture liquidity, not only the investors can exit, but also the management and employees can cash out their stock holdings.

A venture achieves liquidity by going public (i.e., initial public offering) or through an acquisition. A proactive investor plans for venture liquidity at the time of making the investment. Having a plan in place for venture liquidity also attracts future investors more easily. Most often venture liquidity is achieved through a merger with or an acquisition by a strategic acquirer, when the acquirer may be from the same industry or from another industry (when the acquirer would want to enter a new market through an acquisition). Alternatively, a strategic acquirer may want to acquire a specialized technology or specialized human resources. Investors are knowledgeable about the potential strategic acquirers and their acquisition criteria, and can help the venture to achieve the desired growth and reach the critical milestones in order to become an attractive acquisition target.

Venture capital investors thus can add value in at least six key areas, namely in formulating and validating the venture strategy, hiring and incentivizing the management and key employees, acquiring major customers and strategic partners, attracting co-investors and future investors, creating a powerful brand position for the product to dominate a market segment in the industry, and achieving venture liquidity to enable investor exit as well as the management and employees to cash out their stock holdings. Of the six areas, the two activities, namely formulating venture strategy and hiring key management personnel, take more than half of the investor's time spent with a startup.

Building Investor Confidence

Investor confidence can be bolstered by mitigating the venture risks and preparing the venture to be investment-ready prior to approaching the investor for funding. Investor confidence is higher when the entrepreneur has proven the business concept or can demonstrate that the concept is working. For example, the entrepreneur can provide proof of sales and possibly a growth in sales. Investors generally do not invest prior to when the business concept is proven. When the business concept is working and the venture is investment-ready, investors may invest in the growth of the business. The sales growth can be achieved after the customer-value definition and the business model are stabilized. If an entrepreneur approaches the investor too early, prior to proving the concept such that the customer-value definition is yet to be stabilized, the investor may not invest as the degree of uncertainty would require the investor to ask for more than a 100 percent of the equity in the venture. Investors generally do not like to invest when the venture risks warrant the investor to own more than 60 percent of the equity of the venture. The greater the equity percentage the investor owns, the less motivated is the entrepreneur to work hard and provide sustained effort (Mishra and Zachary, 2014).

To bolster investor confidence the entrepreneur must achieve sufficient risk mitigation during the early development stage, and they should be able to demonstrate the risks that have been already mitigated at the time of their pitch to the investor. The entrepreneur must keep the investor's criteria in focus when preparing the venture for funding round. Mishra and Zachary (2014), in their Entrepreneurial Value Creation Theory, proposed that the entrepreneur must develop a certain level of working competence and mitigate the early risks before approaching a potential investor. Mishra and Zachary (2014) showed that when an entrepreneur approaches the investor too early, before a certain level of entrepreneurial competence is developed, either the investor doesn't fund the venture, or if the venture is funded, a high-ability entrepreneur might walk away from the investor's offer. However, a low-ability entrepreneur will always accept the investor's offer, if the investor makes an offer to invest in their venture. Low-ability entrepreneurs will generally approach potential investors too early before their business concept can be proven to work.

Douglas and Shepherd (2002) examined how prospective investors assess whether a venture is investment-ready when the entrepreneur approaches them for capital. Investors often observe that either the venture is not investment-ready, or the business plan cannot demonstrate that the venture is investment-ready. Business plans often fail to recognize the critical risks that may cause a venture to fail. Often, early concept-related risks (i.e., the deal-killer risks) are not mitigated prior to the time the entrepreneur approaches an investor for capital. When the sources of risks are clearly identified (e.g., see chapter 8 for the venture risk profile and risk mitigation plan), the business plan can help facilitate venture funding by enabling the investor to better anticipate and mitigate the venture risks, thus increasing the odds of the venture's survival and growth. In determining the venture's risk profile, the entrepreneur can also acknowledge the need to mitigate the venture risks further. If the risk of investment loss is too high, the investor will not invest in the venture.

Douglas and Shepherd (2002) showed that a venture's investor-readiness consists of three areas, namely product readiness, market readiness, and management readiness. A product or technology is investor-ready when the product actually works, the prototype has been built and tested, and the product can be produced at a unit cost that yields a sufficient gross margin. Investors generally require greater than 50 percent gross margin when considering an investment in a venture. When the product development is yet to be completed, the results of the product tests are not yet known, or the product cannot be easily modified to achieve scale economies at a sufficiently low cost per unit, then the product is not yet investor-ready. An interested investor may want to wait to invest until after these product milestones are met.

A venture is market-ready when the product is beta-tested confirming that the product meets the needs and preferences of the target customers, and the demand for the new product is substantial at the proposed price point. The evidence of the market readiness of a venture can be demonstrated by proof of early sales or through the credible test market results (see chapter 3 for some low-cost market research techniques). If there is an uncertainty whether the market would accept a new product, whether the consumer would switch to the new product, or whether the customer would buy at the proposed price, then the venture is not yet market-ready, and thus the venture is not investor-ready. Successful test market results or a proof of early sales growth can remove the excess early stage risks associated with market uncertainty.

A venture is not management-ready when it doesn't have a competent entrepreneurial team who is familiar with the market and has successful prior operating experience in the industry. The entrepreneurial team includes the founders, the board of advisors, the board of directors, key partners, and management. From the investor's perspective, an entrepreneurial team may not yet have sufficient ability and incentives to execute the business strategy and operate the venture. Startups are often founded by technology-oriented entrepreneurs. Sales and management talents are added later on. In these cases, when the venture is market-ready and product-ready, the investor may invest in the venture subject to a contingency that the investor can bring in outside professionals to provide the management and leadership expertise to the venture.

Furthermore, an entrepreneur may be targeting the wrong investor and thus the investor may not be interested in the venture even though the venture is investor-ready. There should be a good fit between the venture and the investor. Investors specialize in their industries, focus on investing at a certain stage of venture development, limit to a proximal geographic area. When the investor is unfamiliar with the industry or market, they might also reject the investment opportunity, as they believe that they cannot add value to the venture. The investor may have a geographical focus and reject the opportunity if it is not proximal. The investor may reject an opportunity if there is a poor fit between the personalities of the investor and the entrepreneur, whereby the investor expects that their relationship would not be a pleasant one.

Even when the venture is investor-ready, the investor may choose not to invest when the business plan is poorly written or presented. A poorly written business plan or a poor pitch to the investor undermines the investor's confidence in the entrepreneur. Many of the content-related business plan weaknesses can be easily fixed before the investor is given a copy of the business plan. For example, Hirai (2014) identified a number of content-related flaws generally found with a typical business plan that the entrepreneur should guard against and fix prior to presenting their plan to the investor. These content flaws include failing to relate to a true pain point of the customer, inflated customer value, trying to be all things to all people (i.e., lacking focus), absence of a go-to-market strategy, claiming that the business has no competition, the length of the business plan is too long or too technical, lack of risk analysis and mitigation, poor organization of the business plan, forgetting to estimate the working capital needs, unrealistic or overly optimistic financial projections, and estimating insufficient financing needs for the venture.

The greater the customer pain, the more widespread the pain, and the better the product in alleviating that customer pain, the greater is the likelihood of product acceptance in the market (Hirai, 2014). The entrepreneur should clearly define the customer value and prove the relative advantage of the product or service but they should not inflate these claims. Many entrepreneurs believe that more is better and that this mitigates the investment risk, and thus they lack a focus. However, investors prefer a focused strategy and a business plan to execute it. Business plans without sufficient details on the venture's go-to-market strategy may be rejected by the investor. The go-to-market strategy should include who the early customers are, what the initial product features are, what the price point is, how you get the product to the customer, how you create and sustain market awareness, and how new customers can be acquired and at what cost.

An entrepreneur claiming that they do not have competition is not credible. Competition is always present, which may not be direct, but can be indirect from the substitute products or services. There is always competition for the dollars consumers spend on the purchase of goods and services. Moreover, the competition is actually a good thing; it validates the customer pain. Even when introducing new product categories, the entrepreneur should consider the competition from the substitute products that can solve the customer's problem or serve the same need, albeit imperfectly. With new product categories, however, investors know that product acceptance could take a long time, and the venture may need a lot of cash to educate the customer. Strategic partners are often critical to the success of the new ventures introducing new product categories.

Another common flaw often found in business plans is financial projections that are overly optimistic or unrealistic. Furthermore, the venture's working capital need to finance the inventory before the accounts receivable can be collected, is often absent or insufficient. Often, business plans do not list the key assumptions made in arriving at the financial projections, or the entrepreneur makes unrealistic assumptions. Nor do many business plans carry out a sensitivity analysis of these assumptions, identifying the impact of these assumptions on the cash needs of the venture.

Several of these content-related issues within business plans can be easily fixed as the answers to these issues are in the mind of the entrepreneur. However, they need to be laid out in the business plan before it is presented to the investor. The investor must find that the business plan has sufficient information to enable them to reliably predict the chance of the venture's survival and growth. The investor wants to determine the risk profile of the venture and the likelihood of the loss of their investment. Startups are inherently risky, mired with many known and unknown challenges. Although investors know that they are investing in a risky venture, they should be provided with the information to help them evaluate and understand sufficiently the risks and challenges associated with the venture.

Pitching or when making a presentation to the investor is another point at which the entrepreneur must be careful to bolster investor confidence. Crafting the pitch carefully as well as practicing the pitch several times prior to presenting it to the investor is highly recommended. The entrepreneur must anticipate the issues that are important to the investor and gather the data to support their claims made in the pitch. The entrepreneur should thus anticipate the investor's concerns and challenges, and must prepare adequately to address them during their pitch. Investors also want the entrepreneur to know their numbers, such as the customer acquisition cost, gross margin, unit cost, burn rate, market size, and so on.

Mason and Harrison (2003) compared the entrepreneur's pitch to a dramaturgical process, similar to when an actor is auditioning for a part in a movie or play. The pitch, consisting of the value propositions for the investor, involves careful packaging of the content and style such that the investor audience may draw a preferred conclusion. The pitch to the investor is often used in the initial screening stage before the investor will consider conducting a serious due diligence to find out the venture's true potential or the quality of the investment opportunity. Often the pitch entails an immediate reaction from the investor on whether to consider investing in the venture.

Mason and Harrison (2003) studied real-time reactions of a group of angel investors to a pitch made by an entrepreneur who was seeking funding for a software startup. Thirty investors attended the pitch and made 198 separate comments. Three-quarters of these comments were negative, out of which 50 percent were on the issues related to the entrepreneur's presentation. Had the pitch been more carefully crafted and presented, the number of negative comments would have been lower, and there would have been a greater likelihood that more investors might have considered the investment seriously. Investors were critical of both the content and the style of the pitch. The presentation was also too technical, which is a common mistake many entrepreneurs make, especially the technology entrepreneurs, when pitching to investors. Many investors do not have the necessary technical background to understand the presentation and they soon lose interest. A poor presentation also signals entrepreneurial incompetence and poor salesmanship.

The entrepreneur's presentation in the above case also lacked excitement and enthusiasm. Moreover, it lacked structure, thus creating more confusion for the investors. The presentation was technically sophisticated but lacked the essential information on the customer and market that the investors needed most, such as the market size, customer value, relative advantage, pricing, customer acquisition strategy, and so on. Furthermore, the investors were less concerned about the company's financials (Mason and Harrison, 2003). Eighty percent of the investors who attended the presentation chose to reject the investment proposal, and most of these investors attributed that rejection to the weakness in the entrepreneur's presentation. About two-thirds of the reasons given for rejection were the weakness in the content, structure, and clarity of the presentation. Another one-third of the reasons were for the entrepreneur's style of presentation. The entrepreneur's presentation had thus two fundamental flaws. First, the presentation was too technical. Second, the entrepreneur's presentation displayed a lack of understanding concerning the investors' needs and background. Crafting the pitch carefully and practicing it several times prior to presenting it can bolster investor confidence.

Evaluating Investment Opportunities

Macmillan et al. (1985) surveyed a group of investors and found that venture investors use ten essential criteria when investing in a startup. These ten criteria are (1) The team can provide sustained and focused effort; (2) the team must be thoroughly familiar with the target market and industry; (3) the investor can realize a 10x return on the investment in five years; (4) the team's track record includes strong leadership skills; (5) the team has the ability to identify and respond to the inherent risks and challenges; (6) the investor can identify potential exit options to exit in three to five years; (7) the addressable market is large and enjoys a significant growth rate; (8) the team's track record illustrates relevant operating experience; (9) the business model design is articulated well; and (10) the product or the technology is proprietary or otherwise can be protected. The entrepreneurial competence is critical when evaluating a new venture, as entrepreneurial ability comprises five out of the ten investor criteria. The other criteria are related to the market, the business model and venture strategy, and the investment liquidity and investor exit.

In another survey of investors, Feeny et al. (1999) found that the reason for rejecting an investment proposal or a business plan is not simply the converse of accepting one. The main reason for rejecting a business plan is a weakness in the entrepreneurial team. However, the strengths of the market opportunity and the business model design are the main reasons for the investor to accept an investment proposal. Thus, the ability of the entrepreneurial team is certainly a necessary condition when qualifying a venture for investment, but it alone is not sufficient to guarantee acceptance of an investment proposal. Examining the investment proposals rejected by the investors, Feeny et al. found that the attributes of the entrepreneurial team dominated the attributes of the business opportunity. However, when the reasons for investment were ranked, the attributes of the business model and the product market concept dominated the attributes of the entrepreneurial team.

Investors choose to invest in high-ability entrepreneurs and high-quality ventures (Mishra and Zachary, 2014). A high-ability entrepreneur should have at least ten qualities that increase the likelihood of venture success (Zider, 1998): the entrepreneur has the necessary sales and technical ability, can tell a compelling story, recognizes the investor's need for exit, has a good reputation and can provide references, understands the need for a team that can provide a variety of skills and expertise, is focused and works diligently toward achieving a goal but at the same time is flexible, gets along well with the investors, understands the investment structure and is not intimidated by the investment terms and conditions, is sought after by many investors, and has realistic expectations and high integrity. A high-quality venture addresses a customer pain that is real and wide spread, offers a compelling value to the target customer, and promises an attractive rate of return to the investor.

The main reason an investment may be declined is often attributed to the lack of the entrepreneur's ability and integrity. The main attributes of the entrepreneurial team include the team's track record and experience, their familiarity with the market and industry, and their integrity and honesty. The main attributes of the business opportunity include the venture's potential for achieving a high profit margin, a reasonable exit plan for the investors, a risk mitigation plan, and the opportunity for the investors to add significant value to the venture. Thus, the strengths in the entrepreneurial ability as well as the strengths of the market opportunity are important for the investor when considering an investment in a new venture.

Investors also invest in high-margin, high-reward ventures. The basis of the investor's due diligence is the risk-reward structure of the investment opportunity. At the heart of the venture capital investment model is efficient risk mitigation (see figure 1.1). The investor's screening and due diligence criteria are based on the nature of the risks and the return potential of the venture. Venture risks include customer demand risk, product risk, technology risk, market potential risk, competitive risk, management risk, funding risk, liquidity risk, and bailout risk, among others (see chapter 8 for venture risk assessment and mitigation). When the venture is in the early development stage, that is, when the business concept and the product performance are yet to be proven, it can be difficult for investors to ascertain the risk-reward structure of the investment opportunity. It is therefore difficult to find investors in the early development stage. Often, the financing of the early development stage is bootstrapped by the entrepreneur or with funds provided by their family and friends.

Investors invest in high-growth ventures that can achieve scale economies. It is thus difficult to find investors who are willing to invest in low-growth, lifestyle ventures. Lifestyle businesses may provide just enough cash flow to pay for the entrepreneur's personal income; that is, the business is simply an alternative to seeking outside employment by the entrepreneur. The entrepreneur thus buys a job through a lifestyle business. Lifestyle businesses are mostly small businesses, which include gas stations, dry cleaners, restaurants, franchises, and other small businesses. Lifestyle businesses are generally either self-financed or bank-financed. Venture capital investors are not attracted to these businesses because of their low growth potential and often the entrepreneur's unwillingness to support the investor's desire for exit.

Investors thus invest in scalable businesses, the businesses that can achieve $20 million or more in sales in five years or so. Institutional investors (known as venture capitalists), who manage limited partners' money and generally invest in a venture in the later stages, may require an even higher level of sales. Institutional investors might require $50 million or more in sales in five years to qualify a venture for investment. The large venture capital firms would rather invest in a venture that has the potential to achieve a large enough market-share to become one of the top five market leaders in their industry.

The addressable market size and the customer's willingness to pay for the relative advantage of the product are the two most critical areas the investors assess in order to mitigate the customer demand risk. Furthermore, the competitive risk is determined by the product's economic life and the intensity of the competition. The shorter the life of the technology embodied in the product, the shorter is the economic life of the product. Furthermore, the more intense the competition, the shorter can be the economic life of the product. The competition includes existing products from direct competitors, the product substitutes, and potential new products entering the industry.

Investors assess whether the new product has a superior relative advantage over the existing competitive products and substitutes, and whether this relative advantage is sustainable. Investors also consider whether the sustainable relative advantage can create new entry barriers to prevent an onslaught by the potential competitors. Furthermore, investors consider whether the target customer is willing pay for the relative advantage and buy at a price point that affords a sufficiently high gross margin to defray the large fixed costs required to scale the business. Most investors require at least a 50 percent gross margin on a product or service when considering an investment in the venture.

In addition to the customer demand risk, the market potential risk, and the competitive risk, investors also consider the management risk. Is the entrepreneurial team strong in sales and marketing? Can the team work together? Is the team flexible and coachable? Is the team willing to revise the business strategy as the market conditions change and new information is obtained? At the same time, is the team focused on the current priorities and diligent on meeting those priorities? In the early stages of venture development, the business model is yet to be stabilized so the founders should be flexible and willing to adjust the venture strategy when necessary. At the later stage, after the business model stabilizes, a professional management team with more operating expertise in the industry may be better suited to executing a focused business model and strategy to achieve sustained growth and profitability.

Investors also assess the venture liquidity risk or the likelihood that the investors can exit at a desired valuation in a reasonable period, typically in four to five years. There should be more than one exit option for the investor. An initial public offering (IPO) is always a preferred exit option, but IPOs are rare. Most often, the exit option is an acquisition of the startup by a strategic buyer, where the buyer may be an established company in the same industry or from another industry (such that the buyer wants to enter a new market). To determine the potential exit valuation, investors consider comparable exits in the same industry and the valuation multiples offered by the potential strategic acquirers in the past. A proactive investor would prepare an exit plan, including potential exit options and the exit valuation, at the time of investment in a startup.

Investors also consider the bailout risk such that in case the venture performs poorly or the market conditions change rapidly, the investor may want to salvage their investment. Given that startup failure rates are high, the investor should consider a bailout plan as a contingency in adverse performance situations. In high-risk investments such as with early stage ventures, the investor may use a contingency board control provision in the investment agreement to enable the investor to obtain a majority control on the board of directors. By obtaining a majority on the board, the investor then can replace the management team, or may liquidate and sell off the assets of the venture in the event that the venture performance deteriorates substantially.

Investors use a two-stage due diligence process when considering an investment in a new venture (see chapter 8). The first stage is an initial screening stage, during which the investor determines whether the opportunity is a good fit for her, given the investor's industry focus and preference for the stage of venture development. In the first stage, the investor assesses the entrepreneurial ability and the risk of investment loss. Venture investors show a risk preference, in that investors differ in their acceptable level of investment loss. Some investors tolerate a higher level of risk and thus invest in the earlier stages of venture development; others tolerate a lower level of risk and invest in the later stages.

Most business plans are rejected in the initial screening stage. The few that survive the first stage of screening enter the second stage of a detailed due diligence. At the end of the second stage, the opportunity is not only risk consistent but also return efficient. That is, the venture risks are clearly identified and a risk mitigation plan is developed; also, the capital needs are determined and the capital availability is ensured. The investor determines an exit strategy and prepares an exit plan to ensure achievement of a targeted rate of return. Following a successful completion of the second stage of due diligence, the investment may be closed. The investment agreement includes the investment amount and contingencies, the type of venture security and a percentage of equity for the investor, and the investment terms and conditions that are designed to protect the investor in adverse conditions as well as to incentivize the entrepreneur to motivate them to provide a sustained effort and cooperate with the investor in mitigating investment risks and achieving a successful investor exit.

The initial screening stage may take a week to a month. About 80 percent of business plans are rejected in this stage. The second stage of due diligence can take one to three months. Another 15 percent of business plans are rejected in the second stage. The few business plans that survive the two stages of due diligence, that is, about 5 percent or fewer of all business plans received by the investor, may receive an investment from the investor. The closing is typically in four weeks after the term sheet is offered. During this period, the entrepreneur is prohibited, through a no-shop clause, from soliciting additional term sheet offers from other investors. The entire process of the investor's screening and due diligence to closing can take three to six months. The entrepreneur should plan at least four to six months to complete a financing round. The first financing round, however, can take longer up to one year. This time may include the investor's wait-and-see period, up to three to six months, during which time the investor is assessing the progress made by the entrepreneur, and their ability and effort to achieve the projected milestones laid out in the business plan and mitigate the stated risks.

An investment memorandum may be prepared to summarize the investment thesis and the findings of due diligence when investing in a new venture. The investment amount, the use of the proceeds from the investment, and the deliverable milestones are indicated in the investment memorandum. The investment thesis summarizes the reasons for investment and the risks of investment. The investment memorandum may include an efficient risk mitigation plan and a most-likely investor exit strategy, or the risk mitigation plan and investor exit plan are prepared within 90 days after the closing of the investment. The due diligence findings, whether the market opportunity is real and large enough, whether the business model design is efficient and sustainable, and whether the reward is worth the risk and investor effort, are also summarized. In considering whether the market opportunity is real and large enough, the investor assesses whether the customer pain is real and widespread, whether the product or service has a relative advantage over the competing products and substitutes, and whether the customer is willing to pay for this relative advantage and buy the product. Chapters 2, 3, and 4 provide a framework and tools to analyze the market opportunity, and formulate and refine the customer value concept. Entrepreneurs may use the framework and tools to redefine the customer value prior to approaching an investor for funding. Investors may use the framework and tools to analyze the investment proposal and the market opportunity prior to investing in the venture.

We show that the investment return is the product of the operating margin, the operating leverage, and the capital leverage (see chapter 7). In considering whether the business model design is efficient and sustainable, the investor will assess whether the business model can enhance operating leverage, whether the business model can enhance competitive advantage, and whether the business model can provide sustainable scale economies. The investor also assesses what key resources and capabilities are required, what key partnerships are necessary, what the critical risks are, and how the underlying critical assumptions can be tested and the venture risks be mitigated at a low cost. The investor determines the stage milestones and an operating plan, including key performance indicators to be monitored to increase the likelihood of the venture's success. The business model design should provide customer and supplier lock-in capabilities, complementary product market opportunities for the company and its strategic partners, and a differential advantage to achieve sustainable scale economies. Chapters 5, 6, and 7 provide a framework and tools to analyze the desirable qualities of the business model design. The entrepreneur may use these tools to refine and reconfigure the business model design, which increases the chances of getting funded. Investors may use the tools and framework to assess the strengths and weaknesses of the business model design proposed in the investment proposal and its potential to achieve scale economies, sustained positive cash flow, and a higher return on investment.

In considering whether the reward is worth the risk and the investor effort, the investor wants to ensure that the deal structure protects the investor in adverse performance conditions, provides an adequate rate of return to the investor to compensate them for their risk and effort, and enhances the likelihood of investment liquidity. The deal structure should provide sufficient incentives to the entrepreneur and management team, aligning their interests with those of the investors. The deal structure should facilitate investor exit. Investors should prepare an exit plan in addition to a risk mitigation plan at the time of investment. The investor exit plan should estimate an expected exit valuation and identify potential strategic acquirers and develop an investment thesis for the selected acquirers. The investment thesis should then guide the venture strategy. Venture capital investors are actively involved in the risk mitigation of the venture, thereby enhancing the likelihood of the venture's survival and growth. Investors are also value arbitrageurs, as they invest in a startup at a low valuation when the valuation is more uncertain, exit at a high valuation when the business grows to a point large enough for the investor exit, and hedge their investment risk and limit their investment loss by actively participating in the venture development.

The investment agreement summarizes the key terms and conditions of the investment under which the investment can be made, including the percentage of equity for the investor, the contingencies, risk mitigating covenants, control provisions, an incentive structure for the management, and any additional due diligence that may be required prior to the closing. The investor also determines the post-money and pre-money valuations of the venture (see chapter 9), the minimum percentage of equity for the investor, and the maximum investment to be offered commensurate with the stage of venture development and the investor's expected rate of return.

Chapters 8, 9, and 10 provide a framework and tools to analyze the risk and reward structure of the investment, to determine the venture's risk profile and prepare a risk mitigation plan, to prepare an investor exit plan, to estimate a risk-adjusted rate of return for the investor, to determine the valuation of the venture including the valuation of any intellectual property and intangible assets the venture may own, and to determine a minimum percentage of equity for the investor. Investors want the entrepreneur to be familiar with such investment terms and not intimidated by these terms and conditions. A better knowledge of the investment terms and conditions will enable the entrepreneur to understand the investor's needs and offer a creative deal structure minimizing the investment risk and maximizing the investment liquidity, thus increasing the chances of getting funded. An understanding of the investment model also would allow the entrepreneur to be in a position to better negotiate the terms and conditions with the investor in meeting the investor's needs, and work together with the investor in building and growing the business, thereby creating value for all participants.

PART II

Is the Market Opportunity Real and Large Enough?

CHAPTER TWO

Customer Value

A framework is offered to analyze the customer's experience with the product to identify customer pain points. The customer value design involves an analysis of the customer pain points and the competitors' weaknesses, and then selecting the target customers and a set of resonate-focused value propositions in order to lower the barriers to market entry and minimize the inherent resistance from competitors. The opportunity scores are used to rank potential customer-value creation opportunities, based not only on how important a value creation opportunity is to the customer, but also on the level of customer dissatisfaction with the existing products. The customer value propositions can be further disaggregated into three basic elements, the content, the context, and the enabling infrastructure; then these three elements can be reconstructed and re-aggregated to create a more powerful customer value offering. The customer value offering links the customer pain point to the product's capabilities relative to the competitors' weaknesses.

Customer value offered must serve the customer's need and get the customer's job done. Customer value design requires an understanding of the customer experience with the product and the customer pain points. The customer value design process involves selecting the target customer segments and constructing the value propositions to increase the likelihood of product acceptance in a market while minimizing resistance from the competition. An entrepreneur must be familiar with the target customer's needs and desires, the customer's job-to-be-done and their challenges, the customers who might value the new product offering, the existing and potential competitors, the available substitute products or services, and the basis of competition. Without a thorough knowledge of the customer's requirements and the basis of competition, it is not possible to obtain funding from investors.

A startup with limited resources cannot serve all customers. It must carefully choose its target customer segments otherwise its go-to-market strategy and product launch will fail. A careful choice of initial customer segments is key to an efficient and successful go-to-market strategy. The choice of the most valuable customer segments also depends on the creativity of the entrepreneur in segmenting the market and gaining knowledge of the competition. A market can be segmented in several ways: for example, by using customer demographics, psychographics, sociographics, geography, and behavioral characteristics. The entrepreneur may use other creative criteria to profile the target customer. A currently unserved, underserved, or dissatisfied customer segment is an ideal niche segment that the entrepreneur should initially target when entering the market.

A customer segment is a group of customers with common needs and certain shared characteristics. Target customer segments include not only end users, but also buyers, payers, and influencers. Buyers buy a product or service, whereas the payers pay for it. The buyer and the payer may or may not be the same person. The influencers directly or indirectly influence the purchase decision. It is important to understand the buyer's purchasing decision process and their purchasing criteria. The end users are the ultimate consumers who use the product or service. It is important to understand the needs of all customer groups, including end users, buyers, payers, and influencers.

Each customer segment is a homogeneous group of customers. An effective customer segment should be measurable, substantial, accessible, differentiable, and actionable (Kotler and Keller, 2012). A customer segment is measurable when the segment size can be measured. The size of the segment should be substantial so that the marketing efforts targeting the segment are considered worthwhile. The customer segment should be accessible and reachable. The customer segments should be differentiable from one group to another. The customer segment should also be actionable, so that the marketing strategy can be formulated to deliver the customer value and meet the needs of the customer segment.

Customer value definition requires identifying the target customer and determining the corresponding value propositions. The construction of a well-defined customer value concept is critical to the business model design and key to achieving business success. The customer value addresses the customer pain and gets the customer's job done. The customer pain addressed thus determines the target customer segment and the corresponding customer value propositions simultaneously. Defining and identifying the elements of the customer value are critical to the venture's success. The success of the business model design depends on the customer value construction. If the customer value definition is flawed, then the business concept construction is flawed and the business model design will fail. Investors expect a clear formulation of the customer value concept when investing in a venture.

The entrepreneur must be familiar not only with the needs of the target customers, but also with the basis of the current and potential competition in the target market. Often when the entrepreneur has created a new product category, they believe that there is no existing competition. That is not true. Claiming there is no competition almost always guarantees no funding for the entrepreneur. There may not be direct competition for the product or service, but indirect competition from the substitute products or services always exists. Competition is a good thing, whether it is direct or indirect. It validates the existence of the customer need for a product or solution. In the total absence of competition, the customer need may not be real or there may not be an immediate need for the new product or service. When introducing a new product category, often, the customer need exists but the customer may not be aware of their need. It might then require educating the customers on their need as well as the product solution offered.

Know Your Competitors

The product's functionality, or the customer needs the product serves or the customer problem the product solves, determines who the competitors are and how they compete. Competition may be direct, indirect, or potential. Direct competitors of a startup offer the products or services with a similar functionality (i.e., similar solutions), whereas indirect competitors offer substitute products or services that serve the same customer need (or solve the same problem of the customer). Potential competitors are the expected new entrants to the market to serve the same customer need. Potential competitors are thus followers and imitators either with a "me-too" product or a more innovative solution. Businesses in adjacent markets and those who offer complementary products can be potential competitors. Direct competition in a chosen target market may be minimal for a product or service, but indirect competition from the substitute products or services always exists.

For example, consider Zipcar (www.zipcar.com), a car rental company, founded in 2000 in Cambridge, Massachusetts. Zipcar rents a car by the hour and makes the car easily accessible to the customer. Unlike regular car rental companies, the customer at Zipcar, when renting a car for few hours, doesn't have to pay a minimum rental charge for a day and they don't have to travel to the rental company's site to access the car. At the time of its founding, Zipcar did not have any significant direct competition providing hourly car rentals in the United States, although the concept was already proven and popular in Europe. There were then a couple of car-sharing cooperatives in the United States, but they were primarily geared to the environmental mission of reducing pollution and emission from automobiles. Regular car rental companies, such as Budget, Avis, or Hertz, were providing daily and weekly car rentals, but not on an hourly basis.

However, there was indirect competition for Zipcar, including public transportation, personal vehicles, and cabs, which could all solve the same customer problem or get the same job done by providing alternative urban transportation options to the customer. Thus, although Zipcar at the time of its founding had no significant direct competition in the United States, it had significant indirect competition from substitute or alternative transportation modes to solve the same customer problem of travelling a short distance that may take only an hour or two. Besides, the major car rental companies were potential competitors, as they could easily introduce the hourly car rental service. Indeed, today most major car rental companies offer hourly car rentals and make their cars conveniently accessible to their customers.

Direct and indirect competitors may be identified based on the product functionality and the customer problem the product solves. Potential competitors may be identified as those who serve adjacent markets and provide complementary products or services. Once one has a list of direct, indirect, and potential competitors, one can then narrow them down to a short list of three to five close or principal competitors. Some of the competitors are very similar; that is, they provide "me-too" products. In these cases, one representative competitor may be chosen from the list of similar competitors. The idea is to choose three to five principal competitors that are as diverse as possible.

Once one has identified these three to five principal competitors, the next step is to gather as much operating information as possible about them. Figure 2.1 lists these competitor groups and organizes the operating data gathered about them. Talking to prospective customers and distributors, and researching online and secondary data sources, industry and market studies, annual reports, and so on can provide the necessary information on the competitors. There are six key areas in

Competitors: Who are They?	Competitor Group A	Competitor Group B	Summary of Strengths	Summary of Weaknesses
Customer Segments: Who do they serve?				
Primary Benefits: What do they provide?				
Channel Strategy: How do they provide?				
Customer Relationship: How do they acquire and retain customers?				
Pricing Strategy: How do they price the products and services?				
Differential Advantage: What are the sources of their differential advantage?				

Figure 2.1 Know your competitors.

the product-market space we need to understand related to the competition, namely the customer segments they serve, the primary benefits they provide, the channels they use, their pricing strategy, their customer acquisition strategy, and the sources of their differential advantage. Figure 2.1 lists these six areas. The last two columns in figure 2.1 identify and summarize the strengths and weaknesses of the competitors in these six areas.

A competitor may choose to serve a few customer segments depending on the relative advantage with the product or service. Knowing which customer segments the competitors currently serve helps us to know how the market is presently segmented, and more importantly, which of the customer segments are not being served or are underserved. In the last column of figure 2.1, a note is also made to list the currently unserved, underserved, and dissatisfied customer segments. A good strategy when entering a market is to approach a customer segment that the competitors currently do not serve fully or do not find the customer segment profitable, or a customer segment that is currently dissatisfied with the product offering provided by the competitors.

Next, in figure 2.1 one can list the primary benefits these competitors provide to their customers. Primary benefits are the product features and other benefits that the customers value most. Primary benefits include primary customer value propositions, including the points of parity and points of differentiation with the products and services provided by the competitors. These data can help one to uncover the weaknesses in the competitors' customer value offerings, and an opportunity to understand the gap in the market and the unserved and underserved needs of potentially dissatisfied customers. List the summary of the strengths and weaknesses in the competitors' product offerings in the last two columns of figure 2.1.

The third operating data gathered on the competitors is about the channels the competitors are currently using, including the retailers, distributors, wholesalers, online channels, direct sales channels, agents and brokers, and so on. Determine the potential cost and accessibility of these channels as well as the requirements of these channels when qualifying to carry a product or service. Determine the needs and desires of the relevant customer groups, including the end users, payers, influencers, and buyers, and how well the current channels used by the competitors serve these customer groups. Summarize the strengths and weaknesses with the current channels employed by the competitors. The cost of a channel may be prohibitive; however, high cost and inaccessibility can be overcome by introducing a new technology or an innovative business model. The access to a channel may be precluded for the startup, or an opportunity may exist to bypass that channel. The unserved customer segments may not be accessible by the current channels. The customers may be dissatisfied with the service provided by the current channels. List all weaknesses and the areas of potential improvement related to the channels used by the competitors in the last column of figure 2.1. Identify the existing and potential channels that can minimize the cost to bring the new product to market and minimize the potential resistance from the competitors.

Another area to gather data on the competitors is their customer acquisition and retention strategy; that is, how they acquire and retain their customers and what promotional methods they are using. How effective are their promotional methods to reach the customer segments they are serving? How difficult is it for these customers to switch to a new product offering? What might be the incentives these customers need to switch to a new product? How satisfied are these customers with the current offerings? Understand the competitors' customer acquisition costs. Identify the weaknesses in the competitors' customer acquisition and retention strategies and their cost structure. Summarize the strengths, weaknesses, and missing linkages. List them in the last two columns of figure 2.1. Can the customer acquisition and retention strategy be made more efficient? If currently there is no direct competition, because the product or service is in a new category, then understand the methods used by the competitors offering substitute products or services. The data on customer relationship strategies would help identify the customers who are currently dissatisfied with the competitors' offerings. Approaching dissatisfied or unaware customers can minimize the resistance from the competitors for one's product or service and should increase the likelihood of product acceptance in the market.

Another area examined in figure 2.1 is the competitors' pricing strategy and revenue model. When analyzing the competitors' pricing strategy, keep in mind the profile of the customer segments the competitors serve and the primary benefits they deliver to their customers. Customers in similar segments with similar primary benefits would not pay a higher price for one's product. However, the current price point set by one's competitors may be too high in some customer segments. Plot the product prices versus the primary benefits provided by the competitors. The price-benefit graph can help one to understand a competitor's positioning of their product in the market and explain their price point relative to their cost to serve a customer segment. Furthermore, the competitors may be using segment-based pricing strategies. The current price set by the competitors in a certain customer segment may establish an upper limit to the product's price point for a certain customer value offering. There may be potential weaknesses in the competitors' pricing strategy and structure. The pricing structure can be simplified or made more attractive to the customers. Summarize the competitors' strengths and weaknesses in their pricing structure and revenue models in the last two columns of figure 2.1.

The sources of differential advantages of competitors are their scale economies, network effects, customer switching costs, capital requirements, proprietary technologies, preferential access to raw material and talented workforce, favorable geographic locations, established brand names, unequal access to distribution channels, and favorable government regulations (see chapter 5). These drivers of differential advantage may indicate the opportunities for a new entrant to erect and secure new barriers-to-entry against potential competitors and followers in a particular industry. Summarize the strengths and weaknesses of the competitors' differential advantages in the last two columns of figure 2.1.

Figure 2.1 will thus provide a general idea about the market, industry, and how the direct and indirect competitors operate. The data in figure 2.1 helps one identify strengths and potential weaknesses in the market and competition, and determine where the barriers to market entry are low, such that the resistance to market entry would be minimum. Select a few niche customer segments that are currently unserved or dissatisfied to minimize the resistance and attract less attention from one's competitors. Also, identify the unserved and underserved needs of the current customers and the weaknesses in the current offerings by the competitors.

Identify the weaknesses in the competitors' business models and operating strategies, including their served customer segments, product features and benefits, distribution channels, pricing structure and revenue models, key strategic partners, customer acquisition and retention strategy, and differential advantages. The weaknesses thus identified provide the potential areas of advantage for the new venture when formulating the customer value offering and configuring the business model design. Later in chapter 5, we examine the industry structure to determine the critical success factors when entering a new market. The critical success factors are the capabilities the startup should build or acquire in order to succeed in a new market. In chapter 4, we propose a model to develop the customer value concept based on the customer pain points and the competitor weaknesses. The customer value concept links the customer pain points to the new product's capabilities relative to the competitors' weaknesses.

Know Your Customers

One has thus identified a few customer segments that are currently unserved or underserved by the competitors or the customer segments that are dissatisfied with the competitors' offerings, as well as the areas of potential differentiation opportunities for the startup relative to its competitors' weaknesses. Creative market segmentation techniques can be used to identify underserved or missing customer segments. The common segmentation methods use demographic, sociographics, psychographic, geographic, and behavioral variables to identify and profile the customers. Customer demographic variables include age, occupation, income, gender, and education. Geographic variables include country, state, city, or region. Psychographic variables include personality, motivations, and lifestyle. Behavioral variables include customer action or behavior, specifically in how the customers respond to a product or service.

Christensen and Raynor (2003) recommended a market segmentation approach based on the customer's job-to-be-done or the problem-to-be-solved, the notion being that the customer "hires" the product to do a specific job or solve a specific problem. The circumstance in which the customer's job is done or the problem is solved is thus an appropriate basis to segment the market. Christensen and Raynor illustrated this approach to market segmentation with the following example. Consider a quick-service restaurant selling milkshakes. Traditional segmentation methods would use demographic and psychographic variables of customers. However, with the job-to-be-done approach, consider what the customer really wants to get done with the purchase of a milkshake.

Some customers would purchase the milkshake before their morning commute to work to reduce the boredom of the commute. The milkshake makes the customer's time spent going to work less boring. In other times of the day, parents would purchase milkshakes for their children with complete meals. The job the parents are trying to get done is to make their kids happy and quiet. Thus, the job-to-be done segmentation approach results in two customer segments with distinct customer needs, namely the morning commuters and the afternoon parents. The customer value design defines the customer segment and constructs the appropriate value offering. Other creative segmentation techniques may be used to identify the missing and underserved customer segments in the market and to formulate appropriate customer value offerings.

A critical step in defining the customer value offering is to analyze and understand one's customers, the customer segments one may choose to target. Understand the customers' pain points. Consider the experience of all customers, including buyers, end users, payers, and influencers. The customer experience analysis helps one identify the customer pain points and potential value creation opportunities to formulate the customer value offering with the product or service. The customer experience analysis also identifies the points of differentiation the target customers would value the most. The customer experience analysis helps one decide the right customers for the product or service and construct the value creating propositions. The customer value offered, however, when constrained by the product's functional capabilities, should include the complementary products or services that are identified to enhance the new product offering to better meet the customer needs or solve the customer problem.

Figure 2.2 suggests a framework to capture the customer experience with a current product or service (Macmillan and McGrath, 1997). A company may differentiate its product or service at every point the product comes in contact with the customer. Macmillan and McGrath called the customer experience the consumption chain. Each link in the consumption chain provides differentiation opportunities for the

	Category Product	Substitute Product	Complementary Product	Summary of Pain Points
How do customers become aware of their need?				
How do customers find the product or service?				
How do customers consider and select the product?				
How do customers order and purchase the product?				
How is the product paid for and who pays?				
How is the product delivered and installed?				
How is the product stored and handled?				
How is the product used?				
How can the customer return or exchange the product?				
How is the product repaired or disposed of?				

Figure 2.2 Customer pain points.

product or service versus the competitors' products. The analysis of the consumption chain identifies the customer pain points and the unserved needs of the customers (see figure 2.2), as well as the customer segments that are currently dissatisfied with the competitors' products or services. Comparing the primary benefits of the competitors' product offerings (identified in figure 2.1) with the customer pain points identified in figure 2.2 helps one to identify the customer value gaps (to be discussed later in the chapter). The customer value gaps create differentiation opportunities for the startup to position the new product in the market more successfully. The customer pain points identified in figure 2.2 also determine the initial and subsequent product features that may be valued most by one's target customers.

Figure 2.2 lists the ten links of the consumption chain (i.e., the entire experience of the customer with a product or service), namely how the customers become aware of their need, how the customers find a product, how the customers consider and select a product, how the customers order and purchase the product, how the customers pay for the product and who pays for the product, how the product is delivered and installed, how the product is stored and moved around, how the product is used and what help the customer might need in using the product, how the customer can return or exchange the product, and how the product can be repaired, disposed of, or replenished (Macmillan and McGrath, 1997). Figure 2.2 can help a startup analyze the entire customer experience to identify the customer pain points and dissatisfaction with the current product offerings as well as with substitute and complementary products. The analysis also helps to bundle the new product with complementary products to offer a total solution to the customer's problem. Figure 2.2 summarizes the customer pain points in the last column.

From the analysis of figure 2.1, one has three or four niche customer segments that are currently dissatisfied with or underserved by the competitors. These niche customer segments offer the startup, when entering a new market, minimum resistance from the competitors. Those customer segments are further considered in figure 2.2. These customer segments are the startup's potential target customers. Figure 2.2 identifies the pain points of these customers, which in turn helps the startup choose the initial and subsequent product features or benefits to solve the customer problem. Some product features are more important and should be included in the initial and earlier product designs as they alleviate a bigger pain point. Some product features that address smaller pain points may be added in the later versions of the product release. The customer pain points thus identified provide customer value creation and differentiation opportunities for the new product or service. The greater the customer pain, the more valued is the product feature that addresses that pain point. The customer pain point analysis thus helps to identify one or two customer segments whose pain points the new product offering can solve more effectively. Initially one should only target one or two niche customer segments when entering the market.

The first link in the consumption chain is the customer's awareness of the need for the product or how the customers can become aware of their need for the product. The customer may be aware of the problem and is looking for a solution. Alternatively, the customer may not be aware of the exact problem or may be having difficulty in identifying the problem. For example, in the case of Zipcar (www.zipcar.com), the target customer is an urban customer or a college student, a customer who has limited access to transportation options on an hourly basis. The customer need in this example is then to find a cheaper and more convenient transportation solution.

At times, the product or service may include a feature that triggers a need to repurchase the product; the product feature thus creates the awareness of the need for the product. For example, a product warranty may expire in one year and the customer may look for an extended warranty or a replacement product. The product currently used by the customer may become less effective, or the customer's problem may become more complex, triggering a need to look for new products or solutions.

The next two links in the consumption chain are how the customers can find the product they desire and how they select the product that they finally choose to purchase. How do the customers become aware of the several product choices available on the market? How would the customers find the new product offering? How do they decide on a product to purchase? For example, a customer may have a plumbing problem at home. They may look through the yellow pages or go online to find a plumber. They may use some online resources, such as Angies.com or the Better Business Bureau (www.bbb.org) to find plumbing contractors in the local area. They may use an accredited or certified plumbing contractor or may make a decision based on the customer reviews available online. They may ask a neighbor and decide to hire a plumber based on the neighbor's recommendation.

With the Internet, the customer's search process for a product or solution has become more cost effective and time efficient. A customer can now browse through several online resources for customer reviews and testimonials before selecting how and where to buy a product or whom to hire as a service provider. Businesses use several advertising and promotion media, both online and offline, to reach potential customers. The advertising media include online ads, magazines and newspapers, radio, television, word of mouth, and billboards, among others. Businesses may use their salesforce to make the customers aware of their product offerings and persuade them to purchase their products. Several television channels offering home shopping networks demonstrate the use of the product and explain why the new products are superior to the existing products or solutions, thus creating consumer awareness of the new products and educating consumers on how to use these products. Making the consumer's search process for the product or service more efficient and convenient can enhance the customer value offering.

Understand the customer's purchasing criteria and the process of how the customer makes the final selection of the product or service. Consider the needs of all participants in the purchasing of the product, including the buyers, payers, influencers, and end users. What are their economic and non-economic motivations? Who makes the final choice to purchase the product and who influences that choice? Who pays for the product? Is it possible to make the customer's selection process more convenient and less risky, such as offering a trial before the customer purchases the product?

For example, CarMax makes the used car buying process more convenient and less painful. A customer would specify all the features they want in an automobile and CarMax would show them a few cars available for a test drive that meet their needs. CarMax would provide the customer with a complete history of repairs and accidents with the cars. The customer would then select the car to purchase, which is then available at a fixed price without the need for further haggling. The used car buying process is often a nightmare, which is instead simplified by CarMax. Another new company in the car market, Carvana (www.carvana.com) makes the car-buying process even more convenient and less risky for the customer. Customers can choose all the features they want in their automobile from their home. Carvana will then deliver the automobile to the customer's home. The customer has seven days to test drive the car before they decide to purchase it. Furthermore, the customer has thirty days to return the car if they choose not to keep it for any reason. Making the product selection process more convenient and less risky for the customer can be a potential opportunity for differentiation when formulating the customer value offering.

The fourth link in the consumption chain is how the customers order and purchase the product, and who orders and pays for the product. The person who orders the product, the buyer, may not be the same as the end user. Find ways to make the ordering and purchasing experience simpler and more convenient for the customer. For example, mail-order pharmacies through their websites and smartphone apps show how long a customer's prescription supply is remaining and then make it easier for the customer to refill their prescriptions online. Mail-order pharmacies also send reminders to their customers to refill the prescriptions as they might run out soon. Many retail stores, for example, replenish their inventories automatically when their inventory stocks drop below predetermined levels. With the Internet, the customer's experience in making a selection and ordering a product has become more efficient and convenient.

The next link in the consumption chain is how the product is paid for and who pays for the product. This link also can be a potential value creation opportunity. Often the payment process can be cumbersome and a paint point for the customer. Can the payment process be simplified and made easier for the customer? A company may look at its current accounts receivable balance and determine how effective its customer payment policy has been. Is there an opportunity to simplify the customer payment process and reduce the stock of accounts receivable? In large companies, the payment system is managed by their information technology group and often any change in the payment processing system can be difficult. However, in a startup, it can be easier to simplify the customer payment process and improve the receivable collection. Currently there are several online payment-processing companies a startup can use; for example, PayPal (www.paypal.com) or Stripe (www.stripe.com) could make the customer payment processing easier and less risky. Furthermore, when an upfront payment may be financially difficult for the customer, the startup may arrange a suitable credit financing facility for the customer through relationships with banks or other lending institutions. Making the payment process easier and less risky for the customer can be a potential differentiator when formulating the customer value offering.

The next link is how the product or service is delivered and installed. How soon can the product be delivered? How soon does the customer need the product? Can the customer delivery logistics be outsourced so that the startup's delivery expenses can be minimized and the customer can have a more reliable and efficient delivery experience? For example, Amazon (www.amazon.com) offers a prime membership feature to its customers such that the prime members can receive their deliveries in two days after ordering. Amazon charges $99 per year for its prime membership, creating another source of revenue for Amazon. Customer delivery convenience and efficiency can be a potential value creation opportunity to differentiate the customer value offering.

Once the product is delivered to the customer, the installation or assembly of the product may be necessary. This process can be a major pain point for the customer, especially for complex products. A call-in phone number may be helpful to guide the customer and troubleshoot any installation problems. A DVD and a website link may be provided with the product to make the product assembly instructions easier for the customer. Products may be pre-assembled such that very little assembly and installation work is left for the customer to perform. The tools needed to assemble the product may be also included with the product so that the customer does not have to be in possession of the tools. Making the assembling and installation experience of the customer easier and smoother can be a potential differentiation opportunity to enhance the customer value.

The next link in the consumption chain is how the product is stored and moved around. How difficult is it to move the product from one place to another? Can the packaging be designed to make it easier to handle the product? Can the product be made lighter so it will be easier for the customer to carry the product around? The packaging may be designed to help with the product's transportation, especially for fragile and durable products. Can the shape of the product be made easier to hold and carry? Can the product packaging be made such that the storage and handling of the product is easier for the customer? Product packaging and handling is a potential differentiation factor in the formulation of the customer value offering.

How the product is used and what help the customer might need when using the product or service can be a potential differentiation opportunity. The easier it is to use the product and the more reliable the product is when used, the greater is the customer value. The product or service must meet the customer's expectation and, hopefully, even surpass that expectation. It can be an advantage if the product has more usage (i.e., an augmented product) than the only need for which the customer has bought the product. A phone number may be provided with the product for the customer to call in with their usage difficulties. An accompanying DVD can also show how to use a complex product. A company website or YouTube video can also show how the product is used by others.

A risk-free exchange and warranty program can help to alleviate customer worries and encourage the trial of a new or unproven product. Greater customer satisfaction will result in positive customer reviews and a greater product acceptance in the market. Customer satisfaction also builds customer loyalty and helps brand development. Favorable customer reviews and positive word-of-mouth about the new product increase customer awareness and satisfaction, lowering the startup's costs of customer acquisition and retention. Positive customer usage experience with the product provides critical opportunities for differentiating the customer value.

The last two links in the consumption chain are how the customer can return or exchange the product, if needed, and how the product can be repaired, replenished, or disposed of after its use. Many retail stores, for example, provide a thirty-day, no-questions-asked, product return or exchange program. Amazon (www.amazon.com) with its prime membership feature offers to pay for the shipping when the customer returns the product, making the product purchase risk-free. Carvana, an online car dealership, gives thirty days to its customers to return a purchased car if the customer is not satisfied with the purchase decision, or if for any reason they may decide not to keep the car. Customer satisfaction and customer loyalty are enhanced by the after-sales support and service of the product, which increases the customer retention rate and lowers the cost of customer retention. The company can avoid unfavorable customer reviews by giving attention to this part of the consumption chain. Low cost or free extended repair warranties may be offered to give the customer peace of mind and make the purchase less risky. Product replenishment and restocking processes can also be made easier and more convenient for the customer.

In addition to examining the customer experience with the current products for potential differentiation opportunities, one may examine the customer experience with the substitute and complementary products to find new value creation opportunities when formulating the customer value (see figure 2.2). Look for additional value creation opportunities by analyzing across substitute products, product subcategories, complementary products, buyer groups, functional-emotional orientation of the product, and the current social and technology trends (Kim and Mauborgne, 1999). In a purchase decision, buyers compare similar products with substitutes; thus, understanding why the buyers would choose one substitute over another can open up new opportunities for differentiation that the buyers would value. Not all substitute products matter though; only the ones with the greatest usage should be considered. In analyzing the product subcategories, seek to understand why customers trade up or down in a product category when making a purchasing decision.

When studying the buyer groups and the buying process, look for the motivations of not only the payers, but also of the influencers and the end users. By targeting a different buyer group, such as moving the focus from the payers to the influencers or the end users, one may find potential value creation opportunities. One may redefine the customers in new ways. Very few products are used by themselves to solve a customer problem. Customers desire a total solution to address their problem or meet their need. By looking across the complementary products, one may find value creation opportunities in such products or services that detract from the new product. Untapped value in the complementary products enhances the total solution one might offer to the customers. Consider the customer's needs before, during, or after the product or service is used (see figure 2.2). One may thus redefine and enhance the customer value offering and can position the new product differently against the competitors.

Next, consider the functional-emotional orientation of the product as perceived by the customer and try to shift that orientation. If the product is traditionally a functional product, consider adding emotional appeal to it. If the product is traditionally emotionally oriented, simplify it to make a more functional product. Challenge the traditional emotional-functional orientation of a product category. Furthermore, one can, by considering the social, technological, economic, and regulatory trends, especially detecting those trends that are irreversible, find potential customer value-creating opportunities that can unlock a superior value for the customers.

Complete figure 2.2 for current products in the product category, substitute products, and complementary products, and summarize the pain points experienced by the customers. These pain points are the potential value creation opportunities when designing the customer value offering. Not all value creation opportunities, however, are equally important to the customer, nor can the new product have the capability to solve all the pain points identified. Nevertheless, solving some of these critical pain points can lower the barriers to market entry and increase the likelihood of product acceptance in the market. Furthermore, by addressing some of these pain points when formulating the customer value offering, one can create new barriers to entry and discourage potential competitors and followers from entering the market. The product features as well as the start-up's customer acquisition and retention strategy should also address these customer pain points and leverage new value creation opportunities.

In addition to the customer pain point analysis, the entrepreneur or investor should visit with potential customers. There is no substitute for a face-to-face visit to know your customers. By visiting with potential customers in the early stages of venture development, the entrepreneur or investor can identify and validate the customer pain points identified and the potential value creation opportunities, learn how customers are currently dealing with their tasks or problems the product is addressing, explore the customer's likes and dislikes concerning the existing products and solutions, understand the customer's buying decision and criteria, and generate possible ways to segment the market (Cespedes, 2012). Furthermore, customer visits in the early stages can help the entrepreneur identify early adopters, those customers who are already aware of their need, but are dissatisfied with the current product offerings and looking for alternative solutions.

Cespedes (2012) offered a seven-step approach to make customer visits more effective and productive for the entrepreneur or investor. First, clear objectives for a customer visit should be established. In step 2, a sample of potential customers is selected. In step 3, depending on the objectives of the visit, the entrepreneur or investor should decide who in the team should visit with the customer. In step 4, a discussion guide, consisting of specific topics and questions to be covered, is developed (see Cespedes, 2012, for a sample discussion guide). In step 5, conduct the visit. Most customer visits take one to two hours. During the customer visit, the entrepreneur should not try to promote their product, inquire about the price the customer is willing to pay, or ask the customer about the product features they desire. One should also avoid leading questions, which defeats the purpose of the visit to learn the customer viewpoint and identify customer pain points. In step 6, immediately after the customer visit, the entrepreneur or investor should debrief what were the customer's most important points and observations, whether the customer had any unexpected reservations, how the customer is compared to those interviewed earlier, what new ideas the customer visit stimulated, and if there is any aspect of the interview procedure that should be changed (Cespedes, 2012). In the final step, the entrepreneur should send a brief thank-you note to the customer in the week following the visit.

Visiting with potential customers and analyzing customer pain points help one to uncover several value creation opportunities to aid them when selecting the target customers and designing a resonate-focused customer value offering. The customer value differentiation opportunities derived from the customer pain points and the competitors' weaknesses can help a new venture achieve a sustainable competitive advantage and enhanced customer lock-in, resulting in a sustainable growth in scale economies and a higher return on investment for the investor (see chapter 7).

Define Customer Value Propositions

Anderson et al. (2006) offered a systematic approach to develop customer value propositions that resonate with the customers. Customer value propositions are classified into three categories, namely all-benefits, favorable points-of-difference, and resonating-focus. In the all-benefits category, customer value propositions simply include all benefits the company believes its product might deliver to its target customers. In the favorable point-of-difference category, customer value propositions include all favorable points of differentiation a product offers relative to the competing products. In the resonating-focus category, however, customer value propositions consist of two to three key points of difference and one or two points of parity that are most important to the customers and that deliver the greatest value to the customers in the foreseeable future. The resonate-focused value propositions should be the gold standard when formulating the customer value offering.

Resonate-focused value propositions do not list all the benefits or all favorable points of differentiation, but only a few selected (not more than three to five) benefits that matter most to the target customers in the near future. Moreover, resonate-focused propositions contain one or two key points of parity because customers may consider these as the minimum criteria when purchasing the product. Anderson et al. (2006) illustrated the construction of resonate-focused customer value propositions for Intergraph, a provider of engineering software to construction firms. Intergraph's product, Smartplant software, enables the customers to define the flow processes within the plants of the client firms. The product generates piping and instrumentation diagrams for the client firms of construction companies. Intergraph's competitors offer products based on an alternative drafting tool, known as CAD (computer-aided design), whereas Smartplant software offered by Intergraph is based on a relational database platform. Prior to formulating the customer value propositions, Intergraph did customer research and gathered data on what its customers value the most.

Intergraph's resonate-focused value propositions included one key point of parity and three key points of differentiation. The point of parity chosen was that, by using Smartplant, the customers could create drawings and graphics as fast as they would with the CAD-based products (i.e., the competitive products). The three points of differentiation chosen were: (1) Smartplant checks all of the customer's upstream and downstream data so that the customer avoids costly mistakes such as missing design changes or ordering the wrong equipment; (2) Smartplant is integrated with the upstream and downstream tasks, thus requiring no re-entry of data and reducing the margin of error; and (3) Smartplant enables the client to link remote offices during the project planning phase, and these tasks are eventually merged before delivering to the client (Anderson et al., 2006).

Resonate-focused value propositions are difficult to construct as the customer value formulation process involves a thorough understanding of the customer pain points and competitor weaknesses (see figure 2.2). However, resonate-focused value propositions are more effective than simply listing all the benefits or all favorable points of difference. Analyze the customer pain points identified in figure 2.2 and identify potential value creation opportunities to aid in formulation of the customer value offering. Figure 2.3 examines the customer value creation opportunities with the new product and service versus with the offerings of the competitors and substitutes. In the first column of figure 2.3, list the customer pain points identified in figure 2.2. In the next two columns, list the

Customer Pain Points	Competitor Value Propositions	Customer Value Gaps	Product Capabilities	Potential Value Creating Opportunities

Figure 2.3 Customer value creating opportunities.

competitors' value propositions (i.e., the primary benefits offered) and the customer value gaps (see figure 2.2) related to these customer pain points. In the fourth column, list the new product's capabilities related to the customer pain points. In the final column, list the potential value creation opportunities for the customers, given the product's capabilities and the customer value gaps derived from the strengths and weaknesses of the competitors to address a customer pain point.

Value-creating differentiation opportunities must be important to the target customers and profitable for the business. Each differentiation feature can potentially increase the costs of the startup and deplete its limited financial resources. Assess the capabilities of the new product vis-a-vis the competitors' products. A competitor may be strong in some of the value creating areas, moderate in some and weak in some other areas. One will thus determine the relative strengths and weaknesses of the new product offering versus the competitors' offerings. The new product should be at par with the competitors' products with regard to the essential benefits to the customers (or the points of parity) and excel in two to three areas of differentiation.

A value-creating differentiation opportunity should be distinctive, superior, important, communicable, preemptive, affordable, and profitable (Kotler and Keller, 2012). A point of differentiation must be important to the target customer and distinctive from the competitors' offerings. A point of differentiation must be superior, such that the customer cannot obtain the benefit in other ways. The differentiation opportunity must be communicable and visible to the buyers and end users. The differentiation opportunity should be also affordable, such that the customer can afford to pay for the relative advantage or benefit. The differentiation opportunity should be also profitable for the business, in that the point of differentiation can be profitably incorporated in the product's functionality. Furthermore, a value-creating differentiation opportunity should be preemptive, such that it cannot be easily copied or profitably copied by the startup's rivals.

Figure 2.3 will generate a list of customer value creation and differentiation opportunities for the new product relative to the competition. As discussed, in addition to the selected points of differentiation, the customer value definition should include the essential value features required by the customers and those currently offered by the competitors, or the key points of parity. A total of five to six resonate-focused value propositions, including the points of parity and the points of differentiation, may be selected. Note that these value propositions not only target the buyers, but the buyer groups including the payers, influencers, and end users.

In figure 2.4, the customer value propositions and related product features are chosen, and the target customer segments who value these value propositions are selected. We begin with a short list of potential target

Customer Value Differentiation Opportunities	Related Product Attributes	Customer Segment 1	Customer Segment 2	Customer Segment 3

Figure 2.4 Customer value differentiation.

customer segments. Additional potential customer segments who are currently noncustomers of similar products are identified by analyzing customer segments across the substitute industries, broad product categories, and complementary products. It is important to target those customer segments that are not currently served by the competitors or those that are dissatisfied. It is also important to understand why these customer segments are not currently served or dissatisfied. The potential customer segments thus identified are listed in the top row of figure 2.4.

A startup should not initially target the best customers or the most profitable customers of the competitors. The startup needs a focused product solution and a niche customer segment (or a foothold) to enter the market. A niche customer segment is a segment that the competitors find not worthwhile to serve profitably. Moreover, initially, it may not be profitable for the startup to serve this customer segment. But over time, the startup will develop organizational capabilities to serve this customer segment as well as other customer segments efficiently and profitably. The customer value design process thus involves selecting one or two niche customer segments and constructing three to five resonate-focused value propositions in order to lower the barriers to market entry and minimize the resistance from the competitors.

Ulwick (2002) proposed an opportunity score algorithm to rate value creation opportunities. The opportunity score represents how important a value proposition is to the customer and to what extent the customer need is not currently satisfied by the existing products and substitutes. The opportunity score for a customer value creation opportunity is assigned according to the following formula (Ulwick, 2002):

$$\text{Opportunity Score} = 2\,(\text{Importance to Customer}) - \text{Current Level of Satisfaction}$$

Notice that the importance to the customer carries twice the weight compared to the customer's current level of satisfaction with the existing products and substitutes. A company may assess the potential value creation opportunities on the basis of how important they are to the customer on a scale of one to ten (ten being most important) and to what degree the customer is currently satisfied with the existing products or solutions on a scale of one to ten (ten being highly satisfied). Consider, for example, two potential value creation opportunities such that each opportunity is rated nine out of ten from the standpoint of customer importance. However, the first customer value creation opportunity is rated six and the second is rated three from the standpoint of customer satisfaction with the existing products. If one ranks the two potential value creation opportunities according to customer importance alone, it may seem that both opportunities are equally valued by the customer. However, by applying the above opportunity score formula, the opportunity score for the first value-creating opportunity is 12 (i.e., 18–6), and the score for the second opportunity is 15 (i.e., 18–3), which thus suggests that the second value creation opportunity is ranked higher by the customer.

In figure 2.4, the first column lists the potential customer value differentiation opportunities. The second column lists the related product features that are necessary to support a point of differentiation. Make a note of the costs of developing or adding the additional product and service features if the features are not already part of the current product and service. The opportunity scores are then calculated for identified customer segments. The opportunity scores are next totaled for each customer segment and the top one or two customer segments are chosen to be targeted. These customer segments will provide the minimum resistance from the competition and increase the likelihood of the new product adoption. Within each of the selected target customer segments, the opportunity scores are then ranked to select the points of differentiation that are most important to the customer. Thus, in figure 2.4, the target customer segments and the points of differentiation are simultaneously chosen; as well, the product features necessary to support these differentiation opportunities are determined.

Furthermore, the customer value propositions can be analyzed to redefine the customer value offering by disaggregating it into its three basic elements, namely the content, the context, and the infrastructure (Rayport and Sviokla, 1994). These three elements may then be merged in new ways to reconstruct the customer value. Digital assets in the marketspace and information technology can be leveraged to improve the content, context, and infrastructure capabilities embedded in the customer value offering. Marketspace transactions leveraging digital assets are different from the physical market transactions in the conventional marketplace. In the marketspace transactions, compared to the physical marketplace transactions, the content and the context of customer transactions as well as the infrastructure that enables these transactions are different. The marketspace transactions offer lower costs to the customers as well as added convenience and a greater access, enhancing the customer value offered by the new product.

By emphasizing the content (what the company is offering), the context (how the product is used), and the enabling infrastructure (how the company enables the customer transaction), and merging these three elements in different ways the company can reformulate the customer value offering and create new value-added opportunities for their customers. By leveraging marketspace transactions, with or without physical marketplace transactions, the customer value offering can be redefined and recast. The customer needs can be better served, and the customer problem is solved more effectively and efficiently. For a new venture, digital marketspace offers a near-zero marginal cost of the product or service, creating a competitive advantage for the seller and enhancing its profits. As a result of added access and convenience for the customer, the seller can also charge a price premium. With the lower costs and a price premium for its product, the venture can achieve sustainable competitive advantage and earn increasing scale economies by leveraging digital assets in the marketspace (see chapter 7 for the potential of a business model design to generate increasing scale economies). Digital marketspace can also enable the product and market complementaries in the business model design, offering the seller and its strategic partners new opportunities to sell additional products and services in the same market or in new markets (see chapter 7 for product market complementaries).

In the digital marketspace, the three elements of the customer value offering, namely the content, context, and enabling infrastructure, can be separated and reconstructed to formulate an enhanced and powerful customer value offering, thus creating new ways of adding value to the customer. Moreover, the brand value of the product is enhanced and sustained, resulting in an increased customer loyalty. Even in mature industries or with commodity-type products, new value-added opportunities can be created by disaggregating the customer value into its three basic elements, and then re-aggregating them while leveraging the digital marketspace. Niche market segments can be also identified in a mature market, creating new growth opportunities in an otherwise mature or declining industry. Mature industries can be thus transformed and their profit potential can be altered significantly by leveraging the digital marketspace.

A well-defined, resonate-focused customer value design is critical to the venture's success. An ill-defined customer value concept can cause the venture to fail, regardless of how innovative the business model design is and how capable the management team is. In chapter 4, we construct the customer value concept model, and offer the steps to refine an existing customer value concept in order to increase the likelihood of the consumer acceptance of the new product and minimize the resistance from the competitors.

CHAPTER THREE

Market Demand

Market potential is one of the critical risks that investors consider when investing in a new venture. An entrepreneur must exercise care when estimating and justifying the addressable market size of a new product. Low-cost market research techniques can be employed to validate the market size and customer demand. Two methods are provided to estimate the addressable market size, namely, the market factor method and the market buildup method. Demand drivers can be used to estimate the segment market size when using the market buildup method. The market maturity level is critical in determining the key challenges and competitive threats. The Bass Model can forecast the demand when introducing a new product category, when historical market data are not available, or the test market results are not reliable. A startup should make its sales and revenue projections based on the revenue drivers and its sales capabilities.

Investors look for large markets with high-growth potential when qualifying new venture opportunities. In this chapter, we discuss the addressable market size estimation and the industry growth potential. We consider the four stages of the product life cycle: the introduction stage, growth stage, maturity stage, and decline stage. The growth stage of the industry can be further subdivided into the early growth stage and the late growth stage. Investors prefer to invest in an industry when it is in the growth stage, but they might consider the introduction stage when the timing is right and the market potential is large. Investors might also consider investing in the maturity stage of an industry when the product has a technology advantage that can stimulate new demand growth or take away market share from the established leaders in the industry.

Industry definition matters when one is examining the industry. In our framework, an industry includes a broad product category, whereas a market includes a specific product subcategory. A broad product category includes all products that essentially serve a set of basic customer needs in a roughly similar manner, despite their differences in appearance or designs; on the other hand, product subcategories offer distinct customer benefits and are homogeneous groups of products, such that the products in a subcategory are perceived in a similar manner by customers (Capon, 1985). In contrast to product categories and subcategories, a specific product is considered as a brand, and the products within a brand may come in different models or varieties.

Consider the beverage industry, which includes soda drinks, juices, and energy drinks, among other nonalcoholic drinks, whereas an example of a market is for a specific product subcategory such as energy drinks. Within a market category, there can be further subcategories. For example, in the energy drinks market, the product subcategories are energy shots, energy drink mixes, and regular energy drinks. A market may be segmented in several ways, such as using consumer characteristics or channel characteristics (see chapter 2 for market segmentation strategies). For example, IBISWorld (www.ibisworld.com) estimates, in the US energy drinks market, using the channel characteristics, that 60 percent of the energy drinks market constitutes convenience stores, 18 percent grocery stores and supermarkets, 14 percent mass merchandisers, 2 percent exports, and 6 percent other markets. Creative market segmentation strategies can be used to identify unserved and underserved customer segments.

The market potential for a product is the size of its addressable market (see figure 3.1); that is, the size of the market that constitutes all

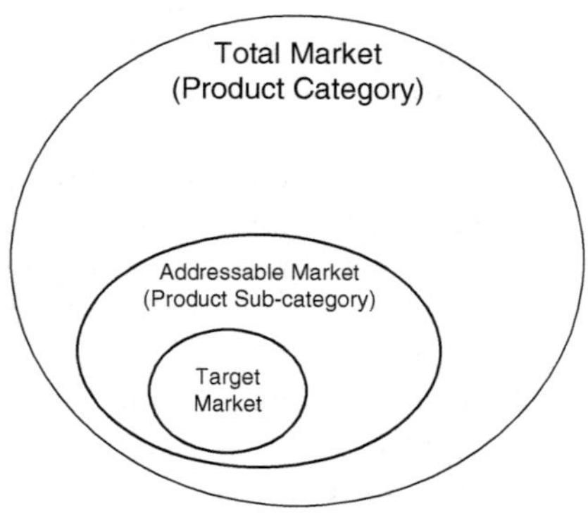

Figure 3.1 Addressable market.

customers who are interested in the product, and who are willing to purchase, 100 percent aware of the product, and fully reachable. The addressable market size for a new product is estimated assuming no competition. The total market includes all product sub-categories when the sub-categories are close substitutes of each other such that the same customer may potentially purchase from any of the sub-categories. Furthermore, a startup may choose a target market that is limited to the customer segments selected within the product's addressable market (shown in figure 3.1). The addressable market size is smaller than the total market size; and a startup's target market size is smaller than the addressable market size (see figure 3.1). The entrepreneur must exercise care when estimating the addressable and the target market sizes.

For example, consider the energy drinks market. According to IBISWorld, the total market for energy drinks in 2014 was $6.8 billion with an estimated annual growth rate of 9.7 percent. The total market size of energy drinks may not include the demand for other beverages within the broad product category including soda drinks, coffee, and other nonalcoholic drinks. Furthermore, the subcategories in the energy drinks category include regular energy drinks, energy shots, and energy drink mixes. For example, the addressable market size of a new product within the energy shots subcategory is $1.22 billion. Within the addressable market, a startup may choose to serve certain target market segments; thus, the startup's target market size is smaller than the addressable market size. For instance, the addressable market for energy shots can be segmented by major channels such as the convenience stores segment, the grocery stores and supermarket segment, the mass merchandiser segment, and the exports segment. Within the energy drinks addressable market, a startup may choose to target the grocery stores and supermarket segments. Now consider the medical devices market. The total market for medical devices in the United States in 2014 was $37.6 billion (IBISWorld at www.ibisworld.com). However, the medical devices market includes several product subcategories such as cardiovascular devices, neuromodulator devices, spinal devices, irradiation devices, respiratory devices, and other medical devices. These medical devices are not close substitutes of each other; thus, the addressable market size should not include all medical device subcategories. Considering a specific product subcategory, such as for cardiovascular devices, the addressable market for cardiovascular devices was 15 percent of the size of the total medical devices market; that is, 15 percent of the total $37.6 billion, or the addressable market size for cardiovascular devices was $5.64 billion in the United States in 2014. One should not inflate the addressable market size estimate when presenting an investment opportunity to potential investors. That will simply indicate that the entrepreneur is not familiar with the product market.

Another common problem when presenting to investors is that the entrepreneurs often claim that the market potential is huge and all they have to do is achieve a 1 percent or less share of the market. This claim is not taken seriously and is often laughed at by investors. It only shows the entrepreneur's unfamiliarity with the market and competition. Several market size estimation and demand forecasting methods are available to calculate the addressable market size. One should exercise caution when using these methods. A careful definition of the product category is critical. Thus, the addressable market that considers a product subcategory is smaller than the total market potential. The addressable market and the target market sizes are the appropriate market sizes that the entrepreneur should provide when presenting the opportunity to potential investors.

There are primarily two methods to estimate the addressable market size for a new product, namely the market factor method and the market build-up method. We discuss these methods in this chapter. Both methods should be used when estimating the addressable market size to gain maximum knowledge of the market and customer characteristics. Each estimation method makes several assumptions and is therefore prone to error. A very precise estimation of the addressable market size is not expected, but a clear definition of the served market and the assumptions underlying the market size estimate should be provided to the investors. An inflated addressable market size estimate and a vague definition of the target market certainly undermine the entrepreneur's credibility when presenting to investors. Furthermore, the demand for a product is driven by several environmental and industry-related factors. Identify the trend variables that drive the market demand and examine the impact of these trends on the market size estimate. One should test and validate the assumptions underlying the estimation of market demand before approaching investors for funding.

Cespedes et al. (2012) summarized several low-cost market research techniques a startup can use when validating the market demand assumptions. These mostly do-it-yourself, low-cost, market research techniques include customer surveys, letters of intent, product usability tests, test market trials, A/B split tests, and the net promoter score of customer satisfaction. In addition, the entrepreneur or investor should visit with potential customers to validate the customer pain points and the market potential (see chapter 2).

Short customer surveys can be used to solicit information from prospective customers on their purchasing intent and preferences, their experience and satisfaction with the existing products and solutions, the frequency of their purchase, and to validate the findings resulting from the customer pain point analysis and customer visits (see chapter 2). Customer surveys are better suited to disconfirm the demand assumptions in the early stages. The surveys are inexpensive and easy to implement. Several inexpensive online survey tools are available. However, the survey questions are often biased and difficult to write. It is also difficult to recruit enough respondents who are representative of the target customers.

A letter of intent (LOI) from a prospective customer is a way to validate the customer demand before the startup has finalized its product offering. In the LOI, a potential customer may agree to try or buy the product at a certain price point with specific features when the product is ready (Cespedes et al., 2012). The LOI is not a firm commitment, nor is it legally binding. If no prospects are willing to sign an LOI, then the customer demand and market size assumptions are flawed. The entrepreneur or investor can also learn more about the customer's needs and preferences by negotiating the product features in the LOI terms.

Product usability tests involve asking current and prospective customers to complete specific tasks with a working prototype (or an initial version of the product) in order to identify potential problems with the ease of use of the product (Cespedes et al., 2012). Product usability tests can be done during the early stages of product development to improve the product design and mitigate the risk that a flawed product design might weaken the market demand. Customer interactions with the product are recorded on a video and later analyzed. Low-cost services are available for a startup to outsource the product usability test.

Test market trials can be used to validate the market demand and refine the customer value concept. A test market trial can be limited to a specific geographic location or a subset of target market. The test offers the consumers an early version of the product at a regular price. When designing a test market trial, the entrepreneur should exercise care in selecting the test customers who are representative of the target market demographics, and consider the time and cost of managing the information flow to and from the test sites (Cespedes et al., 2012). The conversion rate obtained from a test market trial can be used to validate the market demand. The sales and marketing funnel assumes a certain conversion rate at which prospective customers who are contacted with a promotional message or by a salesperson would become paying customers (see chapter 5). A high conversion rate thus validates the market demand. The conversion rates can vary by industry. Test market results also determine the customer acquisition cost and the customer retention rate.

Furthermore, the net promoter score of customer satisfaction can be measured during the test market trial. The net promoter score is a measure to track the level of overall customer satisfaction. The entrepreneur may ask the customers (Cespedes et al., 2012), "On a scale of 0 to 10, how likely is that you would recommend our product to another person?" Those customers who score 9 or 10 are the "promoters"; those who score 7 or 8 are the "passives"; and those who score 6 or below are the "detractors." The net promoter score is then calculated as the percentage of promoters minus the percentage of detractors. Companies with high net promoter scores have low customer acquisition costs and high retention rates.

A startup should go beyond the net promoter score of customer satisfaction and may measure its customer share (see chapter 5). The customer share measure (i.e., the company's share of the customer's total patronage) assesses the effectiveness of the company's customer relationship strategy (Pine II et al., 1995). To calculate the customer share measure, however, the company should have some idea what the customer is buying from the competitors.

Furthermore, a startup may use A/B split tests with different versions of the product offered to separate test market sites to optimize the product design, validate the customer value concept, and determine a marketing program suitable for the product offering (Cespedes et al., 2012). The split tests help to identify key product features and the marketing variables. Most online ventures can easily conduct the split tests with different websites.

A startup should use above low-cost, do-it-yourself market research techniques to validate the customer demand and test the market size assumptions.

Market Maturity

Understanding the life cycle of a product category (i.e., the product life cycle) is critical in determining the key challenges and competitive threats a startup may face when entering a new market. For example, the price sensitivity of the consumer may increase along the stages of the product life cycle, thus influencing the product demand factors and the revenue drivers. The addressable market size and the demand forecasts thus depend on where the product category is in its life cycle.

Other factors that depend on the product life cycle include the need for technological innovation and the introduction of new product features. A startup's go-to-market strategy also depends upon where the product category is at its life cycle. The three critical time metrics the investors consider when investing in a startup—namely, the time to investor exit, the time to bring the product to market, and the time to achieve sustained positive cash flow—will also vary not only with the economic life of the product but also with the product life cycle.

As discussed, the product life cycle consists of the four stages of introduction, growth, maturity, and decline. The growth stage of the product life cycle may be further divided into two sub-stages (see www.ibisworld.com), namely the quantity growth (or early growth) stage and the quality growth (or late growth) stage. The quantity or early growth stage is when there are many new companies in the industry or there is a substantial technology change, whereas the quality or late growth stage is when the technologies and markets are well developed. In the quality or late growth stage, weaker companies leave the industry, whereas the stronger ones survive and prosper. The maturity stage of the product life cycle is associated with major consolidation in the industry. The economic importance of the industry remains stable during the maturity stage. Some companies, however, may introduce new products or processes to stimulate new growth in a mature industry. In the decline stage of the product life cycle, the growth declines and the economic importance of the industry shrinks.

Investors prefer to invest in a product category when it is in the growth stage of its life cycle. The key features of a high-growth product category are (see www.ibisworld.com): the industry revenue grows faster than the economy; many new companies enter the market; evidence of rapid change in technology and processes; a growing acceptance of products by customers; and a rapid introduction of new products and brands. The stage of a product life cycle is determined by the industry's growth rate relative to the Gross Domestic Product (GDP) growth rate, the growth in the number of businesses, the increase in the number of new products in the industry, the rate of technological change, and the level of customer acceptance of the products in the industry.

For example, the energy drinks market was predicted to be in the quality or late growth stage in 2014 (see www.ibisworld.com). Energy drink production was growing at an average annual rate of 10.1 percent in 2014, compared to the US GDP growth rate of 2.7 percent per year. The energy drinks industry thus outpaced the US GDP growth rate by 7.4 percent per year in 2014 (i.e., 10.1% minus 2.7%). According to

Packaged Facts (as reported by www.ibisworld.com), only a small percentage of the US population consumes energy drinks regularly, which was estimated in 2014 to be 5 percent. The high growth rate of the energy drinks industry relative to the US GDP growth rate, the low market penetration rate, and the high growth in the number of establishments in the energy drinks industry placed the energy drinks market in the quality or late growth stage in 2014. In comparison, in 2014, the coffee industry was in the maturity stage and the soda drinks industry was in the decline stage (see IBISWorld, www.ibisworld.com). The wineries industry in 2014 was in the quantity or early growth stage.

The difficulty in the product life cycle analysis is in predicting when the market demand takes off to enter the growth stage and determining when the demand slows down to enter the maturity stage. A study by Golder and Tellis (2004) found the demand takeoff and slowdown points for consumer durable products. A new consumer durable product has a pattern of rapid growth rate of 45 percent per year over the initial eight years, followed by a slowdown in growth as the industry sales decline by 15 percent per year. The demand slowdown occurs roughly at 50 percent of market penetration (also see Bass, 1969). Golder and Tellis also found that the products with a high growth in sales at the demand takeoff phase also experience a high rate of decline in sales at the demand slowdown phase. Leisure-enhancing products and services are found to have a higher demand growth rate lasting shorter time periods than do non-leisure-enhancing products or services. Furthermore, timesaving products tend to have a lower demand growth rate lasting longer time periods than non-timesaving products.

However, a quick growth phase that does not last long is known as a fad. Investors are wary of fads and do not invest in them. A fad is a product that is quickly adopted with great zeal but the demand for it declines very fast (Kotler and Keller, 2012). Fads do not satisfy a strong customer need, nor do they address a customer problem. Fads thus fail to survive in an industry after a short period. In comparison, a genuine fashion product meets a strong customer desire. It is important to distinguish fashion products from fads. A product may go out of fashion and thus the economic life of the fashion product may be short. Although a fashion product may survive for a limited time period, the product may help the startup develop a brand value quickly that can be leveraged later to launch new products. Investors may invest in genuine fashion products, but they will try to recoup their investment return quickly.

The product life cycle begins with an introduction of a new product category. Typically, the sales rise slowly. Then the demand takes off and the sales rise at an increasing rate during the quantity growth (or early growth) stage. During the quality growth (or late growth) stage, the demand continues to rise but at a decreasing rate. In the maturity stage, the demand is relatively constant. In the decline stage, the demand declines.

The introduction stage of the product life cycle begins when a new product category is introduced in the market, before there is a proven demand for the product, and even before the product has been fully proved technically (Levitt, 1965). The introduction of a new product category may follow after years of research and development by one or many organizations (Capon, 1985). Typically, there is one pioneer that introduces a new product category. However, several companies may enter during the introduction stage and jointly develop the new market. Strong research and development is a critical capability that a pioneering company may need when introducing a new product category in the market.

The pioneering company must have large resources to support the product development and market development. Furthermore, during the introduction stage of the product life cycle, there are many product and market uncertainties. Advertising to educate the customers how to use the product and personal selling efforts to inform the customers and distributors about the value of the product are critical for the category creators (Capon, 1985). It is difficult for a category creator to achieve positive cash flow and profitability quickly. The length of the introduction stage of the product life cycle can range from several months to a few years.

The early growth (or quantity growth) stage is characterized by an accelerated growth in the demand for the new product category. Several competitors would enter the industry in this stage, and by their joint marketing efforts, the demand increases more rapidly. New distribution channels may open up and the advertising emphasis shifts to brand differentiation (Capon, 1985). Prices may fall as economies of scale can be achieved with the increase in the sales volume. The quantity growth or early growth stage may not involve intense competition, as there is enough demand in the market to support several competitors.

The demand continues to increase but at a lower rate during the late growth (or quality growth) stage. A few competitors survive. Stronger competitors force weaker companies to leave the industry. The competitors seek differential advantages through market segmentation and product modification. Product variations may proliferate as competitors adapt their products to appeal to specific customer segments and meet their individual preferences (Capon, 1985). The competition may become increasingly price-based and the distribution channels become more selective in choosing the brands they want to carry. Companies use more efficient production processes to conserve financial resources to support the sales promotions and price cuts.

In the maturity stage of the product life cycle, the growth declines and the sales remain relatively constant. Most sales are made to repeat customers. Customers become more price-sensitive. Competitors segment the market based on packaging and promotion rather than on product differentiation; and the entrenched competitors lock-in the distribution channels (Capon, 1985). The scale economies and the market positions achieved by the entrenched competitors make it difficult for a new entrant to enter the market. The maturity stage of the product life cycle may last for several years. New entrants with innovative business models and superior technologies may enter the market and stimulate new demand, and thus turn around a mature industry to reenter the growth stage. An industry may thus catapult to move from a maturity stage to a new growth stage; and thus an industry may never enter the decline stage. A new product may replace an old product, but the product demand may remain stable during the maturity stage or potentially recycle back to the growth stage of the product life cycle.

By turning around a mature industry, the companies may develop new distribution channels to attract new users and stimulate the growth further. A company may re-segment a mature market to find new users and create augmented value propositions to attract the new users. New and innovative technologies may be introduced to reinvigorate the industry. In the maturity stage, thus there can be opportunities for new product introductions and channel innovations stimulating new demand and attracting new users to the industry. A mature industry can potentially recycle back to the growth stage with the rapid introduction of new technologies and innovative business models.

Levitt (1965) suggested several strategies to stimulate new demand in the maturity stage of the product life cycle, such as promoting more frequent usage of the product among current users, developing more varied usage of the product among current users, creating new users for the product, and finding new uses of the product. By shifting the product to a new category, a company in a mature industry can attract new users. Moon (2005) suggested the following two strategies for stimulating new growth in a mature industry. Service companies in a mature industry can simplify traditional complex product offerings (i.e., by reverse positioning) and thus stimulate new demand, recycling back the industry from the maturity stage to the growth stage. Consumer companies selling tangible goods (i.e., packaged goods) may position their products in a radically different product category (i.e., by breakaway positioning) to turn around the industry to shift from the maturity stage to the growth stage.

Addressable Market

Investors require an estimate and validation of the size of the addressable market. The addressable market size is smaller than the total market size (see figure 3.1). The size of the total market is the maximum sales available to a business in a product category at a given time, assuming no competition, with a 100 percent access to all channels and a 100 percent level of customer awareness. However, the size of the addressable market is the maximum sales available to a business within a product subcategory assuming no competition. A company's target market includes served market segments; the target market size is thus smaller than the addressable market size (see figure 3.1). The company's sales forecasts and revenue projections should be based on the target market size. The same estimation methods, although the degree of refinement varies, can be used to estimate the target market size and the addressable market size.

There are primarily two methods to estimate the target market and addressable market sizes for a product or service, namely the market factor method and the market buildup method. The market factor method is based on estimation by elimination, whereas the market buildup method is based on estimation by addition. In the market factor method, one starts with the total population in a geographic area and then adjusts that size by sequentially multiplying several market-qualifying factors to eliminate noncustomers to arrive at an estimate of the addressable market size. Alternatively, in the market buildup method, one decomposes the market into several customer segments and sub-segments and then counts the number of potential customers in each sub-segment and segment to arrive at an estimate of the addressable market size. The market buildup method is difficult but more accurate. One should use both methods to estimate the market size so there is not only some validation of these estimates, but also one can gain maximum insight into the market and customer characteristics. Each estimation method is prone to error and requires several assumptions.

For example, to estimate the market size of energy drinks in the United States, one may start with the total number of households in the United States and then multiply the following market-defining factors, namely the percentage of household income spent on food, the percentage of the amount spent on food that is spent on beverages, the percentage of the amount spent on beverages that is spent on nonalcoholic drinks, and the percentage of the amount spent on nonalcoholic drinks that is spent on energy drinks. The demographic data are available at the US Census, or through online demographic databases such as Gale's Demographics Now (www.demographicsnow.com) or the University of Minnesota's IPUMS project (www.ipums.org). The US Census and the IPUMS data are free. Gale's Demographics Now is available through a paid subscription but most public libraries may have access to these online demographic databases.

Alternatively, one may start with an industry analyst report, such as one from IBISWorld (www.ibisworld.com). As discussed earlier, IBISWorld estimated the total market size of energy drinks in 2014 in the United States was $6.8 billion with an annual growth rate of 9.7 percent for the next five years. The energy drinks market includes product subcategories such as regular energy drinks (i.e., 78% of the total market), energy shots (i.e., 18%), and energy drink mixes (i.e., 4%). For example, if a startup's product belongs to the energy shots subcategory, the product's addressable market size in the United States in 2014 was $1.22 billion (i.e., 18% of $6.8 billion). The energy drinks market can be further segmented by the major channels such that the convenience stores segment accounts for 60 percent, the grocery stores and supermarket segment 18 percent, the mass merchandisers segment 14 percent, and the exports segment 2 percent. Thus, if the startup's target market or served market constitutes primarily the convenience stores channel, then the startup's target market size in 2014 for energy shots was $0.73 billion (i.e., 60% of $1.22 billion). Furthermore, if one chooses initially to target the convenience stores in a particular geographic location, then the initial target market size would be even smaller. Thus, the addressable market size in the above example was $1.22 billion, not $6.8 billion. Alternatively, Packaged Facts (www.packagedfacts.com), a food and beverage industry research firm, estimated that, in 2012, 5 percent of US active adults purchased energy drinks five to seven times a month. Assuming an average retail price of $18 per pack of energy drinks, 60 percent of the US population (316 million) were active adults in 2014, and at a purchase rate of five packs a month by the 5 percent of US active adults, the estimated size of the total market for energy drinks in the United States in 2014 was $10.2 billion. Thus, the earlier total market size estimate of $6.8 billion is validated. The addressable market size, however, would be smaller depending on the product sub-category.

One should exercise caution when estimating the addressable market size, and should not inflate the addressable market size estimate simply by using industry analyst reports without making appropriate market-qualifying adjustments.

In general, the following formula estimates the market size using the market factor method:

$$\text{Market Size} = \text{Total Population} \times \prod_{i=1}^{n} \text{Market Factor}_i$$

In the above equation, Π denotes the multiplication of the market factors, whereas n is the number of market factors. To use the market factor method, one needs to identify the market-defining factors and then multiply them to the total population of customers in a geographic area. A problem with the market factor method is that these estimates are overly optimistic. The market factor method, which is based on a series of eliminating factors applied to the population in a geographic area, may include customer segments that do not have an intention to buy the product. However, the market factor method is simpler to use than the market buildup method.

The market buildup method, in contrast, decomposes the addressable market into several customer segments and sub-segments. Then one counts the number of potential customers in each segment or sub-segment, and then aggregates them to arrive at the market size estimate. A general formula to estimate the market size using the market buildup method is:

$$\text{Market Size} = \sum_{i=0}^{n} N_i * P_i * Q_i$$

In the above equation, n is the total number of customer sub-segments, N_i is the number customers in the ith customer sub-segment, P_i is the average retail price of the product in the ith customer sub-segment, and Q_i is the rate of purchase of the product in the ith customer sub-segment. For example, the energy drinks market may be decomposed into specific customer segments that may include athletes, young professionals, high school seniors, college students, and other active adults. Customer segments and sub-segments may be based on customer demographics, socio-graphics, psychographics, and behavioral characteristics (see chapter 2). A tree diagram can be used to divide the addressable market into the customer segments and sub-segments (Barnett, 1988). The customers in each sub-segment may be then identified by their demographics, and the number of customers can be then counted in each sub-segment to estimate the customer sub-segment size. Finally, the sub-segment sizes are aggregated to find the segment size, and the segment sizes are further aggregated to find the addressable market size.

Furthermore, demand drivers can be identified and used to estimate the sub-segment and segment demand when using the market buildup method. Demand drivers may include economic and industry-specific variables. Identifying the drivers of market demand is critical when estimating the market size (Barnett, 1988). Industry experts and analyst reports may be consulted to identify the demand drivers associated with a customer segment or sub-segment. For example, in the energy drinks market, the two demand drivers are per-capita disposable income and the healthy eating index (see IBISWorld). The trends in these demand drivers influence the market size estimate of energy drinks. For example, in 2014, IBISWorld expected the US per-capita disposable income and the healthy eating index to rise, suggesting that US consumers may consume more energy drinks.

After the key demand drivers related to a customer segment are identified, one may then estimate the segment market demand by using simple or multiple regressions with the historical data on the market demand in a particular customer segment and the data on the corresponding demand drivers. Thus, the regression relation generated can be used to estimate the current and future demand in each customer segment or sub-segment. The sub-segment and segment market demands are further aggregated to estimate the addressable market size. Furthermore, simulation can be employed to forecast a probabilistic estimate of the segment market size instead of a single-point estimate of the market demand (for example, see chapter 8 for an application of simulation software to estimate a probabilistic value of an output variable).

The market buildup method is more difficult to use but the market size estimate is more realistic. The market buildup method also provides more insights into the market characteristics. When the target market segments, channels, and geographies are more clearly identified, the market buildup method is not that difficult to apply. When estimating the market size, one should use both the market factor method and the market buildup method to gain maximum insight into the demand drivers underlying the market demand. Effective segmentation of the addressable market and a careful definition of the target market are essential prior to estimating the size of the addressable and target markets (see chapter 2).

The addressable market size estimate is the market potential of a product at a given time in a given market. However, the company's sales forecasts should be based on its sales and marketing program, and the likelihood of the market acceptance of its product. To estimate the sales forecasts, the top-down and bottom-up methods may be employed. In the top-down method, one has already estimated the market potential. Then, assuming one would achieve a certain percentage of the market potential over a certain time period, the sales forecasts can be made. For example, one may assume to achieve a 1 percent of the $1 billion addressable market in five years. One would then explain their rationale for how they can achieve these sales in the forecast period. Investors, however, do not prefer the top-down method when estimating the sales and revenue forecasts.

Investors prefer the bottom-up approach when forecasting the sales and revenue projections. In the bottom-up method, one identifies the revenue drivers determining the sales forecasts and explains how they aggregate the sales forecasts based on these revenue drivers over the next three-to-five-year period (see chapter 6). The entrepreneur would then explain what resources and capabilities would be needed, in terms of the channel costs, direct sales costs, advertising and promotion costs, and customer acquisition costs to achieve these bottom-up sales forecasts. For example, one may assume that they would make 15 customer contacts per quarter. Assume that the closing rate is 10 percent and an average order size is $10,000 per customer. Thus, the bottom-up sales forecast comes to $15,000 per quarter with the entrepreneur selling directly to customers. If the startup's marketing program can afford five additional salespeople, the sales forecast per quarter may increase by $75,000 (i.e., $15,000 on average per salesperson per quarter at the same customer contact rate and closing rate). If the average purchase order were larger, then the sales forecasts would be higher. Investors would like to see a bottom-up estimate of the sales and revenue forecasts in the startup's go-to-market plan. The entrepreneur should provide the investors with the details of their marketing efforts explaining how the sales figures can be realistically achieved.

It is also important to conduct a sensitivity analysis of the sales forecasts. These estimates and forecasts are based on several assumptions. The revenue drivers underlying the sales and revenue projections should be subject to a sensitivity analysis to gain the maximum insight into the customer and market behavior. The sales forecasts are based on assumptions related to the startup's revenue drivers and marketing efforts. A sensitivity analysis is necessary to gain an insight of the revenue drivers as well as into the time and resources needed to achieve the sales forecasts. Entrepreneurs are generally optimistic in their sales and revenue projections. But realistically, it takes more time and resources than what may be estimated to achieve these sales forecasts. Investors would be rightfully wary of the resources and time needed to achieve the revenue projections; therefore, by doing a sensitive analysis of the critical assumptions underlying the unit sales forecasts and revenue projections, the entrepreneur can boost the investor confidence and increase the likelihood of getting funded (see chapter 1 for building investor confidence).

The market potential risk is one of the critical risks that must be tested and validated very early, and accordingly the customer value concept must be refined (see chapter 4) prior to approaching an investor for funding. The entrepreneur must exercise care when estimating the addressable market size. More than one estimation method should be employed to validate the market size estimate and to gain maximum knowledge of the customer and market characteristics. Moreover, a careful approach to market segmentation and an accurate definition of the served market are required prior to estimating the addressable market size.

New Product Category

Rogers (1962) developed a theory of new product adoption. Rogers divided the potential buyers into five groups, namely innovators, early adopters, early majority, late majority, and laggards. Innovators are most venturesome and daring to try a new product. Innovators and early adopters are the buyers who decide to purchase a new product independently of the actions of other buyers. Early majority (i.e., the early growth stage) occurs when the industry growth takes off and late majority (i.e., the late growth stage) occurs when the industry growth is at its peak. Laggards are the buyers who buy the product after the market reaches the maturity stage. Rogers provided subjective estimates of the sizes of these five groups of buyers. The size of the innovators group is roughly 2.5 percent of the total number of potential buyers for a new product; and the size of the early adopters group is roughly about 13.5 percent of the market potential. Together, the early demand of a new product in the introduction stage of the product life cycle can comprise up to 16 percent of the total market potential. The early majority buyers in the early growth stage comprise roughly about 34 percent of the market potential, the late majority buyers about 34 percent, and the laggards about 16 percent (Rogers, 1962).

According to Rogers (1962), the innovators are thus the first buyers of a new product. These buyers tend to be financially privileged and socially mobile, read magazines and journals regularly, and more willing to try something new (Capon, 1985). Their purchase behavior, however, do not influence others. In contrast, the early adopters, who may be prominent in their communities, are respected for their opinion and their purchasing decisions can influence others. The early majority buyers are slow to try a new product, and these buyers are influenced by the opinions of the early adopters and purchase the product during the quantity or early growth stage. Moon (2005) suggested a stealth positioning strategy for a company in the introduction stage of the product life cycle, to re-position its product from a category that the customers might resist to a more desirable category that is less intimidating. The late majority buyers enter the market during the late growth and maturity stages. The late majority buyers are price-sensitive and wait to purchase a product after the product prices have fallen. The laggards are traditionalists and their purchases are governed by long-established habits (Capon, 1985). Advertising is not needed to persuade the laggard buyers. The laggards purchase the product in the maturity and decline stages of the product life cycle.

Bass (1969) offered a simple model to forecast the number of initial purchases of an innovative product when the product is under development, there is no historical market data available for the new product category, or the test market data is not reliable. Test market data for a breakthrough product category is often not reliable. The number of initial purchases gives the number of first-time buyers of the product category. The Bass Model predicts the timing and likelihood of the purchase of an innovative product, and forecasts a year-by-year demand for the product category. The Bass Model thus estimates the number of potential first-time buyers of a new product category in each period.

Bass (1969) divided potential buyers into two broad groups, namely innovators and imitators. The main distinction between Bass's two groups is that the first group, the innovators, makes the purchase decision independent of the actions of others; whereas the second group, the imitators, is influenced by the decisions of other buyers. Furthermore, the Bass Model provides a forecast of the yearly demand by first-time buyers of a new product category. These yearly forecasts are for the aggregate demand for an innovative product category in a market, and not an individual company's market share or sales forecast for a new product. Market share of individual companies can be estimated from the total market demand based on the company's competitive attributes and the effectiveness of its marketing program. The advantage of the Bass Model is that the yearly aggregate demand forecasts can be made for a new product category without the need of historical sales data.

The total number of potential buyers in an addressable market is one of the inputs into the Bass Model. The total number of potential buyers can be estimated using the market buildup method or the market factor method for a substitute or an analog product (i.e., a product serves a similar customer base as the new product). In the previous section, the addressable market size was estimated in the number of units sold or the dollar value of sales. Using the market buildup formula, without multiplying the average price and the rate of purchase of the product, the total number of potential buyers of the analog product in an addressable market can be estimated. The market factor method can also be used to estimate the total number of potential buyers in an addressable market.

The Bass Model predicts that the likelihood, $P(T)$, of an initial purchase of a new product made at a particular time, T, is a linear function of the number of previous buyers of the product. The likelihood of a first-time purchase by a buyer is (Bass, 1969):

$$P(T) = p + (q/m)*Y(T)$$

In the above equation, $P(T)$ is the probability of a purchase by a first time buyer at time T; $Y(T)$ is the number of previous buyers who purchased the product prior to time T; and p, q, and m are the three parameters of the Bass Model. With these three parameters, the Bass Model can predict the yearly forecasts of a new product's demand without the need for historical market data.

The first parameter, p, is the coefficient of innovation, or the rate of purchases made by the innovator group of buyers who make purchase decisions independent of others. The second parameter, q, is the coefficient of imitation, or the rate of purchases made by the imitator group of buyers whose purchase decision is influenced by the actions of other buyers. The third parameter, m, is the total number of potential buyers in the addressable market, which can be estimated either by the market factor method or by the market buildup method as explained in the previous section. In general, the q value will be greater than the p value; that is, the rate of purchase by the imitators will be higher than the rate of purchase by the innovators. In some cases, however, when the new product category takes off rapidly or the product demand slows down quickly, the p value will be higher than the q value.

The new product demand forecast at time T, or the number of first time buyers who may purchase the new product at time T, is given by (Bass, 1969):

$$S(T) = P(T)*[m - Y(T)]$$

In the above equation, $S(T)$ is the number of initial purchases or the first-time buyers at time T; $P(T)$ is the probability of purchase at time T as defined in the preceding equation; m is the total number of potential buyers in the market; and $Y(T)$ is the number of previous buyers prior to time T. Note that in the above two equations, $Y(1)$ is zero; that is, prior to year 1, there are no previous buyers. The above two equations are simple to use when we have the values of the three inputs to the Bass Model, namely m, p, and q. Furthermore, the Bass Model predicts the number of potential first time buyers when the demand reaches its peak, or $S(T*)$, is:

$$S(T*) = \frac{m(p+q)^2}{4q}$$

Thus, for a new product, $S(T*)$ can be calculated, given the values of the three parameters, m, p, and q. The Bass Model predicts that the market demand would reach its peak at about 50 percent market penetration.

Figure 3.2 shows the values of the coefficients, p and q, for several innovative product categories. These values may be used in the Bass Model equations to predict the demand for similar product categories. Thus, when predicting the demand forecast for a new product, first find an analog product from the product categories listed in figure 3.2, and use those p and q values, along with an estimate of the market potential (m), in the Bass Model to make the aggregate yearly demand projections. Analog products may be chosen based on the product characteristics as well the customer characteristics. If the analog product category is not listed in figure 3.2 but the analog product's historical sales data are available, then the p and q values can be derived with a simple regression of the analog product's sales data over time. There are also several online resources that provide the p and q values for the Bass Model to be used for various product categories.

The first two parameters, the p and q values of an analog product category, can be used in the Bass Model in the $P(T)$ and $S(T)$ equations that were described earlier. The third parameter, m, is the total number of potential buyers, which can be estimated by the market buildup method

Product Categories	Coefficient of Innovation	Coefficient of Imitation
Refrigerators	0.025	0.126
Calculators	0.143	0.520
CD Player	0.055	0.378
Personal Computer	0.121	0.281
Water Softners	0.018	0.297
Power Lawnmowers	0.009	0.338
Coffee Makers	0.017	0.301
Clothes Dryers	0.017	0.357
Black and White Television	0.028	0.251
Cellular Telephone	0.008	0.421
Cable Television Service	0.100	0.060
Handheld Organizer	0.043	0.565
MP3 Player	0.009	0.783

Figure 3.2 Bass model coefficients.

Note: See Bass (1969), Ofek (2005a), and Ofek (2005b).

or the market factor method. In the market buildup method, one will first decompose the market into a number of potential customer segments and sub-segments and then estimate the number of potential buyers in each segment and total them. In the market factor method, one will start with the total population in a geographical area and then eliminate noncustomers by multiplying the market-defining factors qualifying the potential market.

We illustrate the use of the Bass Model with an example (Ofek, 2005b). Ofek provided the data available in 2004 to use in the Bass Model to predict the demand for e-books (or electronic books). E-books can be purchased from online retailers (e.g., Amazon.com), and downloaded to dedicated e-book readers (e.g., Amazon's Kindle), portable tablets (e.g., Apple's iPad), or one's personal computer. To use the Bass Model, we need to find the three values, m, p, and q. Ofek (2005b) provided the data: The US population in 2004 was estimated at 293.7 million; the number of households in the United States was 113.3 million; the internet usage rate in the United States was 67.8 percent; and the US population reading literature and recreational books was 46.7 percent. Furthermore, the likelihood of the US population reading recreational books and literature on dedicated e-book readers was estimated to be 28 percent, and the likelihood of reading the same on other portable devices was 12 percent;

and thus together there was a 40 percent likelihood that the US population would read electronic books either on a dedicated e-book reader or on other portable devices.

The market factor method can be used to estimate the value of *m* in the Bass Model. Thus, the total number of potential buyers for e-books in the United States in 2004 was the total US population (293.7 million) multiplied by the three market factors, namely the percent of the US population reading literature (46.7%), the internet usage rate in the United States (67.8%), and the likelihood that a consumer would read electronic books (40%). The estimated value of *m*, or the number of potential buyers of e-books in 2004, was then 37.2 million. Note that the value of *m* may change in subsequent years and the Bass Model forecasts should be refined later as more information becomes available on the market factors. Alternatively, the market buildup method could have been used to arrive at the total number of potential buyers of e-books or an estimate of *m*.

To select the values of *p* and *q*, one may refer to figure 3.2 for analog product categories. Several choices are available such an MP3 player, handheld organizers, and so on. A careful selection of analog product categories should be made based on comparable product and market characteristics; and if more than one analog product is chosen, then the weighted average values of *p* and *q* can be derived. To keep the calculations simple, we may choose handheld organizers as an analog product. Thus, the selected *p* and *q* values for e-books, using the handheld organizer as an analog, are 0.043 and 0.565, respectively (see figure 3.2). Thus, we have obtained the three parameters, *m*, *p*, and *q*, for the Bass Model equations described earlier, to estimate *P*(*T*) and *S*(*T*).

Figure 3.3 shows the forecasts of *S*(*T*) (i.e., the number of first time buyers of e-books) for 2005–2014, and *D*(*T*) (i.e., the yearly demand forecasts for e-books) assuming an average rate of purchase of three e-books per buyer per year. In figure 3.3, *P*(*T*) is the likelihood of an e-book purchase made at time *T*, and *N*(*T*) is the cumulative number of buyers at time *T*. Note also that the number of e-book buyers was predicted to peak in 2010. These demand forecasts can be revised in subsequent years when the value of *m* or the addressable market size is refined. The Bass Model is simple to use and is recommended for forecasting the demand for an innovative product category.

During the introduction stage of the product life cycle, there are only a few customers who are willing to try the products in a new category. In the introduction stage, as discussed earlier, the companies would spend heavily on educating the customers, increasing customer awareness of the new product category, and promoting the trial of new products. The

Year	P(T)	S(T) (in millions)	N(T) (in millions)	D(T) (in millions)
2005	0.04	1.60	1.60	4.80
2006	0.07	2.40	4.00	7.19
2007	0.10	3.44	7.44	10.33
2008	0.16	4.64	12.08	13.93
2009	0.23	5.69	17.77	17.07
2010	0.31	6.08	23.85	18.24
2011	0.41	5.41	29.26	16.23
2012	0.49	3.87	33.13	11.61
2013	0.55	2.22	35.35	6.67
2014	0.58	1.07	36.42	3.21

Figure 3.3 Demand forecast for e-books.

resources needed for market development and product development are huge. The likelihood of the success of a new product category would depend on the degree of the change needed in the customer behavior and the relative advantages offered by the new product (see chapter 4). Very few venture capital investors are willing to bet on new industries or willing to spend heavily on educating customers to promote the introduction of a new product category, unless the market potential is huge and the investor has sufficient resources to develop the new market.

A startup may introduce a new product subcategory and stimulate growth in a mature industry. For example, Keurig, a manufacturer of coffee makers, created a new product subcategory with its single-cup, pod-style coffee brewing machine, as an alternative to messy coffeepot brewing machines (Yoon and Deeken, 2013). In this case, consumers widely accepted the new product and were willing to pay for the speed, cleanliness, and convenience. Yoon and Deeken examined how lucrative new product categories and subcategories are, and found that thirteen out of the one hundred fastest growing companies in the United States created new product categories that accounted for 53 percent of their revenue growth and 74 percent of their market capitalization growth over the three-year period studied. Product category and subcategory creators with innovative products having significant relative advantage may experience faster growth and receive higher valuations from their investors. Category creators could become smash hits or long hauls (or sure failures), depending on the new product's relative advantages and the product's compatibility with the customer's usage behavior (see chapter 4).

Sometimes, category creators experiment with several products and channels before they arrive at a final innovative product. Redbox, a kiosk-based DVD rental company, which has kiosks placed in grocery stores, started with a vending machine for such products as prepaid credit cards, gift cards, and photo processing services (Yoon and Deeken, 2013). However, when Coinstar, the parent company of Redbox, bought Redbox and put their kiosks in grocery stores to rent movie DVDs, the service became a smash hit. Sometimes the entrepreneur may need experimentation with several products before discovering an innovative product and determining the right channel. To come up with an innovative product, first identify the customer pain points by analyzing the customer experience with similar and substitute products in order to understand how customers become aware of their need, how customers consider and select the product, how the product is paid for and delivered, how the product is used and serviced, and how the product is disposed of and replenished. Identifying the customer pain points using the consumption chain analysis (see chapter 2) and through experimentation with alternative product concepts, the entrepreneur can determine a relative advantage of a new product that meets the customer expectations and that the customer will value.

CHAPTER FOUR

Is the Opportunity Real and Large Enough? Refine the Customer Value Concept

This chapter presents a framework and tools to assess and refine the customer value concept. The three key questions the entrepreneur may ask when reformulating the customer value concept are whether the customer pain is real and widespread, whether the relative advantage of the new product is superior enough for the product to sell, and whether the customer is willing to pay for the relative advantage of the product. The customer value concept should be refined to maximize the likelihood of the new product's acceptance in the market. The target customer group may need to be redefined. The relative advantage of a new product should be superior to compensate for the entrepreneur's self-selection bias and the consumer's loss aversion bias. A framework is provided to determine the competitive price of a product. The seller may charge a price premium for a new product when the perceived value of the product is significantly greater than the cost to serve the customer.

Getting the customer value concept right is critical to the success of the business. The customer value defines the target customers and a set of value propositions to meet the needs of the customers (see chapter 2), and does so simultaneously. If the customer value formulation is flawed or ill defined, the startup is likely to fail. To select the target customers and formulate the resonate-focused value propositions, the entrepreneur must be thoroughly familiar with the target market and the competition, including the customer segments that are currently dissatisfied with the existing product offerings and the customer segments that are underserved with unmet needs. The entrepreneur must have an in-depth knowledge both of the competition, and of the strengths and weaknesses of the competitors. A startup with scarce financial resources cannot serve all customer segments; thus, the startup must choose to target one or two customer segments such that it can maximize the likelihood of its product acceptance in the market and minimize the resistance from the competitors.

A customer segment is a group of customers with shared characteristics. Each customer segment is thus a homogeneous group of customers. Furthermore, customers include not only end users, but also other groups such as buyers, payers, and influencers. Influencers directly or indirectly influence the purchasing decision. The buyer follows the purchasing criteria when buying a product or service, and the payer pays. The end user, the buyer, the payer, and the influencer can be the same person or different persons, and their needs and motivations may also be different. It is important to identify these customer groups in each customer segment and understand the needs and desires of these groups. By understanding the needs of the customer groups and their purchasing criteria, the entrepreneur can appropriately define the customer value concept (see chapter 2).

Market segmentation strategies are used to identify and select customer segments. There are several market segmentation strategies available, based on the customer demographics, psychographics, sociographics, and behavioral characteristics. Other creative segmentation strategies such as customer value-added and job-to-be-done approaches can be utilized (see chapter 2). The idea is to identify one or two customer segments that are currently dissatisfied or underserved by the competitors' product offerings, and then formulate a customer value offering that provides a total solution to meet the needs or solve the problem of these dissatisfied customer segments.

The customer value concept (see figure 4.1) formulated correctly minimizes the customer demand risk and increases the likelihood of the product acceptance in the market. The customer demand risk must be tested early and removed; and the customer value concept must be proven to be working prior to approaching the investor for funding. Positive test marketing results or a proof of sales can mitigate the customer risks, validating the critical assumptions underlying the customer value concept. As shown in figure 4.1, the customer pain point identified is central to the customer value design. The customer value concept links the unit cost of the product (or the cost to serve the customer segment), the relative advantage of the product as perceived by the customer, the selected product features, and the price point, to the identified customer pain points.

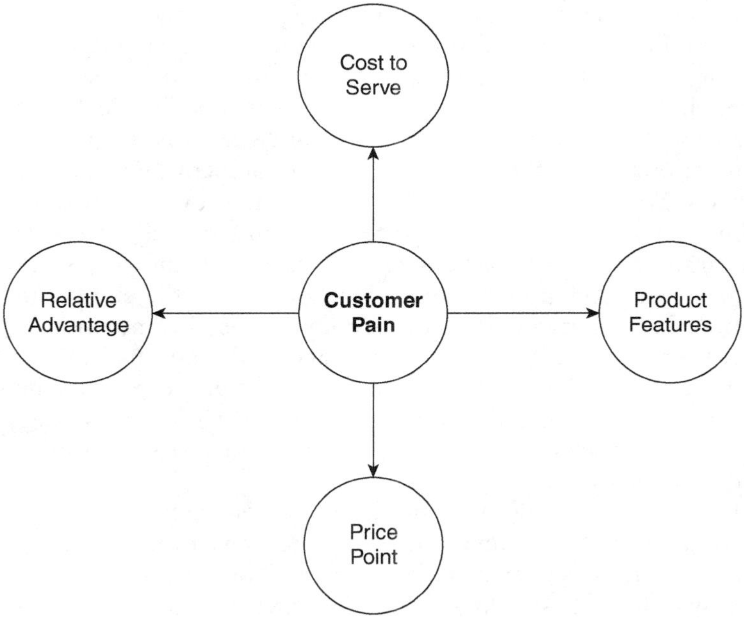

Figure 4.1 Customer value design.

The customer pain points and competitors' weaknesses are identified in chapter 2. The customer experience with the product category, substitute products, and complementary products are analyzed, and the customer pain points are identified (see chapter 2). The customer value concept should address one or two significant customer pain points. These customer pain points selected should drive the relative advantage of the product and the construction of the resonate-focused value propositions. The customer value concept should thus address the customer pain points that are significant and widespread (see the next section). The competitors' weaknesses are also key to constructing the customer value concept. The customer value concept should include a superior relative advantage of the product at a competitive price point determined by the perceived value and the cost to serve (see later in the chapter). The market potential and addressable market are examined in chapter 3. The relative advantage and the likelihood of customer demand for a product are assessed later in the chapter.

Furthermore, the competition risk, which is a dominant risk after the product launch, can limit the demand for the new product and the profitability potential of the venture. Competition always exists, may it be direct, indirect, or potential. Indirect competition arises from substitute products. The direct competition is from the existing similar businesses; and the potential competition is from potential new entrants. Even though a product is a new category and currently there is no direct competition, the startup may have indirect competition from substitute products. The customer need, if it is real, is met by current direct and indirect competitors, albeit imperfectly or inefficiently. The entrepreneur must understand the basis of competition, or the points of parity and differentiation among the products offered by the competitors. To examine and understand the basis of competition, the entrepreneur may choose three to five close competitors and study their business strategy and processes, such as the customers they serve, the primary benefits their products provide, the channels they use, their pricing strategy, and their customer acquisition and retention strategies (see chapter 2 for competitor analysis).

Identifying and understanding the customer segments that are currently served by the competitors is the first step in the selection of the target customers one may choose to serve. The current customer segments give an understanding of how the market is currently segmented. One may then use different segmentation strategies to identify potential customer segments whose needs are not met adequately. Primary benefits or the product features offered by the competitors may not be adequate or efficient in getting the customer's job done or addressing the customer problem. Similarly, the channels used by the competitors may not be efficient or adequate to meet the needs and desires of the customer groups consisting of buyers, payers, influencers, and end users. The underserved customer groups can be identified by the entrepreneur and the new channels can be found to reach the underserved customer groups. It is important to understand the customer acquisition and retention strategies of the key competitors. The strengths and weaknesses of the competitors can be assessed and potential customer value creation opportunities can then be uncovered.

The pricing strategy of the competitors and the price-performance tradeoffs by the target customers can limit the price point the entrepreneur may set for the product offering. The price of the competitive products in the target customer segments must be determined. Understanding the current pricing strategies and revenue models helps the entrepreneur devise a new pricing structure and an innovative revenue model as well. Analyzing the weaknesses of the competition can help the entrepreneur identify where the barriers-to-entry are weak, such that a point of entry can be selected and a go-to-market strategy can be developed by the startup in order to maximize the likelihood of the new product acceptance and minimize the retaliation from the competitors (see chapter 5 for go-to-market strategy).

Creative segmentation strategies can be employed to identify the dissatisfied and underserved customer segments. In addition to looking within a product category to find the underserved or unserved customer segments, one may look across substitute-product industries, product subcategories, complementary product offerings, the functional-emotional orientation of the product, and the current social and technological trends. One may identify potential new customer segments within and across the industries that are not currently served by the competitors' product offerings. A startup should not initially target the best customers or the most profitable customers of the competitors.

In chapter 2, a framework is provided to analyze and understand the customer experience with a product in order to identify the customer pain points. Understanding the customer experience with similar products, substitute products, and complementary products can help the entrepreneur uncover numerous value-creation and differentiation opportunities for the new product offering. Every link in the consumption chain or every step of the customer experience may include customer pain points that can offer value creation and differentiation opportunities in order to reformulate the customer value offering such that the likelihood of the new product acceptance is maximized. The consumption chain captures the entire experience of the customer with a product, namely how the customers become aware of their need, how they find a product, how they consider and select a product, how they order and purchase a product, how they pay for the product, how the product is delivered and installed, how the product is stored and moved around, how the product is used and what help the customer might need in using the product, how the customer can return or exchange the product, and how the product can be repaired, disposed of, or replenished (Macmillan and McGrath, 1997).

Identify the customer pain points from the analysis of the customer experience with similar products, substitute products, and complementary products (see figure 2.2 in chapter 2). Understanding the customer pain points helps the entrepreneur uncover potential value creation and differentiation opportunities. One would then select three to five potential value creation opportunities wherein the new product has the capability to address customer pain points and solve the customer problem effectively and efficiently. Each value creation opportunity can be further decomposed into three basic elements, namely the content, the context, and the enabling infrastructure (Rayport and Sviokla, 1994); and then the three basic elements can be redefined and reconstituted to form powerful and compelling value propositions for the target customers. Digital assets and the Internet can also be leveraged to redefine these three basic elements of the customer value offering.

When constructing resonate-focused value propositions, from a list of three to five potential differentiation opportunities, one may finally choose one to two significant points of differentiation based on the opportunity scores (see chapter 2 for an opportunity algorithm to weigh and rank the potential value creation opportunities). A point of differentiation chosen should be distinctive, superior, important, communicable, preemptive, affordable, and profitable (Kotler and Keller, 2012). The opportunity scores are assigned from the perspective of the target customers. The opportunity scores weigh a customer value creation opportunity not only from the standpoint of customer importance, but also from the standpoint of competitor offerings. The product features can be then selected to deliver the chosen points of differentiation, and the relative advantage thus created may increase the likelihood of the new product acceptance in the market.

Is the Customer Pain Real and Widespread?

Customer value links the customer need to the product capability. Customer value serves the customer need. The first question is thus whether the customer need is real. The customer risk arises when the customer need targeted or the customer pain point identified is not real. If the startup has current sales, then it may be easier to assess the customer risk by analyzing the quantity and quality of the current sales. A potential investor would like to know how much the startup has sold in the last 12 months, who these customers are, what the average purchase order size is, whether these customers reordered, and so on. If the startup has no current sales, it can be more difficult to assess the customer risk.

Often the entrepreneur is passionate about their product, and a friendly focus group put together by the entrepreneur may be encouraging and supportive of the new product. In either case, there is no reliable proof that the customer need exists or the customer pain is widespread. This is a problem of self-selection; that is, if the entrepreneur or their friends and family like the product, they are assuming the market also would like the product and the customers would purchase the product. Indeed, the market and customers may not share the entrepreneur's values, and thus the customer pain identified by the entrepreneur may simply be an outlier. There may not be enough customers with the same need or who share the same values.

Webvan, an online grocery delivery service that went bankrupt in 2001, is a well-known example to understand the self-selection problem associated with the entrepreneurial optimism (Gourville, 2006). Investors invested more than a billion dollars in the company but Webvan failed to attract a sufficient number of customers. A typical grocery customer who enjoyed the selection and shopping experience at a local grocery store didn't share the convenience value offered by Webvan. In comparison, around the same time period, Amazon, another online retailer selling books and music, became a blockbuster success. At Amazon.com store, a wider selection of books and music are available for consumers to sample and purchase, which is not possible at a physical bookstore. In this case, the book buyers share the same values with Amazon. The customer pain was real and widespread in the case of the book buyers.

How would one address the customer demand risk when defining the customer value? The customer demand risk is that the customer need may not be real or the customer may not share the same values as the entrepreneur. One may need to reconsider the product concept and the customer value design. Map the product's capabilities to potential customer needs; one may then choose a customer segment that has the greatest likelihood of product acceptance. The target customer may thus need to be redefined.

Consider Bright Horizons, a workplace childcare provider (Brown, 2001). The childcare industry is one of the most unattractive industries with chronically low operating margins. The childcare industry also uses little proprietary technology, offers very few economies of scale, has very weak barriers-to-entry, and is burdened with heavy government oversight. Traditional childcare businesses target the parents of younger children up to five-year-olds. These parents are skeptical of the childcare facilities and fear the poor quality of services they may receive for their children. The operating margins are so low that most of these facilities have a hard time hiring good quality teachers and staff. There is not enough money available to hire sufficient teachers and thus the teacher-to-child ratio is low, resulting in poor quality of care for the children.

Roger and Linda Brown, a husband and wife entrepreneurial team, ventured to enter the industry, and founded Bright Horizons in 1986. At Bright Horizons, Roger and Linda decided to redefine their primary customers as the workplace employers, not the parents of younger children. They partnered with their customers, who appreciated the value of offering quality childcare to their employees so that the employees do not have to leave early to pick up their children or come late because they have to drop off their children on their way to work. Initially, the partnering corporations feared the potential liability of providing childcare in their premises, but that problem was easily solved by securing a high level of liability insurance coverage, almost fifty times the industry standard level, and indemnifying the partnering corporations. Bright Horizons, by enhancing the operating leverage and capital leverage (see chapter 7), could boost the return on investment for its investors, in spite of a low operating margin, and was able to secure a sizable capital investment from Bain Capital and Bessemer Venture Partners, in an industry not amenable to venture capital investors.

Another example is a nursing informatics software product that was targeted to hospitals offering to improve nursing care and patient satisfaction in hospitals and homecare facilities. The software offers a nurse, while providing care to a patient at a hospital or home, the ability to access information on the best care strategies in a given situation. The nurse also records the type of care she provides to the patient and the hospital records the feedback from the patient as well. The software updates the patient data so that improved care can be provided to another patient in the future in a similar situation. Improved care at a hospital would also boost its reputation and ranking, improving its revenues and patient satisfaction. A satisfied patient will return to the hospital. The entrepreneur was excited about the potential value of the product. However, when contacted, the hospitals did not show a great interest in the product. One problem was the potential liability of the hospitals, as the software would record the good as well as bad care provided by the nurses. Nurses were also reluctant to adopt the product, as they would be penalized for their poor performance when there was patient dissatisfaction recorded by the product.

A solution in the above case was to redefine the customer and thus the customer value offered. Instead of targeting hospitals, the software could be used to train the nurses in nursing schools and provide continuing education to nurses outside the hospital environment. A nursing school may adopt the product to train its student nurses in a simulated environment. Staff nurses, to meet their certification and continuing education requirements, can also use the software to practice in a simulated environment and receive the continuing education credits. Thus, the nursing informatics product had a technology capability but it did not target the right customers. However, after redefining its target customers from hospitals to nursing schools and education and reconstructing the customer value proposition from improving patient satisfaction to aiding nursing education, the likelihood of market acceptance of the nursing informatics product was enhanced.

A business opportunity is not scalable if the customer pain is not widespread or the addressable market size is too small. Investors prefer to invest in scalable, high-growth businesses. According to IBISWorld (www.ibisworld.com), the key features of a high-growth industry are industry revenue growing faster than the economy, many new companies entering the market, a rapid change in technology, a growing acceptance of new products, and a rapid introduction of new product brands. Growth can be also stimulated in mature industries by introducing new technologies and innovative business models. The addressable market size and the industry growth opportunities must be assessed carefully when defining the customer value. The addressable market for a product should be large and growing, such that the market size risk, or the risk that the market size may be less than anticipated, is mitigated.

An industry typically goes through four stages of development, namely the introduction stage, the growth stage, the maturity stage, and the decline stage. The growth stage is further divided into two sub-stages, namely the quantity growth stage (i.e., early growth) and the quality growth stage (i.e., late growth). The quantity growth stage is when there are many new companies entering the market. The quality growth stage is when the products and technologies are well developed and the industry growth is of high economic importance. In the quality growth stage, the weaker companies leave the industry and the stronger ones survive and prosper.

The difficulty in predicting the demand growth is in how to know when the market demand takes off when entering the growth stage and when the demand slows down for the market to enter the maturity stage. Bass (1969) showed that, with a new product, the demand slowdown could occur roughly at 50 percent of market penetration. The new products that experience a high growth in sales at the time of demand takeoff may also experience a high rate of decline at demand slowdown. Leisure-enhancing products and services have a higher demand growth rate lasting shorter time periods, whereas timesaving products tend to have a lower demand growth rate lasting longer time periods (Golder and Tellis, 2004).

The size of the addressable market for a product is the maximum sales available to a business at a given time, assuming no competition, a 100 percent access to all channels, and a 100 percent level of customer awareness for the product. However, the size of the target market is the sales available from the served customer segments. The size of the target market is smaller than the size of the addressable market. The methods used to estimate the market size is similar in both cases; however, the underlying assumptions would be different.

There are two primary methods to estimate the market size: the market factor method and the market buildup method. In the market factor method, one starts with the total population and eliminates noncustomer segments by multiplying the market-defining factors to arrive at the addressable market size. In the market buildup method, the market is decomposed into several customer segments and sub-segments, and then the customers are counted in each segment and sub-segment and totaled to arrive at the addressable market size. The market buildup method is more accurate than the market factor method, since it is difficult to eliminate all noncustomers using the market factor method. Thus, a problem with the market factor method is that the market size estimate is overly optimistic; however, it is simpler to use the market factor method. An entrepreneur should use both methods to arrive at the addressable market size in order to gain maximum insight into the customer and market characteristics and the underlying demand drivers.

During a new product introduction, the market demand is limited as there are only a few customers who are willing to try the new product. To generate demand, businesses may need to spend heavily to educate the customers. Many new products fail, especially the ones known as fads. A fad is a product that is quickly adopted with great zeal but the demand for it declines very fast. Fads do not satisfy a strong customer need. In contrast, a fashion product meets a strong customer desire. Like fads, fashion products experience rapid demand decline, but during this short economic life it can help a startup develop the brand value that can be later be leveraged when introducing new products.

Furthermore, the Bass Model (Bass, 1969) may be used to forecast the demand for a new product category for which historical sales data are not available or the test market data are not reliable. The Bass Model predicts the number of first-time buyers of a new product category. The buyers may be grouped into two categories, namely innovators and imitators. Innovators are the buyers whose purchase decision is independent of others, whereas imitators are the buyers whose purchase decision is influenced by others. To use the Bass Model (see chapter 3), one would need three parameters: the coefficient of innovation (p), the coefficient of imitation (q), and the total number of potential buyers (m). The values of p and q, also known as the Bass coefficients, can be obtained from several online sources for comparable product categories. To estimate the demand for a new product category, one may choose comparable products based on the product and market characteristics. The third parameter, *m*, the number of potential first-time buyers, can be estimated using the market factor method or the market buildup method as described earlier. The Bass Model can be used to forecast the demand for a new product category and estimate the likelihood of a purchase of the new product in a given period (see chapter 3).

Is the Relative Advantage of the Product Superior Enough?

Rogers (1962) developed a theory of new product adoption and proposed five factors to guide the marketing strategy to increase the likelihood of a new product acceptance in a market. The five factors include the new product's relative advantage, its compatibility with the existing usage, the ease of use of the product, the observability of the new product usage, and the new product trialability. Rogers assessed the relative advantage of a new product over the existing products. Compatibility is assessed by the extent to which the new product is compatible with the current usage experience of the customer. The easier it is to use the product, the greater is the likelihood of new product adoption. The other two factors, namely usage observability and product trialability, refer to promoting customer awareness of the product. Furthermore, new product trials encourage new product adoption. The more visible the product usage to potential customers and the greater the number of customers who would try the new product, the greater is the likelihood of the new product acceptance in the market.

Using a normal distribution, Gourville (2006) showed that the value (or the customer value) assigned to a product by a typical consumer falls in the middle two-thirds of the normal distribution, whereas the entrepreneur's estimation of the value of the product may fall in the top 5 percentile of the normal distribution. The behavioral theory postulates that consumers psychologically overweigh their losses (relative to a change in the current usage behavior) when compared with their gains from the relative advantage offered by the new product (Gourville, 2006). For example, Kahneman and Tversky (1979) estimated that the overweighting of losses could be two to three times the gains the consumers may receive from the relative advantage of a product, a consumer bias known as "loss aversion." There are also switching costs the customers may incur when changing from the current product to a new product.

The consumer's gains and losses are measured relative to a reference point, such that the reference point could be the current products the consumer is using or the consumer's expected product.

Gourville (2006) defined the reference point for consumer gains and losses relative to the current product the consumer is using. However, in our framework, we will measure the reference point with respect to the consumer's expected product. When a current product meets the customer expectations, the current product is the same as the expected product. Accordingly, consumer gains and losses are calculated relative to the customer's expected product. With the expected product, a consumer is willing to change their behavior when the current products fall short of meeting their expectations. The expected product definition thus creates opportunities as well as challenges for an entrepreneur when deciding the customer value propositions and the product features.

An expected product is different from the generic product (Levitt, 1980). The generic product includes all tangible or visible product attributes, whereas the expected product, in addition, includes intangible benefits such as the customer's buying and usage experience. In chapter 2, the target customer's buying and usage experience is examined, which helps one to identify customer pain points and the features of an expected product. In our framework, if the customer's current experience with an existing product is painful, the customer is more willing to try a new product. The product benefit differentiation and the customer value creation opportunity thus follow the customer's expectations, and the expected product features includes the selected points of differentiation, in addition to the generic product attributes.

Note that the reference point for consumer gains and losses not only varies by the expected product requirements, but also by the type of customer targeted, in that an expected product for one customer group could be a generic product for another customer group. A reference point for consumer gains and losses is thus determined by the customer definition and the attributes of the customer's expected product. The gains and losses can be assessed relative to the customer's expected product. The consumer may overweigh the losses, relative to an expected product, in an order of magnitude of two to three times the gains. The concept of the expected product provides new opportunities to offer differentiation when the current products fall short of meeting the customer expectations. However, when the customer expectations are met by the current products, a new product must exceed the expected product by an order of magnitude of several times to increase the likelihood of the new product acceptance in the market.

We use the definition of an expected product to determine the relative advantage of a product. Determining the reference point relative to the expected product is critical in assessing how superior is the relative advantage of a new product. Figure 4.2, adapted from Gourville (2006), uses the relative advantage of the product and its compatibility with the customer usage to assess the likelihood of the new product acceptance in the market. The relative advantage of a new product is assessed with respect to the customer's expected product, whereas the product compatibility is assessed with respect to the customer's usage of the current products. Figure 4.2 predicts the likelihood of success of a new product. When the relative advantage of a new product is low and the compatibility with the existing usage is low, the new product will be a certain failure, as shown in figure 4.2. These products not only fall short of the customer's expectations but also would require a significant change in the customer behavior. When a new product falls in this quadrant (i.e., a sure failure), a different customer segment should be chosen and the customer value needs to be redefined (see chapter 2).

When the new product's relative advantage is low but the compatibility with the existing usage is high, the new product is an easy sell. This is a quadrant for a startup to make an initial entry into the market. When

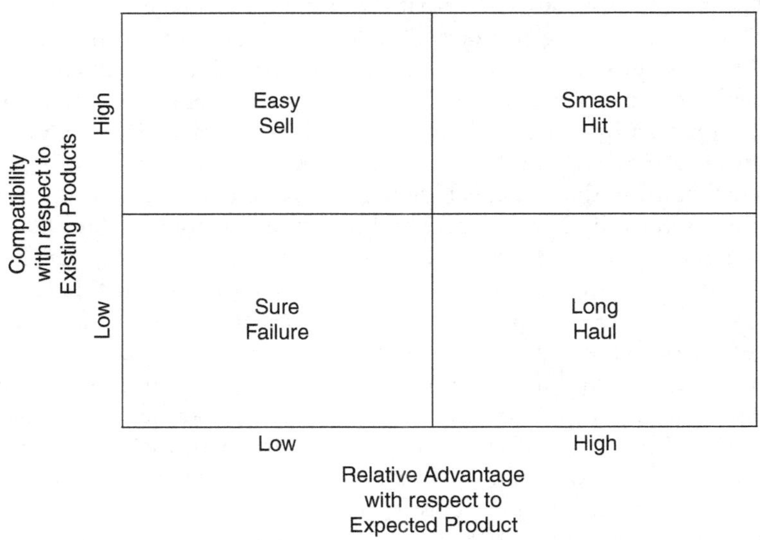

Figure 4.2 Customer demand.

Note: Adapted from Gourville (2006).

the relative advantage of a new product is high but the compatibility with existing usage is low, the product is a long haul. These products would take long time to achieve market acceptance, and would require heavy investment in educating the customers on the value of the product and showing them how to use the product. Several breakthrough innovations and high-technology products we use today, such as satellite television and telephones, fell into this category when they were first introduced. Few investors will invest in the long-haul products unless the market demand is so large that it justifies the investment. The e-book (i.e., electronic books) is another product that falls in the long-haul category (see chapter 3).

The most attractive category of new products, such that the likelihood of product acceptance is maximized, is when the relative advantage of the new product is high and the compatibility with the current usage is high. These products are smash hits, requiring few changes in customer behavior and meeting the customer's expectations significantly. For example, consider Google's search engine. When the product was introduced, a user hardly noticed any difference using Google's search engine when compared to the existing search engines, but the relative advantage of Google's search engine (with respect to the customer expectations) was clearly superior.

Gourville (2006) suggested that the relative advantage of a new product over the existing products should be at least nine times superior for the new product to succeed in the market, which he called "the 9x effect." Consumers overvalue the benefits from an existing product over a new product by a factor of three, and at the same time the entrepreneur overvalues the new product over the existing products by a factor of three; thus arises the "9x effect" of the mismatch between how the entrepreneur values the new product and how the customers value the same product. Consumers undervalue a new product because they are skeptical about the performance of the new product, they are unable to value the need for the new product, they may be satisfied with the existing products, or they overweight the benefits of the existing products. At the same time, the entrepreneur is convinced that their new product works and that there is a need for the new product; they themselves are dissatisfied with the existing products (i.e., the entrepreneur's self-selection bias discussed earlier) and think that the new product meets the customer's expectations better than the existing products.

Consider a startup, Littlewunz, which developed an infrared bottle warmer to heat the liquid in baby bottles. The infrared bottle warmer is more efficient and can provide more consistent heating of the fluid than the existing baby bottle warmers in the market. The current bottle warmers take twenty minutes to warm a baby bottle in the car and about five minutes at home. The infrared bottle warmer can warm a baby bottle in less than five minutes whether in the car or at home. The infrared technology can also provide a consistent heating temperature to the fluid in the baby bottle. The entrepreneur owned a patent to the technology and was excited about the customer value the product offered. But the problem was the entrepreneur's self-selection bias; although the entrepreneur was excited about the technology's potential to be used in a baby bottle warmer, most new parents may not purchase a baby bottle warmer that is heated by the infrared technology. Most parents may not feel that the infrared heating is safe when warming up the baby food (i.e., the perceived value of the product may undermine the product sales).

One way to solve the problem in the above case is to redefine the customer value offered by the consistent heating capability of the infrared technology. A team of students at Florida Atlantic University, who worked on redefining the customer value, identified that the real capability of the product or technology is the infrared heating element that can quickly and consistently heat a liquid. By mapping the technology's capability to potential market needs, the students discovered that redefining the target customers from parents purchasing baby bottle warmers to on-the-go coffee drinkers may offer an attractive customer value and increase the likelihood of product acceptance, as on-the-go coffee drinkers might value the consistent and quick heating advantage of the infrared technology. The consistent and controlled heating capability of the infrared technology can also preserve the flavor when the coffee is reheated.

The customer value, in the above case, was reformulated with a new customer segment (i.e., on the go coffee drinkers) and a set of new customer value propositions, such that there is a greater likelihood of product acceptance in the market. Thus, by mapping the technology's capability to a new customer pain point, one could maximize the relative advantage of the product and thus redefine the customer value. The infrared technology can keep the hot coffee at a consistent temperature for a few hours without the coffee losing its flavor or tasting bad. An infrared warmer can stop heating the coffee just prior to when the coffee reaches the boiling temperature that causes the coffee to lose its flavor. Current coffee warmers in the market cannot provide this value. The relative advantage of the new product must be several times superior to the existing products for the new product to succeed in the market.

Is the Customer Willing to Pay for the Relative Advantage?

The customer pain point may be real and the relative advantage of the product may be superior, but the customer may not find the product's value worth the price. A startup needs to decide a price point for the product when formulating the customer value offering. The price point of a new product is not always set as the lowest price point relative to the competitors' product offerings. Sometimes the lowest price point may signal that the product or service is of a lower quality. It is possible that the consumer may pay for a product directly or indirectly. For example, the product may be free for the consumer, but the usage rate and the size of user base may attract potential advertisers to pay for the product. Google's search engine is free for the users, but the advertisers pay Google to advertise their products and services on Google page views.

Consider Bright Horizons, a workplace childcare provider, an example discussed earlier. Traditional childcare providers competed on price and costs by charging a lower price to parents and reducing the operating costs by paying less to teachers. In comparison, Bright Horizons chose to uphold its commitment to providing high quality childcare, paid its teachers 30 percent above the industry average compensation, and offered a first-rate curriculum to the children. Bright Horizons adhered to the strict accreditation standards set by the National Association for the Education of Young Children. Bright Horizons set its price point higher. To receive a higher price point, Bright Horizons redefined its target customers from parents to their employers and at the same time constructed a customer value offering such that the employers were willing to pay more for the high quality childcare for their employees. The employers valued the relative advantage of high quality childcare as a means to increase employee productivity and retention.

The value received by a customer must exceed the price the customer is willing to pay. Customers compare the price of a new product with the prices of competitive products when purchasing the new product. The competitive price of a product is the maximum price the customer is willing to pay in a competitive market. Suppose V_0 is the perceived value of a new product's benefits to the customer and C_0 is the company's unit cost to serve the customer. The competitive price of a product is limited by the product's value added in a competitive market.

The cost to serve (Shapiro et al., 1987) includes product presale costs, manufacturing costs, distribution costs, and post-sale service costs. Presale costs can vary from one customer account to another, and depend on the nature of the product or service. Some products need a greater time and capital investment in the presale activities before a purchase order is received. The manufacturing cost is the cost of goods, which depends on the order size, product features, packaging, manufacturing location, and inventory requirements. The distribution cost depends on the distribution channel utilized and the location of the customer. Post-sale service costs include the costs of customer service, warranty, repair, customer relationship, and so on.

Let V_c be the perceived value of the benefits with the closest competitive product and C_c is the competitor's cost to serve the customer. The new product's relative value differential (ΔD_0) compared to the closest competitive product then equals, $(V_0 - C_0) - (V_c - C_c)$. Let ΔV_0 measure the new product's benefit differential (i.e., $V_0 - V_c$), and ΔC_0 measure the unit cost differential (i.e., $C_0 - C_c$), relative to the competitive product. By rearranging, the product's relative value differential, ΔD_0, equals, $\Delta V_0 - \Delta C_0$. The unit price of the product cannot exceed $P*$ as given by the following competitive price equation:

$$P* = \text{Min } \{C_0 + \Delta D_0; V_0)$$

The customer will pay a price that is the minimum of two values: (1) the cost to serve the customer plus the product's relative value differential, and (2) the perceived value of the benefits of the product. For example, consider the value of the new product's benefits to the customer is \$10 per unit; thus, the customer is willing to pay a price up to \$10 per unit for the product. The company's cost to serve the customer is \$4 per unit. The cost to serve for a competitive product is \$5 per unit and the perceived value of the benefits offered by the competitive product is \$8 per unit. Then, the benefit differential of the product relative to the competition (ΔV_0) is \$2 per unit (i.e., \$10 minus \$8), and the cost differential (ΔC_0) is −\$1 (i.e., \$4 minus \$5). The new product's relative value differential (ΔD_0) is thus \$3 per unit (i.e., \$2 minus −\$1). The maximum value added by the product cannot exceed the relative value differential or \$3 per unit. In this example, using the competitive price equation as shown above, the customer will not be willing to pay more than \$7 per unit (i.e., \$4 cost per unit plus \$3 value differential), although the value of the new product's benefits to the customer is \$10 per unit. As long as the competition exists, it is difficult to set a price point for the product above \$7 per unit. The competitive price equation thus determines the unit price the customer is willing to pay in a competitive market.

In the above example, the competitive price of the new product exceeds the company's cost to serve the customer. But it is not always the case. Consider another example. Suppose the perceived value of the new product's benefits to the customer is \$6 per unit and the company's cost to serve the customer is \$4 per unit. Suppose also that the cost to serve the customer for the competitor is \$5 per unit, and the value of the benefits offered by the competitive product is \$8 per unit. Then, the benefit differential of the new product relative to the competition (ΔV_0) is −\$2 per unit (i.e., \$6 minus \$8), and the cost differential (ΔC_0) is −\$1 (i.e., \$4 minus \$5). The new product's relative value differential (ΔD_0) is thus −\$1 per unit (i.e., −\$2 minus −\$1). Using the competitive price equation, one may estimate that the customer will not be willing to pay more than \$3 per unit (i.e., \$4 cost per unit plus −\$1 value differential) in a competitive market, although the value of the new product's benefits to the customer is \$6 per unit. In this example, the competitive price point (\$3) is less than the cost to serve the customer (\$4). To increase the customer's willingness to pay a higher price such that it exceeds the unit cost to serve the customer, the company needs to lower its unit cost to serve the customer or boost the perceived value of its product's benefits.

In figure 4.3, the perceived value of the product is plotted versus the cost to serve the customer. The lower the cost to serve and the higher the perceived value of the product, the higher is the power of the seller (see figure 4.3). The perceived value of the product versus the cost to serve determines the power of the seller, but it alone does not determine the price of the new product. The perceived value of the new product is a major determinant of the product price. In figure 4.3, when the perceived value of the product is greater than the cost to serve, the seller has more power in setting the price and the buyer has less power. However, when the perceived value of the product is less than the cost to serve, the buyer has more power than the seller does. The greater the new product's relative value differential (ΔD_0), the greater is the seller power or the lower is the buyer power. In figure 4.3, the space above the breakeven value line is where the buyer has less power and the seller has more power when determining the product price. The space below the breakeven value line is where the buyer has more power, the space the seller should avoid.

When a new product falls in the space below the breakeven value line (see figure 4.3), there would be a need for an investment in educating the customers in order to enhance the perceived value of the new product. Furthermore, the greater the relative advantage of the product and the higher the customer switching costs (e.g., with a proprietary technology

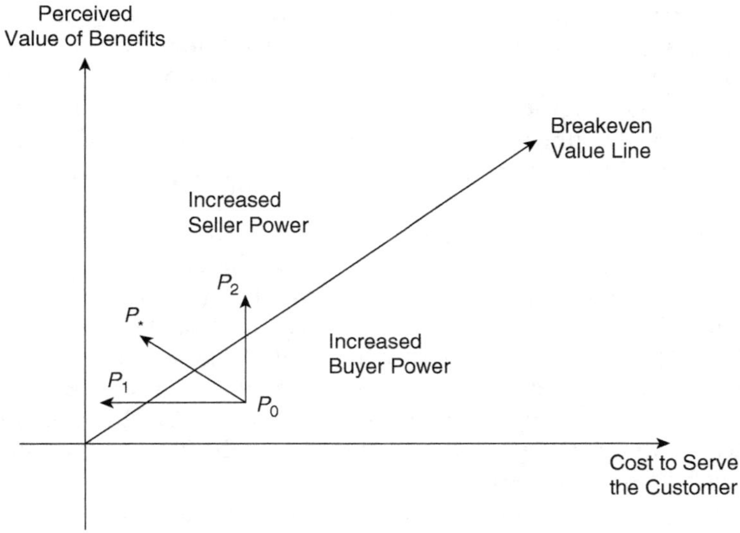

Figure 4.3 Product price determination.

or an exclusive strategic partner), the greater is the seller power and the greater is the relative value differential included in the price of the product. Also, the more price sensitive the customer, the less power the seller has, and the product price will fall below the breakeven value line. Then there is a need to increase an investment in customer awareness of the value of the new product to move the price point to the space above the breakeven value line. Furthermore, lowering the cost to serve by outsourcing the noncritical but costly operations, or boosting the perceived value of the product by bundling with complementary products and services, can help the seller to set the price in the space above the breakeven value line.

Initially, as shown in figure 4.3, a startup might set the price of a new product below the breakeven value line, for example, at P_0. The price point can be later moved to P_1 in the space above the breakeven value line by reducing the cost to serve by outsourcing some of the operations and by achieving operational efficiency and scale economies. The price point can be moved to P_2 in the space above the breakeven value line by an investment in increasing customer awareness of the value of the new product and thus boosting the perceived value. The final price point, P_*, would lie in the space above the breakeven value line, somewhere between P_1 and P_2 (see figure 4.3).

One may not always set the price of a product at par with the average competitive price or the lowest average price in the market. The greater the product's relative value differential and the lower the cost to serve the customer segment, the greater is the price the customer would be willing to pay in a competitive market (see figure 4.3). An entrepreneur may use the competitive price equation when determining the price of a new product in a given customer segment.

Pricing structure is as important as the price point itself. Dolan (1995) proposed an eight-step process to determine the pricing structure for a new product. The steps are: (1) assess value the customers place on the product; (2) consider variation in the perceived value of the product; (3) assess price sensitivity in each consumer segment; (4) identify an optimal pricing structure; (5) consider potential competitive reaction; (6) monitor the pricing terms at the transaction level; (7) consider consumer's emotional response; and (8) analyze whether the revenues are worth the cost to serve the customer.

Fitting the pricing structure to the customer value concept is critical. The pricing structure must be consistent with the business model design, namely the sales and revenue model, the target cost structure, the value chain, and the customer relationship strategy (see chapter 5). When determining the pricing structure, the first step is to assess how the customers would value the product and what value the customers may place on the product (Dolan, 1995). In the second step, look for the variation in the way the customers would value the product. The product may have a higher perceived value in a particular customer segment than for an average customer. An entrepreneur can spot the perceived value difference in the marketplace by assessing whether the customers vary in their intensity of use, whether the customers use the product differently, and whether the product performance may matter more to some customers (Dolan, 1995). In such cases, when the market is large enough, it is better to set customized prices and terms for the separate customer segments. The essential product features may or may not have to be altered to meet the customer value requirements.

The next step is to assess the consumer's price sensitivity. Price sensitivity of a customer segment is influenced by three important factors, namely customer economics, customer search and usage, and the competition (Dolan, 1995). In terms of customer economics, price sensitivity increases to the degree that the end user bears the cost as opposed to a third party, the cost of the product or service represents a substantial percentage of the customer's total expenditure, the buyer is an intermediary who sells their end product in a competitive market, or the customers are able to judge the product performance without using the price as an indicator. Furthermore, the customer's search for and usage of the product can influence the price sensitivity to the degree that the customers can easily compare the relative performance and prices of alternative products, the customer can take the time to find a product or can wait to receive the product, it is easy to make comparisons with alternative products, or the customer can switch to another supplier without incurring additional costs. Finally, with respect to the competition, the consumer's price sensitivity increases when there is limited difference between the performance of the products in a given category, or when a long term relationship with the seller or its reputation are not important considerations in the buyer's decision to purchase the product.

When determining the optimal pricing structure, the company must decide either to price the individual components of the product or service, or to price the product or service as a bundle (Dolan, 1995). With complementary products (e.g., the printer and toner, the razor and blades, etc.), the seller may price an individual component low but lock-in the customer to sell them the higher priced ancillary components later. Furthermore, configuring and pricing a product bundle is critical when the value of the product bundle varies less across the customer segments than do the individual products within the bundle.

The next step is to consider the potential reaction from the competitors. The company should ask itself what it would do if it were the competitor (Dolan, 1995). Any pricing action a company takes would provoke some competitor reaction. The company must consider how its competitors would respond to its pricing strategy. Price wars should be avoided. A brilliant pricing strategy can often be a foolish one if it is going to trigger a price war. The competitors' reaction may not be limited only to a price war; the competitor may bolster its advertising and marketing program to protect its market share. The company must anticipate the competitors' reactions and have an effective response to those reactions when deciding the product pricing.

The product may have a list price, but the final price to the customer varies with a set of pricing terms and conditions the company may offer, such as quantity discounts, early payment discount, special rebates, and other incentives. The seller should also consider the customer's emotional response when determining the product price. Every purchase transaction influences how a customer thinks about the product and talks to others about it (Dolan, 1995). Customer perception of fair pricing of the product is important to the company's reputation and its brand value. If a customer believes that the company's product is unfairly priced, the negative review by the customer can be devastating to the company's future sales.

In the final step when determining the product price, consider whether the revenues are worth the cost to serve a customer segment (see figure 4.3). The customer's perceived value is important when pricing a new product, but the seller should also consider the cost to serve the customer segment, if not initially, certainly after the business model is stabilized. High cost-to-serve customer accounts are sustainable when these customers highly value the product and are willing to pay a higher price.

The following questions may further help an entrepreneur when determining the pricing structure for a new product (Skarzynski and Gibson, 2008): (1) whether the pricing structure can be altered without unprofitably penalizing some customers; (2) whether the pricing structure can be closely aligned with what the customers actually value; (3) whether the pricing paradigm in a particular industry can be broken; and (4) whether the cost to serve the product can be lowered without jeopardizing the perceived value of the product.

The product price is highly correlated with the product's value differential relative to the competition. Pricing decision is critical to the customer value design and to the business model design, but the price point is one of the most difficult aspects of the customer value concept to pin down. The entrepreneur must consider all aspects of the pricing decision as outlined in the above steps to get closer to the "right" price (Dolan, 1995). The company must determine the product price a customer segment is willing to pay in a competitive market. The right pricing strategy is more critical than just getting the price right. An entrepreneur should follow all the above steps when deciding the pricing structure for a new product.

PART III

Is the Business Model Efficient and Sustainable?

CHAPTER FIVE

Business Model Design

A business model creates, delivers, monetizes, and sustains customer value. The more efficient and sustainable the business model, the lower is the uncertainty of the cash flow and the greater is the venture valuation. The greater the customer, supplier, and strategic partner lock-in, the more sustainable is the business model design. In this chapter, a framework is provided to configure the value chain and supply chain configuration to meet the customer demand efficiently and effectively. Activity-based costing may be employed to analyze and estimate the cost structure and identify the cost drivers. The five-force analysis can be used to identify the critical success factors that a startup may consider when configuring the value chain. The more indirect and sustained the attack on the competitors, the more effective is the startup's go-to-market strategy. Several revenue models and their implementation challenges are examined. In a sustained business model, the gross margin on a product must exceed twice the ratio of the customer acquisition cost to the customer lifetime value. A business model design with a high gross margin and high operating leverage is more investable. The customer share measure can assess the effectiveness of the customer engagement strategy.

A business model describes the revenue model, the cost structure, the resources and activities required, and the customer acquisition and retention strategy. The business model is built on the customer value concept. A well-defined customer value concept is therefore critical to the business model design (see chapter 4, figure 4.1). The business model design consists of the underlying value chain (i.e., the value-added activities), the revenue streams and the cost structure, and the strategy to differentiate and sustain the customer value. A business model thus describes how one proposes to create, deliver, monetize, and sustain customer value.

A business model design must be efficient and sustainable for the venture to succeed in a new market.

Investors look for ways to shorten the time to achieve sustained positive cash flow and the path to profitability. Investors want to understand a startup's path to profitability, including the challenges and opportunities lying therein. The time to bring the product to market (including the path to market), and the time to achieve sustained positive cash flow (including the path to profitability) are the key metrics to assess the effectiveness of an efficient and sustainable business model design. The sooner the business model can achieve positive cash flow and profitability, the more efficient and sustainable is the business model design. An important indicator of an efficient business model design is the gross margin (i.e., the net sales minus the cost of goods). A business model with a high gross margin is more scalable. The greater the product's gross margin, the higher is the valuation multiple the investors will pay for the business. Investors look for a high gross margin (in excess of 50%), unless there are opportunities to enhance the business model's operating leverage (see chapter 7). Furthermore, the higher the customer acquisition cost, the higher should be the gross margin of the product.

A new venture can create entry barriers, and thus sustain customer value, by securing scarce resources, investing preemptively in certain capabilities, generating network effects, and developing cost advantages. A new venture needs more than the cost advantage and efficiency to sustain customer value and succeed in a new market. The business model design should provide supplier and customer lock-in. The business model lock-in is achieved when the business model creates strong customer incentives for repeat purchases and increases the customer switching costs for alternative products and substitutes (Amit and Zott, 2001; Mishra and Zachary, 2014).

Furthermore, the business model design should provide product market complementaries. The product market complementaries are achieved when the business model can support the sale of additional products in the existing market, when the adjacent markets can be served with the same product with minor changes in the product features, or when there are present additional channels the company can use to deliver the existing product in the same market or adjacent markets. The business model elements including operating efficiency, differential advantage, supplier and customer lock-in, and product market complementaries are interrelated, and each element of the business model design feeds back positively to reinforce the other elements to create a sustainable competitive advantage and generate sustainable scale economies (see chapter 7). The elements of the business model design should be carefully configured to shorten the time to bring the product to market as well as the time to achieve sustained positive cash flow.

Several approaches to the business model design exist. For example, Kim and Mauborgne (2000) offered a three-step approach to the business model design: (1) which price model should be used; (2) what is the target cost; and (3) who should be the partners. The target cost is set in line with the target price point. To meet the target cost point, the value chain activities can be reconfigured and the supply chain partners can be chosen, such that high-cost, low-value activities can be eliminated, reduced, or outsourced. When setting the price point, alternative revenue models should be considered; if one revenue model does not work, another model can be tried. For example, Blockbuster Video achieved success by changing its revenue model from selling to renting a video. In another approach to the business model design, Yoon and Deeken (2013) proposed that the business model is comprised of three elements, namely a production model (how they make it), a distribution model (how they deliver it), and a profit model (how they make money).

Sometimes the business model is defined as a revenue model; that is, how the business earns revenues. For example, a recently popular business model is the "freemium" model, in which the basic features of the product are available for free or at a low cost, and the premium features are available for purchase. But the freemium model is really a revenue model, not a business model. A survey by the Economist reported in 2005 that 50 percent of senior corporate executives believed that the business model innovation is more important for the product success than the product innovation by itself (Johnson et al., 2008). However, the problem often is in defining and understanding the company's business model.

Johnson et al. (2008) illustrated the business model innovation with an example of Tata Motors' Nano, a compact car at an affordable price as a replacement for alternative motor vehicles such as scooters and motor bikes that were prevalent in India. Ratan Tata, chairman of Tata Group, understood the customer need of providing a safer vehicle alternative to scooters and motor bikes for India's large middle-class families. The smallest car then available in India was five times more expensive than a scooter. Tata's customer value definition was to provide an affordable, safer alternative to families who used a scooter or motorbike for transportation.

Johnson et al. (2008) identified four common barriers that can keep the customers from getting a critical need met. These barriers the customers face are insufficient wealth, access, skill, and time; however, these customer barriers can be overcome through an innovative customer value offering and an efficient business model design. In the case of Tata Motors, the customer's wealth barrier was overcome by offering a car at an affordable price to those who then rode a scooter. Tata set a target price of $2,500 per car, which was less than half the price of the cheapest car then available in India. Tata had to figure out how to make and deliver a car at the target price point. It required a significant change in the product cost structure when making and marketing the car. Tata knew that it would make money by selling to a large addressable market. To make a significant change in the cost structure, Tata had to figure out the changes required in the key resources and processes in making and delivering the car, from how the car was designed and manufactured, to how it was distributed.

Tata Motors thus set a target price point of $2,500 per car. Next, Tata figured out a cost structure to make and deliver the car at that price point, and found the partners from whom the parts were outsourced. A company does not have to possess all resources and capabilities necessary in making and delivering a product to its target customers. Some of the resources and capabilities can be obtained from strategic partners and supply chain partners. Thus, an efficient business model can be designed to create and deliver powerful customer value by reconfiguring the existing value chain, supply chain, pricing model, and cost structure. Tata reconfigured its value chain to save on the costs by eliminating the unneeded features of the car and outsourcing most of the parts, and so could offer an affordable competitive price to its target customer base.

The business model innovation can be also combined with product innovation. Yoon and Deeken (2013) proposed that a business that combines product innovation (what they serve) with the business model innovation (how they serve) creates new product categories and can achieve faster growth and greater profitability. The category creators experience a faster growth and receive higher valuations from investors. Yoon and Deeken found that only 13 percent of Fortune 100 companies would be classified as category creators, but these companies accounted for 74 percent of Fortune 100 companies' total market capitalization. When senior executives of large companies were asked why they wouldn't pursue a category creation (i.e., product innovation combined with business model innovation), their answers were: (1) startups are better at creating breakthrough innovations; (2) we cannot afford to do this; or (3) our market is mature or our customers don't want to try new things.

However, startups as well as large companies can become category creators, as seen in the cases of Apple's iPod/iTunes product and Microsoft's Xbox live gaming system. Microsoft's Xbox Live created an online gaming service using a subscription-based pricing model. Microsoft offers a better customer experience and a great customer value, an online gaming experience such that players can play and compete with one another at a low annual subscription price, which is about the price of a single video game. Microsoft partners with several content providers—such as Netflix, YouTube, Hulu, ESPN, and so on—to provide more content through its Xbox system. Microsoft makes money from the sale of Xbox consoles and annual subscriptions.

Apple's iPod/iTunes was another example of a breakthrough product and business model innovation. Apple took a great technology innovation and combined it with a great business model (Johnson et al., 2008). Apple was not the first company to bring digital music to market. Diamond Multimedia introduced a similar product in 1998 and Best Data in 2000. Both of these products were also innovative and stylistic; however, these products didn't succeed in the market because of their poor business model design (i.e., the way the customer value was delivered). In comparison, Apple's iPod/iTunes product became a spectacular success. Apple sold $10 billion in three years after the product launch in 2003. The product success was not only because of an innovative and stylistic product (i.e., iPod), but also because of an innovative business model design, specifically how the music was delivered online to the devices (using iTunes), by making downloading music easy and convenient through the iTunes platform.

There are primarily two types of business models: the faster-better-cheaper model and the brave-new-world model. The faster-better-cheaper model is for technologies with incremental innovation and serves the market segments with a known demand for products; on the other hand, the brave-new-world model is for technologies with breakthrough innovation and serves the market segments with an unknown demand for products. The brave-new-world business model is often used for introducing new product categories in unproven markets, which is inherently riskier than the faster-better-cheaper model. With brave-new-world business models, it is even more difficult to assess the entrepreneur's ability and incentives to execute the business strategy.

Many investors prefer to invest in faster-better-cheaper business models coupled with the entrepreneurs' known abilities. Brave-new-world business models are riskier but they provide increasing scale economies and a high rate of return to the investor, in that there is a first-mover advantage with these models due to high customer switching costs and positive network effects (see chapter 7 for business model scalability and increasing scale economies). Brave-new-world business models with first-mover advantage can yield high rewards. However, these ventures are unprofitable for a long period of time, so the investor must have enough capital or an access to a network of investors with enough capital to fund the venture.

A flawed business model design can cause business failure. Furthermore, a business model design based on an ill-defined customer value concept can lead to business failure. The operating margin (i.e., the operating cash flow divided by the net sales) and the time to achieve sustained positive cash flow are key performance measures to assess and monitor the business model efficiency and sustainability. The more efficient and sustainable the business model design, the less uncertain is the operating cash flow and the greater is the venture's valuation. Cash flow is important to the survival and growth of the business, and is an important metric for investors to monitor venture performance. The value of a business is a function of the cash flow, the timing of the cash flow, and the risk of the cash flow. The business model design explains how the venture cash flow is generated, when the cash flow is generated, and how the cash flow risk is mitigated. Investors place a value on a business based on the capability of its business model to generate and sustain positive cash flow, and thus the business model design is key to the investor's valuation of the business. A key metric of the quality of the business model of a startup is the time to achieve sustained positive cash flow. Investors, when investing in a startup, consider how soon the startup can achieve positive cash flow. The sooner the startup can achieve sustained positive cash flow, the faster is the time to investor exit and the greater is the venture's current valuation.

The business model is configured after the customer value is clearly defined. Customer value is defined by the customer value concept (see chapter 4); that is, it is defined by the target customers and the value offered to the target customers. The business model design then explains how the customer value is created and delivered, how the business makes money in the process, and how the business sustains and grows the cash flow. How the business sustains and grows the cash flow is often considered the role of business strategy. However, the business strategy, in our framework, is an integral part of the business model design. The business strategy determines how a business model can respond to potential competitive threats and market opportunities to secure a competitive advantage, sustain, and grow the operating cash flow.

In this chapter, we determine the critical success factors to increase the likelihood of a new product acceptance, and for the startup to erect new barriers to secure a competitive advantage. We examine the five market forces and the current trends to determine the critical success factors for a startup in a given industry (Porter, 2008). The five-force analysis uncovers positive and negative factors impacting the profitability potential of a new venture. The five competitive forces and the current trends help the entrepreneur to identify potential competitive threats and opportunities for a startup. The critical success factors drive the business model design. The critical success factors are also important when preparing the investor's risk mitigation plan and the venture's operating plan, and in choosing the key performance indicators to monitor the venture performance (see chapters 6 and 8). A risk mitigation plan increases the likelihood of the venture's survival and growth (see chapter 8 for how to prepare a risk mitigation plan). The venture operating plan determines the stage milestones for the venture and the key activities and resources to achieve these stage milestones (see chapter 6 for how to prepare an operating plan and determine the startup's operating and capital budget).

Figure 5.1 explains the configuration of a business model design, from formulating the customer value concept to determining the value chain configuration to the business model design. The four components of the business model design, based on the underlying value chain, are the revenue model, the financial model, the customer engagement model, and the cost structure. The four components of the business model design are built on the customer value concept and the corresponding value chain. The value chain determines the key activities and the resources and capabilities necessary for those activities. The critical success factors drive the business model design including the value chain configuration and the four components of the business model design (see figure 5.1). The customer engagement model component describes the venture's market entry strategies or the customer acquisition and retention strategies. The value chain configuration also determines the cost structure. The sales and revenue model is an integral part of the business model design. The business model design should be cost and capital efficient and support sustained scale economies (see chapter 7). In this chapter, we discuss the value chain, the customer engagement model, the revenue model, and the cost structure. Financial model and operating plan are discussed in chapter 6. The drivers of scale economies and sustained competitive advantage are discussed in chapter 7.

In our framework, the business model design includes the venture strategy to sustain the customer value, in that the venture determines how it differentiates from its competitors, how the customers experience this differential advantage, and how the customer value can be sustained. The differential advantage is necessary for a startup to succeed in a new market and generate a sustained positive cash flow. A business model can

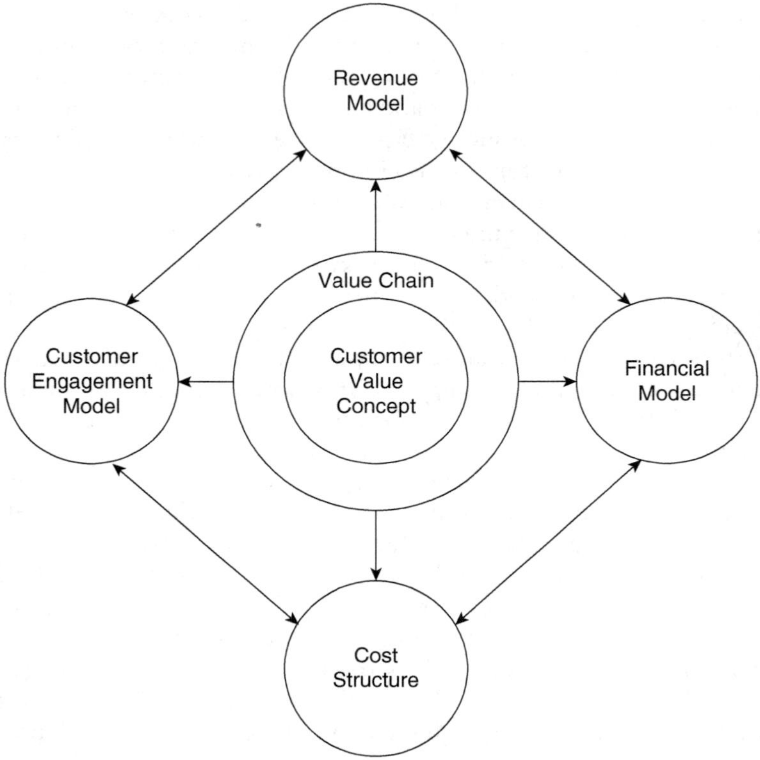

Figure 5.1 Business model design.

differentiate in several ways, as, for example, in customer value offering, customer selection, pricing structure, cost structure, value chain and supply chain configuration, product and process technologies, human resources, key partners and resources, and so on.

To sustain positive cash flow, a business model must have a differential advantage. To formulate the differential advantage to succeed in a new market, the startup should determine potential threats and opportunities, and evaluate the strengths and weaknesses of its resources and capabilities. The startup may complete the five-force analysis, the trend analysis, and a SWOT analysis (i.e., strengths, weaknesses, opportunities, and threats) relative to the critical success factors identified or the critical capabilities necessary for success.

To identify the threats and opportunities, examine the industry structure and the current trends, namely the economic, social, political, technological, and regulatory trends. To identify the strengths and weaknesses, a startup should evaluate its resources and capabilities, such as the product capabilities, process capabilities, and people capabilities. To overcome the weaknesses and mitigate the potential threats, and to increase the likelihood of venture success, leverage the existing strengths and capabilities, and form new strategic partnerships. Furthermore, reconfigure the value chain (i.e., the value-added activities in a business) and supply chain configuration to achieve operational efficiencies and scale economies (see chapter 7). Industry best practices and technological advances may be adapted to improve the venture's operational efficiencies and organizational capabilities. Finally, establish a market niche such that the target customers value the customer value offering and are willing to pay for the differential advantage and product features (see chapter 4).

A startup should determine the critical success factors to configure the value chain and the components of the business model design (see figure 5.2). Critical success factors are the key activities and capabilities that the startup must focus on and monitor regularly to succeed in a given market. Critical success factors are derived from an analysis of the industry structure and trends—that is, from the positive and negative forces that influence the market demand. For example, in the food processing industry, the critical success factors include key activities and capabilities such as new product development, distribution capabilities, and effective advertising (Leidecker et al., 1984). In the automobile industry, the critical success factors include key resources and capabilities such as a strong

Market Factors	Favorable Forces	Unfavorable Forces	Critical Success Factors
Barriers to Market Entry			
Buyer Power-Consumer Price Sensitivity and Switching Costs			
Supplier Power-Cost Structure			
Product Price-Performance-Threat of Substitutes			
Price and Non-Price Competition			
Social, Economic, and Regulatory Trends			

Figure 5.2 Critical success factors.

dealership network, automobile body styling, control in manufacturing costs, and the ability to meet the regulatory standards.

Hofer and Schendel (1978) defined the critical success factors as the key decisions that can affect significantly the overall competitive position of a business in a given industry. The critical success factors can vary from one industry to another. Leidecker et al. (1984) characterized the critical success factors as the conditions and variables that, when properly sustained and managed, can have a significant impact on the success of a business competing in a given industry. Once the critical success factors are identified, a business's strengths and weaknesses may be assessed based on these critical success factors; and the resources and capabilities must be found to overcome the business's weaknesses and mitigate the potential threats. The business should also leverage its strengths and capabilities to take advantage of the available opportunities.

Leidecker et al. (1984) offered several methods to identify the critical success factors for a business, including the industry structure analysis; the environmental analysis of social, economic, political, and technological trends; the analysis by industry experts; and the analysis of the business practices of the dominant firms in the industry. Industry reports available from industry research analysts, such as one from IBISWorld (www.ibisworld.com), can provide a current analysis of the business practices of the dominant firms in the industry, as well as of the social, economic, political, and technological trends in the industry. These industry reports include the opinions of the industry experts and observers. Below we present a framework of the industry structure analysis that was developed by Porter (see Porter, 2008). A thorough analysis of the industry structure and the competitive forces impacting the performance of a new venture is necessary to identify the critical success factors that will allow the venture to succeed in that industry.

Porter (2008) presented a framework for how to identify and evaluate the competitive forces within an industry and to determine how these forces can affect the industry profitability. These competitive forces are positive and negative forces a startup has to reckon with eventually. These competitive forces not only determine the barriers to market entry but also can erode the profitability of a new venture. The Porter framework includes five forces, namely the bargaining power of the buyers and end users, the bargaining power of the suppliers and strategic partners, the threat of new entrants, the threat of substitute products, and the intensity of rivalry among the existing competitors.

Analyzing the threat of new entrants uncovers the potential barriers to entry. A startup wants to position the business in a market where the barriers to entry are favorable. Analyzing the power of the buyers and end users uncovers other market factors such as the price sensitivity and the switching costs of the buyers. A startup wants to choose a customer segment that is less price-sensitive and likely to be more loyal. A startup should not want to enter in a price war with the established competitors. Furthermore, the power of the suppliers and partners impacts the cost structure. Accordingly, the startup wants to position itself within the industry and along the supply chain such that the suppliers and strategic partners are more flexible and have less power. Otherwise, the suppliers and strategic partners may eat away the startup's profits.

Analyzing the threat of substitute products uncovers how the customers tradeoff the price versus the performance of the product, indicating potential pressure on the price point. Analyzing the intensity of rivalry among competitors uncovers the basis of competition or the key points of differentiation that are valued by the customers. Customer value creation opportunities should be identified; and the most valuable differentiation opportunities should be included in the customer value concept (see chapter 2).

Porter (2008) suggested several contributing factors driving the five forces underlying the market success. A startup should analyze the sources of those five forces and determine whether the forces are working in its favor or against its success. The barriers-to-entry advantages of existing businesses are their scale economies, network effects, customer switching costs, capital requirements, proprietary technologies, preferential access to raw material and talented workforce, favorable geographic locations, established brand names, unequal access to distribution channels, and favorable government regulations. These factors also indicate the opportunities for a new entrant to erect and secure new barriers-to-entry against potential competitors and followers in a particular industry. The sources of barriers-to-entry are also the key areas where potential investors can add value with their industry expertise and connections (see chapter 1).

Economies of scale is a cost advantage the existing businesses have such that the fixed costs can be spread over the volume of production; and thus the unit cost of production and distribution will be lower with the increased volume. With economies of scale, the gap between the unit price and the unit cost will be wider, providing a greater competitive advantage to an existing business and erecting a barrier to entry for new entrants. As a new entrant, to overcome this barrier, the startup may need a new technology or an innovative business model to lower the costs of production and distribution. However, it generally takes time to achieve economies of scale. In the meantime, a startup may need product protection with a proprietary method or technology to minimize the retaliation from the competitors. A startup should examine its business model and reconfigure the value chain underlying the business model to achieve sustainable scale economies (see chapter 7). A company's value chain is a series of value-added activities, the primary and supporting activities that the company undertakes in its operations to create and deliver customer value. Chapter 7 discusses how to reconfigure a value chain to increase the operating efficiency and enhance competitive advantage. By analyzing a value chain one can identify the opportunities for building new barriers to entry to sustain a competitive advantage.

Existing businesses also enjoy positive network externalities with their established brands and strategic alliances. Customers recognize these brands and trust them. As the startup is a new entrant to the industry, customers are not yet aware of the startup's product or brand; they may be skeptical about the product performance. Furthermore, a startup may not have the resources to launch a large-scale marketing campaign to create customer awareness and build trust for the new brand. Thus, a startup should identify and target a specific customer segment that is currently dissatisfied with the product offerings of existing businesses. The acceptance of the new product by the early customers who are currently dissatisfied with the products of the existing businesses may open up new opportunities for further penetration in the target market. Customer switching costs are another source of barrier to entry. High switching costs can discourage the early customers from switching from the competitors' offerings to the new product. A startup's product offering must have superior customer value such that the customer value offered exceeds the sum of the price of the new product and the customer switching costs. Customer value design and customer incentives must be reviewed to surmount this barrier (see chapter 2).

Capital requirements are another barrier, especially in capital-intensive industries. Initially a startup is capital constrained. Capital is required not only to secure physical assets and develop the product, but also to pay for the operating expenses including employee wages, marketing and sales expenses, and inventory and distribution expenses. It is important to identify an initial customer segment that can be accessed and served more efficiently as well as to configure a business model that is more capital efficient (see chapter 7). Lower capital requirements can lower the barrier to entry for the startup.

Existing businesses also have other advantages such as preferential access to distributors and suppliers, proprietary technologies and brand identities, and favorable geographic locations, among others. It is difficult for a startup to bypass these barriers initially. The startup may look for strategic partnerships to help bypass some of these disadvantages. An investment from a known investor can provide credibility and connections in an industry to facilitate the acquisition of strategic partners. Existing distribution channels may be monopolized by the competitors. A startup may consider using new and emerging channels including direct marketing to access the customers. The online channels and smartphone apps are also new channel innovations that are available to a startup at a low cost. Existing businesses sometimes find these emerging channels at conflict with their existing channels; thus, they are slow to utilize these channel innovations, creating an opportunity for startups. Furthermore, government policies may also work against or in favor of the startup. Current and potential regulations by local, state, and federal governments may create barriers or opportunities for a startup.

Several industry analysts, such as IBISWorld (www.ibisworld.com), provide a checklist of the barriers to entry in a particular industry. Consult these checklists. For example, IBISWorld uses a checklist of seven variables to assess the barriers to entry in a particular industry. These barriers to entry include competition, market concentration, life cycle stage of the industry, capital intensity, technology innovation, regulation and policy, and industry assistance. The strengths of these seven factors are assessed by IBISWorld for an industry (as low, medium, or high) to indicate the areas where the barriers to entry are strong and where they are weak. Accordingly, a startup may position itself for success where the barriers are weak in its industry or by acquiring the resources and capabilities to overcome the barriers, or build new barriers.

Related to the above checklist, IBISWorld defines the competition to include the existing competition in the industry. The market concentration is the market share concentration of the dominant players. The life cycle of the industry refers to whether the industry is in introduction stage, growth stage, maturity stage, or decline stage. Capital intensity refers to the need for capital for fixed assets and operating expenses. Technology innovation in an industry refers to the rate of technology change in the industry. Regulatory policy refers to the burden of current and impending government regulation in an industry. Lastly, industry assistance refers to the level of assistance provided by trade associations to their members in an industry, as a unified voice for all industry participants.

For example, for the energy drinks market, IBISWorld barriers-to-entry checklist indicates high competition, high market share concentration, growth stage of the industry life cycle, high capital intensity, moderate changes in technology, heavy regulatory burden, and low industry assistance. In the energy drinks markets, most barriers to entry are high except two, which may be in favor of a new entrant, namely the rate of change in technology innovation and the growth stage of the industry life cycle. Thus, a startup with new innovative technology might successfully enter this market. Consider another market. For smartphone apps, the IBISWorld checklist indicates high competition, low market share concentration, growth stage of the life cycle, low capital intensity, high rate of change in technology, moderate regulation, and low industry assistance. Thus, in the smartphone apps market, there are several opportunities where the barriers to entry are low for a new entrant. Low capital intensity, high rate of technology innovation, the growth stage of the industry life cycle, and a low market share concentration are all opportunities for a startup to enter the smartphone apps market.

In the second and third columns in figure 5.2, list the positive forces (in the startup's favor) and the negative forces (against the startup), respectively; and then in the last column, list the critical activities that a startup can undertake and the capabilities the startup must build or acquire in order to minimize the impact of the negative forces and maximize the impact of the positive forces. Also, identify and list the weakest barriers to entry, dissatisfied customer segments, and the opportunities to build new barriers-to-entry advantages.

Powerful suppliers, a skilled workforce, and strategic partners can lower the profitability potential of a new venture by either increasing its operating costs and the costs of raw materials or by sharing the profits of the venture. For example, in the personal computers industry, two major costs of personal computer manufacturers are the cost of the Windows operating system supplied by Microsoft and the processor chips supplied by Intel or AMD. These key suppliers have a tremendous power over the cost structure of personal computer manufacturers. Strategic partners may lower the capital requirements but they eat away most of the startup's profits. Channel partners can also appropriate or take away most of the startup's profit margin. A skilled workforce increases the operating costs, lowering the profitability of a new venture.

Porter (2008) listed six potential sources of the power of suppliers and strategic partners in an industry. A supplier is more powerful when it is concentrated in the industry to which it sells, when its revenue does not heavily depend on one industry, when there is a heavy switching cost to change the suppliers, when the supplier offers a product that is highly differentiated, when there are no or few substitutes for the component or raw material offered by the supplier, and when the supplier can credibly threaten to vertically integrate to become a potential competitor. One can find a list of key suppliers and channel partners in an industry report provided by industry analysts (e.g., see IBISWorld). For example, in the energy drinks market, key suppliers and channel partners are supermarkets and grocery stores, convenience stores, pharmacies and drug stores, sugar processors, syrup and flavoring producers, vitamin and supplement producers, and plastic and aluminum can manufacturers. For energy drinks, the average cost of purchases and supplies is 51.5 percent of the revenue, according to IBISWorld. Identify the major costs and assess the six sources of the power of suppliers and partners to determine the positive forces and negative forces and enter them in figure 5.2. List the key activities and capabilities that can minimize the negative impacts and maximize the positive impacts from the power of key suppliers and partners.

Similarly, the power of the buyers can lower the revenues, especially when the buyers are price sensitive and the customer switching costs are low. Price sensitive buyers pressure for price reductions. High customer switching costs increase the customer acquisition costs. A buyer has greater power when there are few large-volume buyers, when the products are more standardized or commoditized, when the buyers have low switching costs to change the suppliers, and when the large-volume buyers can credibly threaten to backward integrate to become potential competitors (Porter, 2008). Identify the buyer groups and analyze their purchasing power and price sensitivity. A buyer is more price-sensitive when the buyer's purchase amount represents a significant fraction of its cost structure, when the buyer's profit margin is low, when the buyer is strapped for cash, and when the product performance is less important to the buyer or its downstream customers. The power of market intermediaries and channel partners can be reduced by direct marketing or through a marketing campaign directed to the end users. In figure 5.2, list the positive and negative impacts on the startup arising from the power of the buyers. In the last column, identify the critical success factors or list the actions the startup may take to minimize the power of buyers and channels.

The threat of substitute products, similar to the threat of new entrants, can raise the barriers to entry in a market. A substitute product performs a similar function or solves the same problem of the customer, although by different means. A customer compares price-performance tradeoffs with substitute products when considering the purchase of a new product. It is important to understand the price-performance tradeoffs and the forces driving these tradeoffs. Product substitutes lower the revenues of the startup by limiting the price the customer is willing to pay and reducing the number of units that can be sold.

The threat of a substitute product is high when the substitute offers an attractive price-performance tradeoff or when the buyer's cost to switch to the substitute product is low. For example, in the market for energy drinks, the substitute products are soda drinks, coffee, juices, bottled water, and so on. It is important to understand the structure of these industries as well (see chapter 2 for an analysis across substitute industries to identify new customer segments). Compare the factors driving the price-performance tradeoffs between the new product and the substitute products, and list the favorable and unfavorable factors in figure 5.2. For example, a change in customer tastes and preferences, or a change in the technology or social structure, might favor one product over its substitutes. List the critical success factors or the actions that the startup can take to drive the price-performance tradeoff in its favor.

Finally, the intensity of rivalry among the existing competitors can limit the profitability potential of a business in an industry. The intensity of competition is greater when the competitors are numerous and roughly equal in size, when the industry growth is mature or declining, when there is excess capacity in the industry, and when the industry is using highly specialized assets such that the barriers to exit for an existing business are high (Porter, 2008). The competition may be based on price or non-price differentiators (see chapter 2 for the basis of competition). Analyzing the customer experience with the product, as done in chapter 2, uncovers potential price and non-price differentiators as the basis of competition. The price-based competition is more harmful to the industry profitability than the non-price-based competition. Price-based competition is more likely when the products or services are nearly identical, when customer-switching costs are low, when the unit cost of the product is low, when there is excess capacity in the industry, when the product is perishable, and when the technology can become rapidly obsolete. Price competition can also distract the customers from non-price differentiators.

List the positive and negative impacts of the competition in figure 5.2, and list the critical actions necessary to enhance the startup's competitive advantage. Furthermore, list the positive and negative impacts of the social, economic, and regulatory trends, and the critical actions the startup must take to achieve success in figure 5.2. The analysis of the five forces and the current trends, the drivers of these forces and trends, and their impact on the startup's success can lead to a list of critical success factors that guide the business model design and venture strategy, the choice of key performance indicators (see chapter 6), and the risk mitigation plan (see chapter 8). A niche customer segment can be then identified, or a customer segment with the weakest barriers to entry and less price sensitivity may be targeted when entering a new market. The impact on the startup's cost structure can be minimized by lowering the power of key suppliers and strategic partners. The price-performance tradeoff of the product versus the substitute products can be improved. The likelihood of price-based competition can be avoided, and the non-price based differentiators can be enhanced. The startup should also position itself to enable the opportunities and mitigate the threats arising from the current social, economic, and regulatory trends.

The following sections develop the four components of the business model design (see figure 5.1). We consider how a startup can enter a well-guarded market, and acquire and retain customers; how the startup can create and deliver customer value efficiently; and how the startup monetizes and sustains the customer value. The value chain and supply chain configuration, and the associated cost structure and cost drivers are considered; that is, we consider the value-added activities in making and selling the product, such as product development, production, marketing and sales, distribution and delivery, customer support and relationship. To monetize and sustain the customer value, we examine several revenue models and their implementation challenges.

How Do You Create and Deliver Customer Value?

Creating and delivering customer value requires figuring out the underlying value chain activities of the business model, namely how to design, test, manufacture, distribute, and provide support for the product or service. The value chain design also determines the cost structure, outsourcing choice, supply chain partners and strategic alliances, and channel choice. A generic value chain in an industry can be reconfigured within a business model to create a competitive advantage for the company and secure an entry barrier to prevent potential competition or new entrants from entering the industry. A value chain can be configured to create and deliver the customer value efficiently and competitively.

Magretta (2002) proposed that a business model is a variation of the generic value chain. The underlying value chain can be reconfigured to refine and improve the business model design. Indeed, most business model innovations come from a reconfiguration of the underlying value chains. Magretta described the business value chain as consisting of two parts, all activities associated with making the product and all activities associated with selling the product. The first part of the value chain, the activities associated with making the product, includes product testing and development, sourcing raw materials, manufacturing, inventory control, and so on. The second part of the value chain, the activities associated with selling the product, includes customer acquisition and retention, transacting sales, distributing and delivering the product, customer relationship, and so on. A new business model may offer a better way of making or distributing a proven product, or a better way to meet an unmet customer need.

Alternatively, the value chain within a business model is divided into two groups of activities (Porter, 1985), namely primary activities and support activities. Primary activities include the manufacturing and distribution of the product, whereas support activities include infrastructure activities, technology and systems, human resources, procurement, customer relationship, and so on. Primary activities include inbound logistics, operations, outbound logistics, marketing and sales, and service. Furthermore, inbound logistics includes securing and warehousing raw materials and components; operations include processes for transforming raw materials and other inputs into finished products; outbound logistics includes the warehousing and distribution of finished products; marketing and sales includes demand generation, customer acquisition and retention, customer relationship, and sales; and service includes customer support, after-sales service, warranty, and repair. Support activities include human resource management such as hiring, training, retaining, and developing human resources; infrastructure management and organizational leadership such as internal control, strategic planning, and raising capital; product development such as R&D, product testing, and technology management; and procurement management such as purchasing supplies, components, and raw materials.

Whereas the value chain lists the key activities within a company, the supply chain links these activities across companies, namely, the activities of the partners, suppliers, and distributors. There is potential for value creation by reconfiguring not only the value chain within a company but also the supply chain network, such that the system as a whole can benefit from the value-added coordination and cooperation, enhancing the competitive advantage. A key objective of a supply chain strategy underlying the business model design is to meet the customer demand efficiently and effectively through the most effective use of its resources and processes.

Similar to the value chain, the supply chain performs two distinct functions, namely a physical function and a market-making function (Fisher, 1997). The physical function of a supply chain includes cross-company activities such as procurement, production, distribution, and so on, while the market-making function ensures that the product reaching the marketplace matches what the customers want to buy and when. Each of these functions of the supply chain incurs distinct costs. The cost of the physical function includes the costs of production, inventory, and transportation across companies; whereas the cost of the market-making function is an opportunity cost a business incurs when the product supply mismatches the customer demand, resulting in either a lost sales opportunity or an increased inventory forcing the business to sell at a loss by marking down the prices.

When the customer demand is more predictable (e.g., in the case of commoditized products), the cost of market-making function is minimal; a business then focuses on its operational efficiency, minimizing the cost of the physical function across the supply chain. In the case of commoditized products, customers are price sensitive; it is thus crucial to improve the cost and operational efficiency of the supply chain to serve these customers. Here the use of information technology and enterprise planning software can help the company manage its supply chain more efficiently, minimizing inventory costs and maximizing production and distribution efficiencies. For commoditized products, suppliers, manufacturers, distributors, and retailers within a supply chain configuration must coordinate their activities to meet a more predictable customer demand at the lowest possible cost.

The supply chain configuration depends on whether the product is a functional product or an innovative product. Minimizing the cost of the physical function may be an appropriate objective for a functional product, but not for an innovative product. Functional products satisfy basic needs and do not change much over time, such as groceries, oil and gas, and basic staples; they have long product life cycles, but low profit margin. Functional products also have less variety available in a product category. In comparison, innovative products have high profit margins, shorter product life cycles, and a greater customization and variety within a product category.

Within the same product category, there can be functional products as well as innovative products. For example, in the automobile industry, functional products include standard, low-cost vehicles, whereas innovative products include high-end, luxury vehicles. Similar combinations can be found in other industries as well. Supply chain strategies, or how you make and deliver products across a supply chain to meet the customer demand, can vary significantly between a functional product and an innovative product.

The key challenge in delivering an innovative product is the unpredictability of the market demand, whereas the key challenge with a functional product is the price-sensitivity of the buyers. Cost minimization and improving operational efficiency are appropriate goals to serve the needs of customers purchasing functional products. However, with the short life cycle of innovative products and the associated unpredictable demand, the opportunity cost of not meeting customer demand, or the cost of the market-making function, can be very high. The goal when designing a supply chain configuration for innovative products is to minimize these opportunity costs by making the supply chain more responsive to the changing market needs and customer demand. The supply chain design then entails selecting reliable partners and suppliers and requiring an appropriate action from these partners to be collectively responsible for meeting an unpredictable demand in the marketplace.

The supply chain strategy for innovative products, which is geared to respond quickly to an unpredictable market demand, requires excess inventory, excess manufacturing capacity, shorter lead time for delivery, and the use of modular product design (Fisher, 1997). High profit margins are required from the sale of innovative products to compensate for the cost of market-making activities. In the case of innovative products, the profit margin the investors require can be higher than 60 percent. Innovative products thus need a different production and distribution strategy, or a different supply chain configuration.

Raz (2008) summarized the key questions to be addressed when configuring a supply chain and identifying the key partners: (1) who provides the raw materials and components, and where are these suppliers located; (2) what distribution channels are currently used to deliver the product to the end users; (3) how the relationships are built with the key suppliers, distributors, and strategic partners; (4) how the information flows are coordinated; and (5) how the incentives of all partners in the supply chain are aligned. The answers to the above questions would differ for functional products versus innovative products. These answers can help a business when designing a supply chain configuration, by identifying the key partners who may participate in creating and delivering customer value more efficiently, effectively, and on time. Thus, when designing a business model, in deciding how to create and deliver customer value, the value chain activities and the supply chain configuration need to be clearly understood and may need to be reconfigured to achieve the specific objectives appropriate to the nature of the product and its process.

To select channel partners and design a customer-driven distribution system (Stern and Sturdivant, 1987), the following steps may be used: (1) find out what the customers want and desire; (2) identify all possible outlets and channels; (3) construct and assess the market clusters; (4) determine the channel costs; (5) compare the channel options and costs; and (6) choose the appropriate channel partners. The first step, when choosing a channel, is to understand what the customers want and desire. Prepare a catalog of customer wants and desires but exclude the too grand desires or preferences. Understand the customer's buying process—including price and delivery preferences—and potential add-on products in which they may be interested. Then, group these customer wants and desires into market clusters, so that the market clusters are based on customers' delivery and service preferences. Note that customer wants and desires are often intangible and thus might be difficult to visualize.

In the second step, identify appropriate distribution channels and retail outlets to serve the market clusters determined in the previous step. Use well-known retail outlet names to label the choices. When there are no existing outlets for certain market clusters, use short descriptions of hypothetical outlets and coin new names to label these outlets. The outlet labels, either existing or hypothesized, are simply the points of reference. One may not use exactly the same outlets but may choose the outlets with similar characteristics.

In the next step, given the channel availability, assess the market clusters determined in step one (i.e., the clusters of customer desires and preferences) to determine whether the clusters are indeed feasible. Thus, the implausible market clusters can be eliminated in this step. Next, determine the distribution partners needed to support the outlets identified in step two for the remaining market clusters; determine which downstream supply chain partners can support the outlets to serve each market cluster. Furthermore, determine the channel cost to support each outlet for each market cluster.

Next, review the channel strategies of the existing competitors (see chapter 2) and then determine the feasibility and constraints that may limit the choices of the channels for each market cluster. Some channel strategies may not be feasible or cost effective for the company. In the previous steps, the ideal channels and outlets were determined to serve a market cluster. But in this step, those channels and outlets are compared with the channel strategies of the competitors. This comparison will reveal opportunities and limitations when choosing a feasible distribution system to serve each selected market cluster.

In the final step, talk to distribution experts and retail executives to determine if there are further constraints and opportunities in using the distributors and outlets for each selected market cluster, and whether these challenges can be overcome with the company's available financial and human resources. And last, choose the channels and outlets to serve the market clusters. Note that different channel partners may be chosen to serve the wants of customers at various stages of the buying process. For example, a customer may use an online retail store to read customer reviews to assess a product but go to a physical store to try the product, and then go to another online or physical store to actually purchase the product. Thus, the customer's wants and desires at each stage of the purchasing process, including purchasing support, education, trial, service, and so on, should be considered when choosing the channel strategy and partners (see chapter 2 for the consumption chain analysis).

Alternative business model designs and their underlying value chains require different cost structures to create and deliver customer value to their customers (see chapter 4 for an analysis of the perceived value of the product versus the cost to serve the customer). The cost structure and the underlying cost drivers associated with the business model design determine the efficiency and scalability of the business model. To understand the cost structure and the cost drivers, analyze the value chain activities and processes.

The activity-based costing method is a great tool to identify the cost drivers and estimate the resources required to create and deliver customer value. The traditional product-costing framework, such as absorption costing, does not account for all critical activities related to making and delivering a product or service. For example, the sales and marketing costs are not part of a product cost under the traditional costing framework. However, for a startup, the business development and the product development costs can be high. The activity-based costing method helps to identify the major activities underlying a product's cost structure and the related cost drivers, and determining the cost of each activity and the resources needed to support those activities. A fishbone-type diagram can be also used with the activity-costing method to break down the product's cost structure into distinct cost components and their underlying cost drivers.

The following example illustrates the use of the activity-based costing method. Consider a key activity such as marketing and sales. Suppose the startup's current cost of marketing and sales is $2,000 per month. Let the associated cost driver be the number of purchase orders received per month. Suppose the company currently receives 20 purchase orders per month. Then, the customer acquisition cost (or the cost of sales and marketing per purchase order) is $100 per order (i.e., $2,000 cost per month divided by 20 purchase orders per month). Thus, if the company expects

50 purchase orders in a future month, then the company can expect to spend $5,000 for marketing and sales (i.e., $100 cost per order times 50 purchase orders in the given month). Thus, one may use the activity-based costing method and the cost drivers underlying the cost structure to estimate the major costs (see chapter 6).

The activity-based costing method, when used to analyze and estimate the cost structure associated with the value chain activities, uncovers not only the true cost of the product but also identifies where the resources are available in excess and where the resource bottlenecks might arise. The company may then take measures to alleviate the resource constraints, such as by outsourcing certain activities or raising additional capital to build the required resource capacity. The activity-based costing method is useful to plan the resource requirements and determine the financing needs of a startup (see chapter 6).

Skarzynski and Gibson (2008) provided a checklist to understand and analyze the current value chain activities underlying a business model design to determine how the key processes can be refined or improved upon to shorten the time to achieve sustained positive cash flow. The checklist includes the following questions for the entrepreneur: (1) what distribution channels are currently used by the competitors; (2) how is the supply chain configured in the industry; (3) who are the key partners and suppliers, and how can they help in creating and delivering customer value; (4) whether the product delivery and customer support processes can be made easier and more enjoyable for the customers; (5) whether the customer experience with the product or service can be reinvented in ways to create a stronger sense of affiliation the customer has with a business; (6) whether there are opportunities to improve efficiency and effectiveness of the value chain activities and processes; (7) whether the startup can reposition itself in the supply chain to create a competitive advantage against the existing competitors, or to create an entry barrier against potential competitors; and (8) which strategic partners can help the startup to create and deliver customer value more efficiently and effectively.

Furthermore, when refining and reconfiguring a generic value chain or a currently in use value chain, the company needs to weigh the costs and benefits to any changes in the activities and the need for additional resources and partners to implement those changes. The company also needs to decide to build internal capabilities or outsource, and most importantly, determine the effects of the changes on the company's cash flow both in the short term and in the long term, including the effects on the time to achieve positive cash flow and its path to profitability. A change in a value chain activity or process that shortens the time to positive cash flow and the path to profitability, that might reduce the uncertainty of the cash flow, or that is cost efficient and capital efficient, should be considered (see chapter 7).

How Do You Acquire and Retain Customers?

As a new entrant, a startup should consider the market entry barriers and then secure an entry where the barriers are the weakest. Barriers-to-entry are advantages the existing businesses have that are difficult for a startup to surmount. A startup should use a sustained force strategy to attack the weakest barriers to make a successful entry in the market. In figure 5.2 discussed earlier, we analyze the five forces and current trends, and determine their potential positive (opportunities) and negative impact (threats) on the venture's success. One should further evaluate the venture's strengths and weaknesses and identify the critical actions and capabilities that the venture must consider when entering a new market.

To crack a well-guarded market and to succeed when entering a new market, a startup may leverage the existing resources and capabilities, reconfigure the value chain, or establish a market niche. It may form strategic alliances to mitigate competitive threats. It may employ a single strategy or a combination strategy. Reconfiguration of the value chain, by eliminating or outsourcing certain activities, or by rearranging the sequence of activities, can result in an efficient and sustainable business model design. To reconfigure the value chain, a new entrant must understand how the competitors are serving their customers, how new technologies can be used, how a business model from another industry can be adapted, and how a generic value chain in a given industry can be modularized by combining activities or substituting those from several other value chains (Bryce and Dyer, 2007). Figure 5.3 shows alternative market entry strategies. The startup may leverage its existing capabilities to exploit the market opportunities, establish a market niche when faced with competitive threats, reconfigure the value chain to overcome its weaknesses to exploit the opportunities, and form strategic alliances in areas of its weaknesses in order to mitigate competitive threats.

Selecting a niche market segment and staying away from mainstream customers will not attract the attention of current competitors, in that the competitors would not realize that they have competition. Initially, do not target the best customers or the most profitable customers of the competitors. In the long run, however, one may reach out to these profitable customers once an initial foothold has been established in the

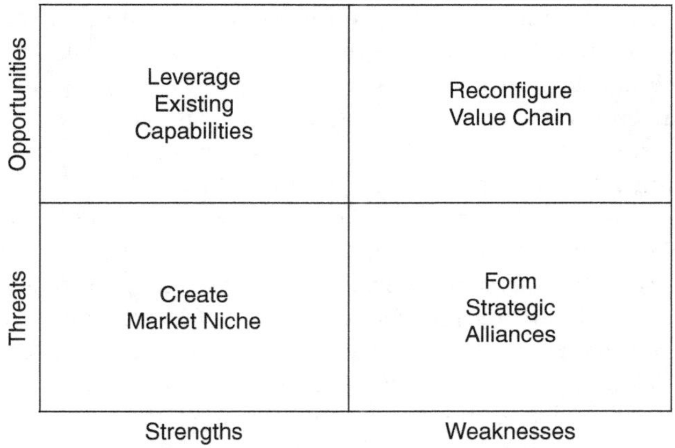

Figure 5.3 Market entry strategies.

market. The more indirect the attack on the competitors, the more effective and sustainable is the go-to-market strategy. The indirectness of the competitive strategy depends on the nature of the industry and the capabilities of the new entrant. To establish a market niche, a new entrant must determine whether the customers care more about specific product features, whether the customers vary significantly in their needs and preferences, and if there are rebel customers who avoid mainstream products. The startup must also identify the customer segments that are not well served by the competitors.

For example, consider Skype (Bryce and Dyer, 2007). To differentiate themselves from other telecom competitors (such as AT&T, Verizon, Sprint), Skype let people make free or inexpensive calls over the Internet. Skype reconfigured the value chain by using resources such as the Internet instead of the fiber optic cable network that was used by the competitors. Skype's initial target market was a niche segment of more price-sensitive customers, not the best customers of the competitors; those customers did not mind the minimal inconvenience of calling over the Internet. The telecom competitors ignored Skype, which gave the company the time to scale and build a sustainable competitive advantage.

To leverage existing resources and capabilities, a new entrant must determine whether there are underutilized resources that can be deployed to enter the new market and whether there are intangible assets the company can leverage. Assets with high fixed costs should be leveraged to achieve scale economies. An example is Walmart (Bryce and Dyer, 2007). Walmart introduced its private label of soft drinks, Sam's Choice.

Walmart chose to outsource the production and bottling operations from a strategic partner, Cott Corporation, in Canada. Walmart leveraged its shelf space and cost-efficient distribution system to overcome the barriers from entering the soft drinks market. Walmart thus leveraged its existing resources and capabilities, and reconfigured its value chain by outsourcing certain key activities, to enter into a fiercely competitive industry. Unlike the major competitors such as Coke and Pepsi, Walmart sold the soft drinks in its own stores, not through grocery stores, vending machines, soda fountains, or convenience stores, the mainstream channels used by the competitors. Another example is Costco, which succeeded in leveraging its strengths and capabilities to enter and succeed in a new market. Costco leveraged its brand name and supply chain network to introduce private labels in several product categories.

Another example is Toys-R-Us (Bryce and Dyer, 2007). Toys-R-Us entered the apparel market by opening its Babies-R-Us stores. By targeting a niche segment and leveraging its existing brand asset and distribution capabilities, Toys-R-Us became the largest baby products retailer in the world. Another example is Sketchers, which broke into the shoe market by first offering a niche product, a sport utility logger boot in 1993. Sketchers then introduced a lace-free line of sneakers for a niche customer segment, the young and hip crowd. Sketchers thus avoided the mainstream lines of shoes to successfully take on its direct competitors such as Nike, Reebok, and Adidas.

Jakks Pacific is another example (Bryce and Dyer, 2007) of a company succeeding in a new market when entering the gaming market. Jakks reconfigured a generic value chain by embedding the software into the game controller, and outsourcing the game content from the game makers. Jakks also targeted a niche customer segment of young children who found the games offered by Nintendo's Wii and Sony's PlayStation more difficult to play. Jakks Pacific also leveraged its brand asset known for its familiar television shows and game shows.

How can a startup acquire and retain customers efficiently and effectively? A startup with scarce financial resources can afford low-cost customer acquisition and retention strategies. The startup should know its customer acquisition cost. Initially the startup's customer acquisition cost may be high but the cost declines with an increase in the sales volume. After the business model is stabilized and sustainable, the average customer acquisition cost should be below the average customer lifetime value. Customer lifetime value is the present value of the cash flow from all purchases and transactions made by an individual customer. Moreover, in a sustained business model, it can be shown that the gross margin on a product must exceed twice the ratio of the average customer acquisition cost to the average customer lifetime value. Initially, for a startup, the customer acquisition cost would be greater than the average customer lifetime value; but the average customer acquisition cost declines with the sales volume.

A customer acquisition strategy involves creating customer awareness, generating leads, and converting the leads into paying customers, also known as the marketing and sales funnel. Hoffman and Novak (2000) offered several customer acquisition and retention strategies for a startup, such as word-of-mouth, public relations, affiliate programs, online advertising, strategic partnerships, and broadcast and print advertising. Broadcast advertising such as radio and television advertising is the most expensive customer acquisition strategy. The word-of-mouth strategy involves no direct costs but is the most powerful medium to acquire customers. Online banner ads are less expensive but click-through rates and conversion rates can be low. An advantage with online banner ads is that the customer acquisition rate can be tracked. Strategic partnerships are exclusive relationships, in that the partners place banner ads on each other's websites, and such mutual relationships are more efficient in channeling customers to each other.

Public relations are less expensive than media advertising and can generate word of mouth. Another less expensive customer acquisition strategy is through an affiliate program, in that a company pays an affiliate a commission on the sales or a fixed cost to direct the customer to the company's website. A startup with limited financial resources may pursue less expensive customer acquisition strategies such as an affiliate revenue sharing program, word of mouth, public relations, and online banner ads. At a later stage, when more resources are available, a company may consider print and broadcast media and strategic partnerships.

Customer acquisition cost as a percentage of sales should decline with an increase in the sales. Customer acquisition cost can be calculated based on the cost of media and the conversion rate. For example, for online ads, suppose the cost per thousand impressions (CPM) is $5 or the cost per impression is 0.5 cents. If the click-through rate is 0.5 percent, then the cost per click is $1 per click (i.e., the cost per impression divided by the click-through rate). If the conversion rate is 2 percent, then the average customer acquisition cost is $50 per customer (i.e., the cost per click divided by the conversion rate).

Suppose, in the above example, an average customer stays with the company for six months and makes a total purchase of $200 (i.e., the purchases by the customer are discounted back to the present value).

Thus, the company's average customer lifetime value is $200, which is greater than the average customer acquisition cost of $50. Furthermore, the ratio of the average customer acquisition cost to the average customer lifetime value is 25 percent (i.e., $50 divided by $200); thus, this product's gross margin must be higher than 50 percent for the startup to be investable. In a sustained business model, the gross margin must exceed twice the ratio of the customer acquisition cost to the customer lifetime value.

By cultivating learning relationships with customers a startup can increase the likelihood of customer retention (Pine II et al., 1995). Through learning relationships with customers, the customers teach the company more about their needs and preferences, which ensures customer lock-in and customer loyalty, increasing the customer switching costs and thus making it difficult for the customers to switch to the competitive products and substitutes. Learning relationships with customers give the company a sustainable competitive advantage. A startup may leverage the capabilities of the Internet and information technology to cultivate learning relationships with the present and potential customers. Learning relationships can become smarter as the startup interacts more with its customers. The more the customers teach the company what they want and how they want it, it becomes more difficult for the competitors to entice away the customers (Pine II et al., 1995). Even when a competitor offers a similar product, the customers are already invested in the learning relationships with the company and thus are less likely to switch to the competitor's product.

In the learning relationship model, the entrepreneur is the chief customer relationship manager, not a product manager. A product manager pushes the product into channels and into customer's hands; whereas a customer relationship manager knows their customer's preferences and needs by cultivating learning relationships with the customers, and develops the product and process capabilities to fulfill the customer needs effectively. Pine II et al. (1995) recommended a learning relationship model with four components, namely an information gathering strategy for initiating dialogs with customers and remembering their preferences, a production and delivery strategy for fulfilling what the company learns about the needs and preferences of the customers, an organizational strategy for managing customer relationships, and an assessment strategy for evaluating the effectiveness of learning relationships.

A company may use the Internet and other interactive technologies to elicit and manage information about the customer needs and preferences. The company should use the information gathered from the customers to build its production and delivery capabilities. A company should track the customer share measure (i.e., its share of the customer's total patronage) to assess the effectiveness of the learning relationships and customer retention strategy (Pine II et al., 1995). To calculate the customer share measure, the company should have some idea what the customer is buying from the competitors. The company must go beyond the customer satisfaction surveys and the net promoter score measure (see chapter 3), and develop the customer share measure to assess the effectiveness of its customer relationship strategy.

How Do You Monetize Customer Value?

The investor's valuation of the venture is determined by the cash flow, and its timing and risk. Furthermore, the timing and risk of the cash flow is determined by the business model design. Cash flow equals revenues minus costs. Revenues may come from a single source or multiple sources such as subscriptions and advertising. A startup's costs and expenses may be fixed, variable, or semi-variable. Fixed costs do not vary directly with production volume, but variable costs do. Semi-variable costs have both a fixed component and a variable component.

Understanding the revenue model and the cost structure is key to determining how and when a startup can generate and sustain cash flow. An entrepreneur should understand how the competitors make money and to examine the strengths and weaknesses of their revenue models and cost structures when doing a competitor analysis (see chapter 2). Is there an opportunity to increase the revenues and lower the costs? In this section, we discuss alternative revenue models and the revenue drivers built into the business model design. An entrepreneur should understand the revenue model choices available and their implementation challenges when monetizing the customer value. In a previous section, we discussed how to employ the activity-based costing method to determine the cost structure and analyze the underlying cost drivers to determine the required resources.

Osterwalder and Pigneur (2010) described several revenue models, including the freemium model, bait and hook model, insurance model, advertising model, long-tail model, inside-out and outside-in models, integrated models, and platform models. A revenue model must be appropriate to the customer value definition (i.e., the customer segment, the relative value proposition, and the price point); that is, the revenue model should be aligned with the customer value definition. Each revenue model has its implementation challenges, including the formulation of a go-to-market strategy, the associated sales and marketing costs, and the need for resources and strategic partnerships. Disparate customer segments may require the use of different revenue models; thus, a company may use more than one revenue model, or integrated models.

Osterwalder and Pigneur (2010) illustrated the freemium model with an example of the company, Flickr, a photo-sharing website, which was acquired by Yahoo in 2005. In a freemium model, the basic features of a product or service are offered at no cost or at a minimal cost to the customer, but the premium features are available for purchase at additional cost. In this revenue model, a small base of paying customers subsidizes free users. The freemium revenue model is appropriate when the marginal cost of serving free users is low. In the case of Flickr, free users can have a basic account that allows them to upload and share images. However, free use comes with certain constraints such as limited storage space and a limited number of uploads per month. With a paid annual subscription, the customer can enjoy full service features including unlimited storage space and uploads. The freemium model is thus aligned with the needs of two customer groups, in that casual users would use the free services and the paying users with high-volume photo uploading would use the premium services.

Typically, the conversion rate from free users to premium users is less than 5 percent. The freemium revenue model is used by many Internet service companies, including Dropbox, Spotify, Match.com, and LinkedIn, to name a few that are well known. However, several challenges are existent when implementing the freemium model. A startup should ask six questions before choosing a freemium model: (1) what features should be free; (2) will the customers fully understand the premium offer; (3) what is the target conversion rate; (4) is the startup prepared for the conversion life cycle; (5) are the free users becoming evangelists; and (6) whether the startup is committed to the need for ongoing product innovation (Kumar, 2014).

It is sometimes difficult to choose which features should be offered as free. The goal of making free features available in the freemium model is to attract new users. Thus, the incorrect choice of free features will cause the freemium model not to work. Clearly, there are at least two sets of value propositions: one set directed to free users and the other set to premium users. Sometimes for the second set of value propositions, the incremental value added for the premium users is poorly understood by the target customers. As a result, the conversion rate from free use to premium use can be lower.

Two key metrics should be watched when using the freemium model, namely the average cost of serving a free user and the conversion rate at which the free users convert to become paying customers. The target conversion rate is critical to the design of the freemium model; too low a rate means there is not enough monetization and too high a rate means there are not enough new customers. Kumar (2014) found that most companies using the freemium model have a conversion rate between 2 percent and 5 percent. Furthermore, conversion rates dip when the customer base expands beyond the early adopters and begins attracting more price-sensitive users. Some companies then may stop using the freemium model and simply switch to offering a limited-time free trial of the product. The use of the freemium model also requires constant product upgrades and the addition of new features to increase the value of the premium services in order to retain and grow the number of premium users. It is also important to keep the free users happy so that they continue to refer the product to more customers, thereby increasing the user base (i.e., the free users act as evangelists and thus help the product to go viral).

In a freemium model, a small base of premium users subsidizes a large base of free users. In comparison, in the insurance revenue model, a large base of users subsidizes the cost of servicing a small base of users. The insurance model offers peace of mind to the customers, in that the risk is transferred from an individual user to a pool of users who share the risk and the costs. Insurance companies, healthcare companies, and alarm monitoring companies, for example, use the insurance revenue model. A large base of customers who pay for the service may not use the full features of the service. The costly features of the service are only used by a small group of customers in low-likelihood, demanding situations.

In a bait and hook revenue model (also known as a loss leader model or razor-and-blade model), the initial product is available at a low cost (i.e., at a subsidized price), but the business makes money by selling the related products in the future to the same customer. The bait and hook revenue model is applied to the same customer who buys a "bait" product and subsequently makes repeated purchases of the "hook" product. The hook product subsidizes the cost of the bait product. For example, a printer is sold at a low price but the related products, such as toners and cartridges, are sold to the same customer at a higher price. Free cell phones with two-year service contracts are another example. Gillette, in another example, sells the razor handle at a low cost but the blades are sold at premium prices. The bait and hook revenue model ensures customer loyalty and the business model lock-in by increasing customer switching costs (see chapter 7).

In the advertising revenue model, the use of the product is free (or available at a low cost), but the advertisers, who want to reach these users, pay for the cost of the product or service. For example, Google's search engine is free to the users but the company earns its revenues by selling online ad space to advertisers. Newspapers, radio, magazines, television, smartphone apps, and so on, are many examples that use the advertising revenue model by itself or in conjunction with a low-cost subscription model. Facebook is another example that uses the advertising revenue model, allowing free accounts to its users but selling ad space to advertisers. In the advertising revenue model, the larger the user base, the greater is the cost of ad space and the greater is the company's revenue. The advertising model thus requires attracting two types of customer groups, namely users and advertisers. The advertising model needs two sets of customer value propositions for the two groups of customers. The free product attracts the user traffic, which makes the media space more attractive to advertisers.

The advertising model is a type of platform revenue model. A platform revenue model is used by an intermediary who serves two or more customer groups. These customer groups are distinct but interdependent. The success with one customer group feeds back positively to the success with other customer groups (which is known as the network effect), yielding increasing returns to scale (see chapter 7). The platform model enables the interactions between the separate customer groups. Furthermore, as discussed in the case of the advertising revenue model, the platform is of value to one customer group, only if the other customer groups are present (Osterwalder and Pigneur, 2010).

Apple's iPod/iTunes is an example of the platform revenue model. The success of Apple's iPod was due to the success of its iTunes platform allowing iPod users to buy and download digital music. The music artists can upload their music onto the iTunes platform. Similarly, Apple's App Store is another example of the platform model. The iPhone users can buy and download apps from Apple's App Store; and app software developers who build smartphone apps can upload the apps on Apple's App Store platform. The apps are then available for download to the iPhone users. With the App Store platform, Apple has two separate customer groups, namely software developers and iPhone users, who interact on the App Store platform. Apple is thus an intermediary, earning a percentage of revenue the software developers make on their apps that are sold at the App Store. Other examples of platform intermediaries are Visa, MasterCard, and eBay, to name a few well-known companies.

The long-tail revenue model is appropriate for low-margin, high-volume products. Netflix and YouTube are examples of companies using the long-tail revenue model. A long-tail revenue model is used with a large number of niche products or contents, each of which sells relatively infrequently (Osterwalder and Pigneur, 2010). Some products sell well and some do not, but in aggregate the company earns positive revenue. Book publishing companies also use the long-tail revenue model. The long-tail model requires value propositions targeting a large number of less-profitable customer segments.

Lulu.com, an online book publisher, uses the long-tail revenue model (Osterwalder and Pigneur, 2010). Lulu.com offers thousands of authors the ability to publish and sell their books using its online platform. The books are printed on demand (i.e., when there are actual purchase orders). Lulu.com helps niche and amateur authors publish and sell their books. The likelihood of the failure of a particular book title is less relevant for Lulu.com, as the marginal operating cost of such a failure is negligible.

The inside-out and outside-in revenue models are royalty-based revenue models, which are used in technology licensing and business franchising. In technology licensing, a technology is licensed out to a licensee for a predetermined royalty stream for the licensor. Technology licensing can be in-licensing or out-licensing, depending on whether the company receives a license or it licenses out, respectively. In business franchising, a business process and the brand name are franchised to a franchisee in lieu of predetermined royalty payments to the franchisor. A franchisee leverages the franchisor's brand and customer relationship to assemble or sell the final product to a customer.

In chapter 6, we will describe several customer-funded revenue models a startup can use in the early development stage; namely, matchmaker model, deposit model, subscription model, standardize-and-resell model, and scarcity model (also see Mullins, 2013). The advantage in using these revenue models is that they not only can generate early cash flow, but they also generate early demand for the product or service. The matchmaker model is used by an intermediary, carrying no inventory. The deposit is model, also known as the retainer model, is used by professional service firms. The subscription model requires the customer to pay a monthly or an annual membership fee in advance to use the product or service. In a standardized-and-resell model, a product or service created for one customer can then be standardized and offered to a larger customer base. The scarcity model is used by businesses offering products that can become rapidly obsolete or are perishable (see chapter 6).

CHAPTER SIX

Financing Stage Milestones

An entrepreneur must be able to articulate a path to sustained positive cash flow to the investor, at the lowest cost and in the shortest time. A startup is a series of stage experiments, and each stage requires sufficient funding to test the critical assumptions and mitigate the stage risks efficiently. An entrepreneur should nail the customer value concept first before approaching the investors for funding. A startup should not lock into key hires and partnerships too early, and the investment in the startup should be kept at a minimum before the path-dependent risks are mitigated and the business model is stabilized. This chapter presents the seven rules to bootstrapping a startup, including consumer-funded and crowdfunding models, a framework to estimate the critical resources and operating budget, and a framework to estimate the venture's financing needs and the time to achieve sustained positive cash flow. A framework is also provided to develop a milestone-based operating plan. A startup must first complete an operating plan prior to estimating the financing needs. The experience curve effect and a sensitivity analysis of the critical assumptions should be considered when determining the financing needs of a startup.

A startup is viewed as a series of stage experiments, in that each stage requires achieving certain milestones. To achieve the stage milestones, certain activities and resources are required, and funding is needed to finance these resources and activities. Several assumptions are made at the beginning of each stage, which are then tested and validated at the completion of each stage. The results are then used to refine the business model and operating plan. The required activities and resources, and the funding needed to finance them, are then updated. The results of the stage experiments may cause the startup to pivot the product market concept, reformulate the customer value offering, and reconfigure the business model design, or completely abandon the venture.

A startup is not a small business; managing a startup can be more intense than managing an established business. Moreover, a startup is different from an established company. Little is known at the inception of a startup. There is much uncertainty with a new venture, in that there are many known and unknown challenges and risks. In contrast, an established company has a history of operating results, such as the resources utilized, the activities that are successful and not successful, the cash flow surplus or the existent deficit that needs to be financed, and the track record of the management. However, much is unknown in the case of a startup. A startup mitigates the risks by efficiently managing a series of stage experiments. Certain hypotheses and critical assumptions are made at the beginning of each stage; and these hypotheses can be tested and validated, the results of which can then be used to manage the uncertainty inherent to the startup, mitigate the risks, increase the likelihood of survival of the startup, and further refine its business model going forward.

The amount of money a startup will need to finance each stage is an important decision for the entrepreneur. Available capital is scarce for a startup. Raising more capital than necessary to complete the stage milestones not only dilutes the entrepreneur's equity, often at a lower valuation, but more importantly, the excess capital in the early stages may be squandered in noncritical activities, making future financings more difficult to obtain. The entrepreneur should raise just enough capital to fund the next stage plus a small cushion for contingencies. If the results of the stage experiment are favorable, such that the stage risks are successfully mitigated, then another round of financing may be obtained at a higher valuation to finance a subsequent stage. Otherwise, the venture may be abandoned or overhauled. The cost of venture failure is contained by raising just enough capital to finance one stage at a time.

The critical assumptions and risks should be identified at the beginning of each stage, and the entrepreneur must have a plan for how to test these assumptions and mitigate the venture risks efficiently (see chapter 8 for a risk mitigation plan). The entrepreneur should raise enough money to finance each stage experiment and test the stage hypotheses. The financing amount raised should be enough to mitigate the stage risks and stabilize the business model. The business model should be stabilized prior to making key hires and locking into key partnerships.

ONSET, an early stage venture capital investment firm, in its research on startups, found that the startups that delayed hiring key managers until after the initial rounds of experiments had proved successful and enjoyed a greater likelihood of venture survival and growth (Sull, 2004). For example, hiring a CEO too early may lead to a wrong CEO who is not able to execute the revised business model that results from the completion of the early stage experiments. Founders need not have expertise in a particular area of knowledge, but they may seek out advisers and mentors to fill the gaps in their knowledge. However, hiring key executives and forming key partnerships too early, before the business model is stabilized, is not recommended.

The scarce resources in the early stages of a startup should be used to mitigate the critical risks and uncertainties. All noncritical functions should be outsourced when possible. For example, some critical functions in the early stages of a startup are customer acquisition, product development, and raising capital. A new venture may initially outsource such functions as product manufacturing and distribution. If the early stage results are favorable, and after the business model is stabilized, some of the outsourced functions may be internalized to achieve scale economies and growth. Achieving scale economies and rapid growth are goals for the later stage of a venture, not in the initial stages for most ventures, certainly not prior to the proving the customer value concept. Furthermore, a new venture should not become locked into long-term relationships with key partners in the early stages prior to the business model being stabilized. The relationship with a key partner should be based on the critical activities at hand at a given stage.

The startup founders should be flexible, although passionate and focused, during the early stages. A startup should pivot its customer value concept and reformulate the value offering to meet the customer demand (see chapter 4). Pivoting the customer value concept may require abandoning the old product line and introducing a new product that the customers want. Zoosk, an online dating site, for example, had initially introduced a software product to facilitate market research data gathering; but after it found the customers liked its dating game app on Facebook, Zoosk chose to scrap the initial product concept and pivoted its strategy to build a dating app on the Facebook platform. Thus, in the initial stages of a startup, the entrepreneur needs flexibility in terms of customer value concept formulation.

An entrepreneur should not approach investors too early, before the venture is investor ready. Investors with their rigid expectations of the venture performance might cause some inflexibility and may create a bottleneck. Furthermore, a venture is not investor ready until after the deal-killer risks (associated with the customer value design) are mitigated and the customer value concept is proved (see chapter 8). When considering an investment in a startup, investors require proof that the customer value concept is working and the business is ready to scale, in addition to the startup having a solid team of founders and some proprietary advantages. In the very early stages, the entrepreneur is still trying to figure out the details of the customer value concept. Thus, the entrepreneur should nail the customer value concept prior to approaching the investors for financing.

Approaching investors too early not only may risk a rejection but also may foreclose on future financing options. Furthermore, a premature funding of a new venture, especially in the customer value formulation and testing stage, may lead to potential conflicts and disagreements between the investor and the entrepreneur, which may lead to the entrepreneur being fired or the investor not making further investments in the venture. An entrepreneur when unable to prove the product performance and the consumer acceptance of the product should not approach investors for funding. The product performance and the consumer acceptance of the product are the deal-killer risks that must be mitigated and the assumptions underlying them must be tested prior to the entrepreneur approaching the investors for funding. During these initial stages when the deal-killer risks are mitigated, the startup is often bootstrapped by the entrepreneur.

The Rules of Bootstrapping a Startup

An entrepreneur often bootstraps and manages the early stages of the startup without the aid of external capital. The entrepreneur uses their personal savings and, possibly, funds from their family and friends. The rules of bootstrapping a startup are (Bhide, 1992): (1) get operational early; (2) forget about an A+ team; (3) keep the venture growth in check; (4) focus on cash, not on profits or market share; (5) look for quick cash-generating opportunities; (6) offer products requiring direct personal selling; and (7) initiate and cultivate early relationships with potential investors and financiers.

Bootstrappers often start with a copycat idea targeting a niche market (Bhide, 1992). Large companies often do not show interest in competing with the startups entering a small, niche market. Using a proven idea or concept requires less money for market research and validation. Once the entrepreneur is in business, better opportunities may turn up and they may discover a more improved product design or process advantage. The entrepreneur can then pivot their strategy to suit the new opportunity.

Don't wait to get operational until after the idea is fully refined. Get operational quickly. Much of the learning and refining of the concept occurs during the experimentation with an early idea. Starting with a proven idea keeps the cost of early stage experimentation low.

Second, look for some quick cash-generating opportunities. Such quick cash-generating businesses may be considered distractions for a more mature business; yet, at the very early stage, any cash generated raises the entrepreneur's self-confidence and helps build credibility with the suppliers and partners. The early cash generated from these small opportunities can help pay for the product development and customer acquisition, thus relying less on outside capital. For example, a software company may offer software-consulting services and the cash thus generated finances its product development and market testing efforts without the need for external capital. During the early stages, when the customer value concept is yet to be proven, it is difficult to raise external capital, and the entrepreneur's personal savings may not be enough. When there is opportunity to generate cash, it can help pay for the initial activities related to proving the customer value concept. It is easier to raise external capital when the customer value concept is proven, or the customer risk and the product risk are mitigated. Furthermore, a startup can generate quick cash and test the market by starting to sell the product online either on its own website or on another company's website such as at Amazon.com.

Crowdfunding platforms are another source for a startup to raise early cash from a large number of contributors, each contributing a small amount. Crowdfunding platforms can also be used to test and validate the market demand for a product or service. There are five types of crowdfunding models (Harrison, 2013), namely donor models, reward models, pre-purchase models, lending models, and equity models. In donation models, the donor receives nothing in return except some name recognition. Donation models are used by nonprofit and charitable organizations. In reward models, the contributor is offered a nominal token gift (e.g., a tee shirt) in return for their contribution. The pre-purchase model is similar to the reward model, but instead of a token gift, the contributor is promised to receive the product the entrepreneur is making at a price less than the market price. This model not only provides the consumer-funded seed capital to the entrepreneur but also validates the demand for the product. The last two models are peer-to-peer lending and equity models. In the lending model, the contributor is promised a return of their principal plus an interest charge. In the equity model, the contributor is provided an equity share in the venture or promised a profit share from the future cash flow of the venture. The last two models are subject to federal government scrutiny and regulations in order to protect the general public from investment frauds and scams.

In the early stages, when bootstrapping, customer cash can be used to finance a startup (as in the case of the pre-purchase crowdfunding model). Mullins (2013) identified five revenue models that can be customer funded early on, without the need for much external capital. These bootstrapped revenue models include matchmaker model, deposit model, subscription model, standardize-and-resell model, and scarcity model. These customer-funded revenue models not only can generate early cash but also generate early demand for the product or service. The matchmaker model is used by an intermediary, connecting buyers and sellers. These startups carry no inventory and their cost of goods is very low, thus reducing the need for working capital. Initially, a small, niche market is tested and if the concept works, then the startup expands into a larger market. However, if one finds a lack of interest from buyers and sellers, then one might have overestimated the market demand.

The deposit model, also known as the retainer model, is a popular customer-funded model used by professional service firms, which requires a customer to pay a small amount upfront for an ongoing service or transaction. Similarly, the subscription model requires the customer to pay a monthly or annual subscription fee or membership fee in advance to use the product or service. For example, Costco collects annual membership fees from its members. Netflix requires customers to pay a monthly subscription fee. Subscription fees have been traditionally used by newspapers and magazines. The subscription model user can initially offer a low-cost or free trial subscription, and then it is renewed at the regular rate. Poor renewal rates indicate the demand is weak. Several online services are subscription-based, where customers pay a predictable amount in advance. Customer-funded subscription and membership fees reduce the amount of external capital needed by a new venture.

In the standardize-and-resell model, a product or service created for one customer can then be standardized and offered to a larger customer base. The initial one or two customers thus pay for the product development. Microsoft's initial alliances with IBM and Apple Computers financed the development of its early products such as MS-DOS and Windows. In the scarcity model, a startup may use the scarcity of a product to motivate the customers to pay in advance to purchase the product. Zara, a fashion apparel maker, which creates more than 10,000 styles a year with limited-edition designs, does not offer the same assortment of styles at all times; thus, the customers need to pay in advance to secure their order (Mullins, 2013). The scarcity model should be credible to the customers; when an item is gone, it should be gone, thereby creating a sense of scarcity among the customers. The scarcity model is generally used by businesses offering products that can become rapidly obsolete or are perishable.

Another rule of bootstrapping a startup is to offer high-valued products or services that require direct personal selling. Compelling a customer to switch from a familiar product or service to a new product or service offered by a startup requires a convincing and superior relative advantage. An incremental advantage may not sway the customer to switch to the new product. Furthermore, direct selling to customers reduces the initial costs of marketing and sales. Bhide (1992) found that only 10 percent of the startups studied in his research used distributors or brokers initially. Indeed, most entrepreneurs are initially their company's chief sales officer. Furthermore, it is easier for a company to overcome customer inertia and motivate the customer to switch to a new product when the company offers a tangible advantage, rather than implicit or intangible advantages. Concrete product features offering the customer tangible benefits will also require less investment in marketing and sales.

A bootstrapper should not worry about recruiting an A+ team initially. Their resources are scarcely enough to pay for most sought-after talents. A new venture does not have enough credibility initially to attract A+ talent. In his research, Bhide (1992) found that those startups that attracted employees by providing them the opportunities to build their resume and upgrade their skills were more successful. A startup's challenge is to find and motivate diamonds in the rough. Passion and strong motivation in employees are crucial in the early stages of venture development, not strong credentials. Often employees with strong credentials, who are persuaded to leave a large company with established systems and structure, may find a startup's unstructured environment unappealing, thus wasting the startup's limited financial resources and precious time.

Bootstrappers should keep the growth in check. High growth requires more working capital and capital expenditures. Many startups do not have the capital to finance the high growth initially. Successful bootstrappers are careful to pace their growth; that is, monitor the rate of growth they can afford financially and control (Bhide, 1992). Bootstrappers tend to invest in resources and not in advance of growth, but only when there is no other alternative available to complete the activities. Successful startups may outsource the noncritical activities initially. When the startup is ready to scale and the financing is available to fund the growth, some of the early-stage outsourced activities may be internalized within the venture. Furthermore, in the early stages, the customer value concept is yet to be proven and the business model is not yet stabilized; thus, investing too early in people and resources may be a wasted effort. The refined customer value concept or the revised business model may require a different set of employee expertise and resources. The entrepreneur should nail the customer value concept first, and then scale it with an efficient business model design. The rapid growth and expansion come at a later stage, after the business model is stabilized.

A startup should not initially target the best customers of the competitors. Furthermore, initial customers are not always the startup's best customers or most profitable customers. Once there is some traction in the marketplace and the customer value concept is working, then the startup may target better and more profitable customers. In some cases, for example, when the product's economic life is short or the customer switching costs are high, there may be a first mover advantage requiring an initial investment in high growth (see chapter 7). Nevertheless, in most cases, a first mover advantage is not real and may be short-lived. Even when a product's economic life is short, an ongoing investment in the product development program with controlled growth may be the right strategy. Bypassing the initial wave of competition and the need for investment in customer education, the followers may overtake the first movers in establishing leadership positions within the industry.

Another rule for bootstrapping is not to lose focus on cash. Initially, a startup is not expected to be profitable. It may take a few years or more to achieve profitability. Moreover, initially a controlled growth is more desirable than achieving a higher market share. Thus, profitability and market share expansion are not the best initial focus of a startup's strategy. Rather, the startup should focus on cash and conserve cash. Outsource all noncritical activities when possible. The performance of a new venture in the early stages is best measured by how well it is managing its cash, not in terms of profitability and the growth in market share.

Favorable terms from suppliers, early payments from customers, and a faster inventory turnover improve a startup's cash position, requiring less working capital. A bootstrapper tries to finance the early stage capital needs with personal savings and the credit available from suppliers and customers. When the customers pay earlier, before the suppliers have to be paid (i.e., when the days' accounts receivable is less than the days' accounts payable), the startup's working capital is negative (Mullins and Komisar, 2009). With negative working capital, the need for external capital is reduced.

The days' accounts receivable is defined as the number of days the customers take on average to pay after the goods are shipped. For example, the customers may take on average 60 days to pay after the goods are shipped. The days' accounts payable is defined as the number of days of credit extended from the suppliers. For example, the suppliers may give credit for 30 days between the time when the startup receives the materials and when the suppliers are paid. Furthermore, the days' inventory is defined as the number of days between the receipt of the unfinished materials and the shipping of finished goods. For example, it may take 15 days between the receipt of raw materials from the suppliers and the shipping of finished goods to the customers.

The days' operating cycle of a startup is the sum of the days' accounts receivable and the days' inventory. In the above example, the days' operating cycle is 75 days (i.e., 60 days plus 15 days). The days' operating cycle minus the days' accounts payable is the days' working capital. In the above example, the days' working capital is 45 days (i.e., 75 days minus 30 days). In most companies, the days' working capital is positive, which needs to be financed with external capital. However, with negative working capital, the days' working capital is negative; that is, the days' operating cycle is less than the days' accounts payable. In effect, the days' operating cycle is financed by the credit from the suppliers. A startup with a negative working capital is more capital efficient. A more capital efficient venture provides a higher return on investment (see chapter 7).

For example, when the customers pay with a credit card at the time of placing the order, the days' accounts receivable is typically three days. Suppose a startup holds the inventory on average for a week (i.e., the days' inventory is seven days). The days' operating cycle is then 10 days (i.e., the sum of the days' accounts receivable and the days' inventory). Suppose the days' accounts payable is 30 days; that is, the company pays its suppliers on average in 30 days. Then, the company has a negative working capital, as the days' working capital is −20 days (i.e., 10 days' operating cycle minus 30 days' accounts payable). In this case, the credit from the supplier finances the working capital needs and there is cash left to finance a part of the operating expenses. Negative working capital reduces the amount of external financing. The business models of many Internet companies such as Amazon and Dell, for example, utilize negative working capital; that is, their working capital needs are funded by the credit from their suppliers, with cash left to pay for some of their operating expenses.

Another rule for bootstrappers is to initiate and cultivate early relationships with potential investors and financiers. It may be too early to ask for funding but a relationship can be initiated early with potential investors, and their advice may be sought when formulating the business strategy. The investors should periodically be sent an update with regard to the progress of the startup and its key achievements. Investors typically monitor a startup's progress for some time before deciding to make an investment. A startup should also keep the company records and accounting books organized, which gives the investors the impression that the entrepreneur will be more careful with their money.

The rules of bootstrapping apply to a startup in the early stages of development, reducing its need for external capital. However, at a later stage, when it is time to scale the business and pursue growth, the startup may have to abandon some of the above rules. The startup would then need to hire a professional management team and acquire the critical organizational capabilities necessary to achieve growth and scale economies (Mishra and Zachary, 2014), pursue a large customer base and expand the market share, in order to be cash-flow positive and achieve sustained profitability.

Stage Milestones and Resource Requirements

Investors fund a startup in stages to mitigate the risk of investment loss. Each stage financing tests and validates the stage assumptions and mitigates the stage risks before the next stage is financed. If the results of a stage experiment are not favorable, the investor may not provide additional funding and may liquidate the venture. The results of a stage experiment help to mitigate the risks and refine the assumptions of the subsequent stages. By financing a startup in stages, investors mitigate their risks and limit their investment loss.

The venture development cycle is divided into five stages, namely early development, early operations, expansion, major expansion, and investment liquidity. In a typical startup, the related financing rounds corresponding to the first four stages are Seed, Series A, Series B, and Series C, respectively. However, during each stage of venture development, there may be more than one financing round. For example, during the major expansion stage, a venture may have Series C, Series D, and so on. Each financing round is tied to certain milestones that are expected and must be achieved with the financing provided. Each round of financing prepares the venture for the subsequent financing round.

The amount of money funded depends on the stage of venture development. In a seed round, if external capital is available, as the early development stage is often bootstrapped, the capital is provided to finance the product development and market testing. Thus, in the early development stage, the expected milestones are to complete a working prototype and an initial version of the product, and receive some feedback from the early customers. A seed stage funding round may be as little as $100,000 or less. A startup may be in pre-revenue or has a small amount of revenue in the early development stage. The next stage is the early operations stage when a startup has the product ready for beta testing and may achieve some revenue. The early operations stage may be funded by a Series A round, which may be a bigger angel round, or probably be the first institutional round, in the amount of $1 million or so. In the early operations stage, one or two major customer accounts are acquired, and the startup team is expanded. In each stage of venture development, there may be more than one round of financing. Typically, the amount of early stage funding is for 12–18 months of the operating and capital expenses.

The next stage is the expansion stage. The startup has now an efficient and stabilized business model and an expanded team in place. The revenue growth or the size of the user base expands, but the startup is yet to achieve profitability. The amount of funding in the expansion stage could be as high as $5 million or more. Several financing rounds may be needed to complete the expansion stage. The next stage in the venture development cycle is the major expansion stage. In this stage, the startup has proven products, a sustainable business model, and a complete management team. The revenues are high. A major expansion round can be in the size of $10 million or more. Several rounds may be needed to complete the major expansion stage. In the investment liquidity stage, the investors exit when the venture valuation is high enough to meet the investor's anticipated exit valuation, which occurs in most cases after the venture has achieved a sustained positive cash flow. The venture risks are mitigated and the venture valuation increases as the startup progresses from the early development stage to the investment liquidity stage. Thus a startup would exchange less equity for more money, when raising capital, as the venture matures from an early stage to a later stage.

Each stage of venture development may use multiple rounds of financing to achieve the stage milestones and mitigate certain risks. Each stage development may take six to eighteen months. Moreover, the time to complete each financing round can take three to six months or more. However, the earlier rounds can take even more time. In the early development stage, most of the financing needed is bootstrapped by the entrepreneur. The entrepreneur funds the venture with their personal savings or an investment from their family and friends. Some angel investments may be available toward the later part of the early development stage, after the prototype testing results are favorable, to complete the initial product development and for early market testing. In the early operations stage, after completing the initial product development and successful test marketing, most of the funding needed comes from angel investors; but toward the later part of this stage, an institutional venture capital round may be possible. The expansion stage and the major expansion stage are typically funded by institutional venture capitalists.

In each stage of venture development, with the financing provided, the startup mitigates certain critical risks and achieves certain milestones. Milestones are the expected outcomes at the end of a stage. Each milestone requires the completion of certain activities. These milestones vary from one industry to another and from one business model design to another in the same industry, depending on the nature of the product, the market, and the business model design. Block and Macmillan (1985) identified some generic milestones for a typical startup. In the early development stage, the expected key milestones are to prove the product market concept, to build and test the prototype, and to develop an early version of the product. In the early operations stage, the key milestones are to complete beta testing and secure one or two major customer accounts. In the expansion stage, a startup faces major competitive action, which may require a product redesign and a change in the business strategy.

Prior to the expansion stage, the business model needs to be stabilized. In the expansion stage, the management team is expanded and key strategic partners are in place. Some of the operations that may be previously outsourced may need to be internalized, and the organizational capabilities are expanded to achieve sustained growth and scale economies. Then, in the major expansion stage, the venture pursues rapid expansion, but only after it successfully achieves a sustainable competitive advantage during the expansion stage. A complete management team is needed to pursue major expansion.

The venture achieves sustained positive cash flow prior to the investment liquidity stage. Toward the end of the major expansion stage (i.e., in the investment liquidity stage), the venture may have secured a valuation high enough for the investors to exit either through an acquisition by an established company or through an initial public offering. The investor exit or a liquidity event may also occur during the expansion stages, after the venture has stabilized the business model and achieved a sustainable competitive advantage, although the venture valuation offer may not be high enough to entice the investors to exit. Sustained positive cash flow can obtain a high enough valuation that may exceed the investor's anticipated exit valuation.

During the early development stage, which may be bootstrapped or funded by a seed round, the least amount of financing is available, as the venture valuation is low and the venture risks are high. The target milestones in the early development stage are to complete the product market concept testing, develop and test the product prototype, and launch an initial version of the product. The product market concept may be tested by talking to potential customers, industry experts, key channel partners, and key suppliers (see chapter 3 for test market design). Concept testing validates certain critical assumptions made regarding the product functionality, customer value offering, and market demand.

A product prototype will be built and tested, and the assumptions made about the product development time and the product manufacturing costs are validated. The initial product features and the target price point are determined based on the customer feedback and a validation of the customer need (see chapter 2). The initial product design should include the product features that are most desired by the early customers and that are critical to the product functionality. The goal is to have a functional product that can be manufactured at a low cost and is acceptable to the initial target customers. Prototype development and testing, as well as the initial manufacturing, may be outsourced when proving the customer value concept.

Outsourcing the manufacturing initially validates the material and labor costs, the process specifications, the unit cost of the product, and the product quality achievable, before a large investment can be made to install a manufacturing and operations facility. A startup should outsource the pilot operation needs instead of making a large investment in the manufacturing plant and operations. A batch of finished products from the pilot operation can be tested in a small market to validate the customer value and market assumptions, including the consumer acceptance of the product, the perceived value of the relative advantage, the price point, and the size of the addressable market. Product quality and customer support expectations are also tested at this time. In the early operations stage, the manufacturing operation may be outsourced when the unit cost of the outsourced product is lower than the unit cost of manufacturing the product in-house. The manufacturing batch size and the inventory size should be kept small, as the product design may require a change depending on the customer feedback and the market acceptance of the product.

During the early operations stage, the startup should have secured one or two major customer accounts. The first major customer account could be a sale to a major distributor or retailer. By securing major customer accounts, a startup validates the assumptions related to how the product compares with the competition, whether a major customer finds the relative advantage of the product to be superior, whether the product quality and customer service standards meet the projected expectations, and whether customer acquisition costs are acceptable. Furthermore, the startup tests and validates the potential for growth and scale economies when it receives purchase reorders from these major customers. A host of problems and issues may be discovered in the early stages, which should be addressed prior to making major investments in the operations and hiring key personnel. By the end of the early operations stage, a startup has proved that its business model design works.

In the beginning of the expansion stage, a startup might experience retaliation from major competitors, and may face competition from new entrants. Depending on how the competitors respond and how the market accepts the product, the startup may need to redesign the product, or add additional product or service features. The startup may need to change its business strategy and product pricing. Additional product features may be needed for the startup to maintain its competitive advantage in the market, retain the existing customer base, and attract new customer segments. In the expansion stage, a product moves from the early adopters to the early majority customers in the mainstream market. The needs of these mainstream customers can be different from those of the early adopter segment. The product may need to be redesigned to suit the needs of the mainstream customers.

In the expansion stage, the competition may force the company to re-examine the pricing structure, and the revised price point may require the company to restructure its operations to lower the manufacturing and distribution costs. By the end of the expansion stage, the startup has installed the necessary organizational capabilities such as manufacturing, distribution, leadership, and key partnerships. The startup has also achieved a sustainable competitive advantage. The startup thus has a competitive product in the market and a stabilized business model in place to achieve further growth in scale economies. The company may not yet be cash flow positive, but it has achieved a sustainable competitive advantage. In the subsequent stage, that is, the major expansion stage, the startup will achieve sustained positive cash flow.

Following the expansion stage, a major ramp-up begins as a stable business model and a sustainable competitive advantage are in place. The startup may leverage its current success to enter new markets and target additional mainstream customers. Additional revenue streams may be sought. New products or product features are introduced to sustain the competitive advantage and protect the market share. During the major expansion stage, the startup may contact their investment bankers and potential strategic acquirers to prepare the venture for the investment liquidity stage when the investors exit. In the investment liquidity stage, the startup is ready for the investor exit, and may complete a merger with a strategic acquirer or goes public (i.e., an initial public offering). A bridge financing round may be needed at this time, just prior to the investor exit in some cases when the liquidity event is delayed. Large amounts of funding are needed to finance further growth, which can be obtained from the proceeds of an initial public offering or from a strategic acquirer. An established company may acquire the venture at an attractive valuation. At this stage, most investors cash out and exit. In case a potential acquirer is not found or the startup cannot go public (especially when its growth potential is limited), other exit opportunities such as a management buyout or a share refinancing arrangement are sought to facilitate the investor exit (see chapter 9).

Next, a framework is presented to develop an operating plan and estimate the resource requirements of a startup at each stage of development (see figure 6.1). The milestone-based operating plan presented in figure 6.1 is similar to the material resource-planning framework (in which the production forecasts are translated into the demand for materials and component parts for the forecast period). Similarly, in the milestone-based operating plan, the stage milestones are translated into the forecast of personnel and non-personnel resources. Furthermore, the operating plan is also analogous to the time-driven activity-based costing model, where the sales forecasts are translated to the demand for resources (Kaplan and Norton, 2008). The startup's operating plan estimates the amount and cost of the resources necessary to execute the business model, from the early development stage to the investment liquidity stage. Thus, the milestone-based operating plan estimates the resources required and generates an operating budget. The operating plan also generates a dashboard of key performance indicators to monitor the startup's performance and progress. The milestone-based planning framework may utilize the activity-based costing method of determining the unit cost of the product and estimating the resource capacities (see chapter 5).

The milestone-based operating plan estimates the recurring operating expense budget and the non-recurring capital expense budget for a startup, which are then used in the financial model developed in the next

	Early Development (Bootstrap/Seed)	Early Operations (Seed/Series A)	Expansion (Series B/Series C)	Major Expansion (Series C/Series D)
Stage Milestones				
Time for Completion				
Key Activities				
Key Partners				
Staffing Needs				
Plant and Equipment				
Recurring Monthly Operating Budget				
Non-Recurring Capital Budget				
Key Performance Indicators				

Figure 6.1 Milestone-based operating plan.

section, when determining the financing needs of the startup. The operating plan includes the key activities and operating processes, and estimates the associated costs. The operating budget includes recurring operating expenses, while the capital budget includes non-recurring capital expenses. The operating expenses are deducted on the income statement; whereas the capital expenses are shown on the balance sheet as fixed assets, which are amortized and the amortization amount is deducted on the income statement. The operating plan also utilizes a dashboard of key performance indicators (similar to a balanced scorecard) to monitor the performance of the startup and resource utilizations at each stage of development. The operating plan is a prerequisite to determining the financing needs of a startup.

The operating plan, shown in figure 6.1, requires the following steps: (1) identify the key milestones for each stage of venture development and the time required to complete them; (2) translate each milestone to a set of activities; (3) choose which activities can be outsourced; (4) identify key partners and suppliers for the outsourced activities; (5) determine the staffing needs for each stage; (6) determine the non-staffing, plant and equipment needs for each stage; (7) estimate the monthly operating budget and non-recurring capital budget to complete each stage; and (8) determine the key performance indicators, both financial and nonfinancial, that need to be monitored for each stage. The key performance indicators provide a dashboard of performance metrics to monitor the progress of the startup at each stage of development. The milestone-based operating plan thus begins with the stage milestones and ends with the operating and capital budgets and a performance dashboard. The operating and capital budgets are then used in the financial model to determine the financing needs (see the next section).

The activity-based costing model can be used with the milestone-based operating plan to estimate the capacity and costs of the personnel and non-personnel resources necessary at each stage. The activity-based costing model identifies the activity drivers and the type of resources required to complete each activity (see chapter 5 for an example); and then for each resource, it determines the resource cost rate and the resource consumption rate. The product of the resource consumption rate and the time to complete an activity determines the amount of resource needed for the activity. The product of the resource consumption rate and the resource cost rate provides the cost of the resource. The cost of the resource is included in the operating budget or the capital budget, depending on whether the activity is recurring or non-recurring, respectively.

Furthermore, the resource consumption rates and resource cost rates should be used as key performance indicators to monitor the operating performance of the startup. A startup should also consider the experience curve effect and take into account early stage operating inefficiencies when estimating the operating resource requirements. Leave a cushion of an extra capacity of resources so that the startup will not run out of the resources. A startup should not assume 100 percent resource utilization when developing the operating plan and estimating the resource requirements.

Cash Flow Burn Rate and Time to Sustained Positive Cash Flow

Determining the financing need of a startup requires estimating the following (see figure 6.2): (1) operating income, (2) capital expenditures, (3) operating working capital, and (4) net cash flow to equity. The initial projections in figure 6.2 are for the most likely operating scenario. In addition, high-growth and low-growth scenarios are modeled and their effects on the net cash flow and the financing needs are considered. It is better to have a financial model based on two growth plans in order to mitigate the funding risk, such that in case the funding is delayed or not available, the startup can switch to a low-growth plan (see chapter 8). The recurring operating expenses and non-recurring capital expenditures are estimated when preparing the milestone-based operating plan (see the previous section). The go-to-market plan also provides the sales and revenue forecasts, and an estimate of the cost of sales and marketing program (see chapter 5).

The financial model, as shown in figure 6.2, should be developed only after completing the startup's go-to-market plan and operating plan. In figure 6.2, a monthly forecast of revenues and costs is recommended, at least for the first two years. If the monthly forecasts are difficult, then the quarterly forecasts may be utilized. The entrepreneur should provide at least three years of monthly or quarterly forecasts based on the company's operating plan at the time of raising money. The three years of forecasts are necessary to understand the needs of the startup at the time of current financing round and for the subsequent financing round. The key assumptions underlying the financial model in figure 6.2 should be listed separately and provided to the investors. These assumptions may vary from one industry to another and from one business model design to another.

Step 1: Operating Income (Thousands of Dollars)
Sales Units
Net Sales
- Cost of Goods Sold

Gross Margin
- Sales and Marketing Expenses
- General and Administrative Expenses
- Miscellaneous Operating Expenses

Operating Income (EBITDA)
- Depreciation and Amortization Expense
- Interest and Lease Expense

Earnings Before Taxes
Taxes Payable

Step 2: Capital Expenditures
Capital Expenditures

Step 3: Operating Working Capital
Accounts Receivables
+ Inventory
- Accounts Payable
Net Working Capital
Increase in Net Working capital

Step 4: Cash Flow to Equity
Operating Income (EBITDA)
– Interest and Royalty Payments
– Capital Expenditures
- Increase in Net Working Capital
– Debt Repayments
- Taxes Payable
Net Cash Flow
Cumulative Cash Surplus (Deficit)

Figure 6.2 Estimating financing needs.

In the first step, to estimate the operating income, the number of units that can be sold and the revenues are forecast. The number of units to be sold can be estimated based on the size of the initial market and the number of sales calls that can be made with the available resources. In the initial period, when the product is being developed and tested, there may not be any sales revenue. However, the startup still incurs operating and capital expenses. Forecasting the revenues is more difficult than forecasting the costs. A driver-based revenue forecasting method can be used, in that the revenue drivers are first identified, and then the revenue drivers are used to predict the sales and revenues in the future period. The revenue drivers may include product and market characteristics such as market demand, industry growth, the relative advantage of the product, competitive factors, advertising and promotional spending, the likelihood of product acceptance, and the repeat customer purchase rate. The revenue drivers would vary from one industry to another and from one business model to another. Each company must list the key assumptions underlying their revenue projections. The sales and marketing resources available, and the customer acquisition and retention strategy determined in the go-to-market plan, drive the startup's forecasts of the sales and revenues (see chapter 5).

A startup may develop its sales and revenues forecast using six revenue drivers (Kaplan and Norton, 2008), namely product performance, advertising performance, sales promotion, price performance, product trial performance, and distribution. The product performance driver estimates the percentage of the target market population who are willing to try the new product and switch to the product even before the startup makes a major marketing investment. The advertising performance estimates the impact of the advertising spending on new and repeat customer purchases. The sales promotion factor estimates the impact of in-store promotions on the product sales. The price performance factor determines the impact of price changes on product demand. The product trial performance estimates the impact on product demand of delivering product samples directly to end users. Finally, the distribution factor estimates the impact of available distribution channels and retail outlets on product sales. The revenue drivers may vary by the customer's willingness to purchase the product, and thus vary with the company's customer value propositions, revenue model, distribution model, and the economic factors (see chapter 5).

Note that the net sales revenues are net of the distribution costs, customer discounts and incentives, and product returns. After the unit sales and net sales revenues are forecast, the cost of goods and operating expenses are estimated. The monthly operating expenses are estimated in the operating plan (see figure 6.1), which are based on the stage milestones, key activities, staffing plan, and go-to-market plan. The operating expenses include the sales and marketing expenses, and other general administrative expenses such as rent, insurance, utilities, travel, legal and accounting expenses, officers' salaries, payroll taxes, consultation fees, license and permit fees, etc. The next step is to provide a detailed schedule of the operating expenses by month. An entrepreneur should note that investors are wary of excessive officers' salaries and consultation fees. Consultation fees, if possible, should be avoided or kept at a minimum and officer salaries should be reasonable for the industry and the stage of the venture.

The cost of goods or the cost of sale includes the direct costs, such as the materials cost and direct labor cost, and certain overhead expenses that can be directly related to the production and distribution of the product or service. Initially the cost of goods will be higher; but with experience and scale economies, the unit cost of goods will decline. It is important not to use a low estimate of the cost of goods initially. A startup should also allow a cost margin for initial operating inefficiencies and lack of scale economies. The cost of goods will generally decline with the sales volume, and a greater efficiency can be achieved over time due to the effect of the experience curve.

One may use the industry average cost of goods as a percentage of sales, as a starting point to estimate the startup's cost of goods or sale. Industry-average financial ratios are widely available; and one may find these publications online or in public libraries. Alternatively, the cost of goods can be estimated by aggregating the various direct costs related to the production and delivery of the product. Although industry averages for firm sizes and geographical locations are widely available, it is not always easy to find the exact industry match for the product or service. Thus, when estimating the startup's cost of goods as well as other operating expenses, the industry norms and ratios may be referenced but these average ratios should be adjusted for the startup to account for the initial inefficiencies and a lack of initial scale economies. Finally, the initial inefficiency factor must not be neglected, as the initial cost of goods can be higher than the estimate suggested by the published industry norms and averages.

Next, the capital expenditures for non-recurring and depreciable fixed assets are to be estimated. The capital budget is estimated when preparing the milestone-based operating plan (see the previous section). The timing of the capital expenditures is determined dependent upon when the resources are necessary. The level of capital expenditures depends on which resources can be outsourced and which resources should be developed in-house. Initially the capital expenditures of a startup should be kept low, and most of the non-critical resources, if possible, should be outsourced. As discussed earlier, a startup should not commit major investments in fixed assets until its business model is stabilized. The startup will be thus more capital efficient and risk efficient (see chapter 7).

In the third step, the operating working capital is estimated (see figure 6.2). There are two ways to estimate the operating working capital need. One alternative is to use published industry guidelines to estimate the working capital requirement as a percentage of sales. The operating working capital is the accounts receivable plus the inventory minus the accounts payable. Industry norms can be referenced to estimate the accounts receivable, the inventory, and the accounts payable, as a percentage of sales. The problem is, however, finding the exact industry match. Initial inefficiencies and differences in business model design should be considered when extrapolating the industry ratios for use in estimating the company's operating working capital requirement.

Another approach to estimating the operating working capital requirement is to determine the days' accounts receivable, the days' inventory, and the days' accounts payable; and then the days' working capital is the days' accounts receivable plus the days' inventory minus the days' accounts payable. Next, the average net sales per day multiplied by the days' working capital gives the amount of operating working capital needed. For example, if customers pay in 30 days, then the days' accounts receivable is 30 days. The days' inventory, that is, the number of days the inventory is held between the receipt of unfinished materials and the shipping of finished goods, is determined. Suppose, for this example, that the estimated days' inventory is 15 days. Next, the days' accounts payable is estimated. For example, if the suppliers give a credit of 30 days then the days' accounts payable is 30 days. In this example, the operating working capital needed is 15 days of sales (i.e., 30 days of accounts receivable plus 15 days of inventory minus 30 days of accounts payable). Furthermore, a margin of safety should be added to the estimate of the days' working capital. In the above example, adding an additional seven days for a margin of safety, the operating working capital required is 22 days of the net sales. If the net sales projection in a given month is \$100,000, then the operating working capital needed in that month is estimated at \$73,000 (i.e., \$100,000 divided by 30 days, multiplied by 22 days).

The net cash flow is reduced by the increase in the operating working capital amount. In the above example, the initial operating capital based on the initial sales of \$100,000 for the first month is \$73,000. But suppose the second month's sales projection is \$150,000. Then, as per the estimated operating working capital of 22 days of sales, the second month's operating working capital need is \$110,000 (i.e., \$150,000 divided by 30 days, multiplied by 22 days). However, as the level of the operating working capital in the previous month was \$73,000, then the additional working capital needed, or the increase in the operating working capital in this month, is \$37,000 (i.e., \$110,000 minus \$73,000). Thus, there is an additional investment of \$37,000 in this month in the operating working capital. The net cash flow in that month is then reduced by \$37,000.

This approach to estimating the operating working capital required as the days' working capital times the net sales per day is simpler. However, a more precise estimate of the operating working capital requirement would be to estimate the accounts receivable based on the days' accounts receivable multiplied by the sales per day; and the inventory by the days' inventory multiplied by the cost of goods per day, and the accounts payable by the days' accounts payable multiplied by the cost of goods per day. Then, the accounts receivable plus the inventory minus the accounts payable gives the operating working capital needed. In the preceding example, the accounts receivable would be 30 days of net sales, the inventory 15 days of the cost of goods, and the accounts payable 30 days of the cost of goods. Then, the accounts receivable plus the inventory minus the accounts payable gives the operating working capital needed. The operating working capital estimate should not be ignored or underestimated when estimating the financing need. Seasonality should be also considered when estimating the monthly or quarterly accounts receivables and inventories. Startups often run out of working capital and may cease to operate. Often business plans do not give adequate consideration to estimating sufficient operating working capital.

In the fourth step, the net cash flow to equity is calculated (see figure 6.2). The net cash flow to equity is the operating income minus the sum of the capital expenditures, the increase in the operating working capital, and the priority cash payments (including interest expenses, debt repayments, royalty payments, and taxes payable). The net cash flow determines the cumulative cash surplus or deficit, and the cumulative cash deficit determines the timing and amount of the financing needed for the startup. The time to sustained positive cash flow is when the net cash flow turns positive and remains positive. The financing needed and the timing of the financing rounds can be determined from the cumulative cash deficit. The initial amount of financing should cover the cumulative cash deficit of 12–18 months. Then, the subsequent financing rounds may cover the cash flow deficit of 6–12 months. The initial financing round can take six months or more to close. The follow-on rounds may take three months or more.

The time to achieve sustained positive cash flow and the remaining months of liquidity are two important cash flow metrics the investors should monitor when financing a startup. The remaining months of liquidity is simply the number of months a startup has cash available before running out of cash. Finally, a scenario analysis can be employed with the financial model developed in figure 6.2 to examine different growth assumptions including high-growth and low-growth scenarios.

The financial model is developed using Microsoft Excel, so it is easier to recalculate the cumulative cash surplus or deficit under different growth assumptions. A sensitivity analysis of other critical variables and assumptions may be employed. Simulation software such as Crystal Ball (www.oracle.com) may be used. Simulation of the financial model developed in figure 6.2, using Crystal Ball, is discussed further in chapters 8 and 9.

Crystal Ball is an Excel add-in tool to carry out simulations of the key operating and financial variables. A probability distribution is assigned to each critical input variable of the financial model. The assumptions underlying the financial model should be reviewed when selecting the critical variables and assigning probability distributions to these variables. For example, the unit price of the product, the number of units sold per period, or the cost of goods may be chosen as the critical input variables, and a triangular distribution may be assigned to each of these input variables. The triangular distribution requires providing three values of the variable, namely the most likely, the maximum, and the minimum values. Crystal Ball then generates a probabilistic estimate of the selected output variable, such as the cumulative cash balance in figure 6.2.

The probabilistic estimate is more meaningful to the investor than a deterministic, single point estimate of the cumulative cash balance. Crystal Ball simulation also can provide the likelihood of and when the startup might run out of cash; and similarly, the likelihood of and when the startup would achieve positive cash flow. In addition to high-growth and low-growth scenarios, the goal-seek tool available in Microsoft Excel can be used to determine the revenue growth rate achievable with the available financing. The growth rate achievable with the capital available is known as the fundable growth rate. The startup growth should then be carefully adjusted and monitored so that the startup would not run out of cash.

The results of scenario analysis can further determine the critical variables and the key risk factors that are critical to the success of the venture. At the minimum, a scenario analysis of the financial model by recasting the sales and costs for optimistic, most likely, and pessimistic growth scenarios should be employed when determining the financing need of a startup (although this approach is not sufficient to manage the cash flow uncertainty in a startup; see chapter 8).

The timing and amount of financing determined in figure 6.2 should be reconciled with the operating plan developed in figure 6.1. The initial funding needs, which should be kept low and may have to be bootstrapped by the entrepreneur, should cover most of the activities of the early development period. The next round of funding should be adequate to cover the activities of the early operations period. The subsequent stages and the activities may be funded in several rounds. Rarely does a startup receive more than three or four rounds of external funding before the investors exit. Each financing round must be tied to the milestones necessary to complete each stage of venture development. It is important to raise sufficient capital in each financing round to cover the activities appropriate to that stage of development, and to achieve the milestones needed in order to qualify for the subsequent financing round. At the same time, it is important not to raise too much capital, as raising too much capital too early will give away the precious equity in the venture at a lower valuation. Moreover, before the product market concept is proved, investors and entrepreneurs may want to keep the investment amount as low as possible. During the early operations stage, before the business model is stabilized, all noncritical activities should be outsourced when possible.

In figure 6.3, the startup's cash flow curve is shown for the high-growth and low-growth scenarios. The cumulative cash balance is on the y-axis of figure 6.3 and the time is on the x-axis. The time to sustained

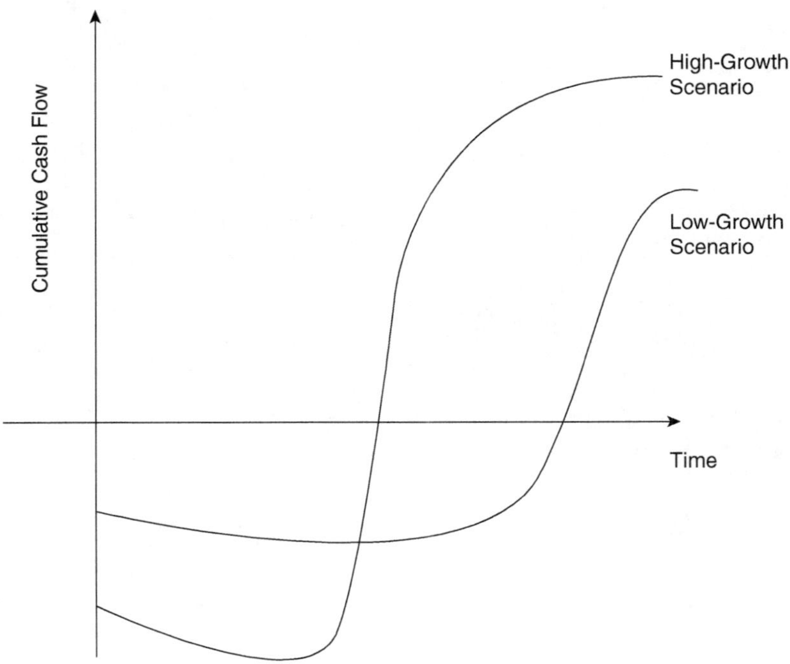

Figure 6.3 Time to sustained positive cash flow.

positive cash flow is when the cash flow curve intersects the x-axis and remains positive. The net cash flow turns positive earlier, but the cumulative cash balance turns positive only after the cash flow curve intersects the x-axis (see figure 6.3). Furthermore, a high-growth scenario would require more capital outlay but less time to achieve sustained positive cash flow, whereas a low-growth scenario requires less capital outlay but more time to achieve sustained positive cash flow.

With potential first-mover and customer lock-in advantages (e.g., when the customer switching costs are high), the investors may choose a high-growth strategy and invest additional capital early to implement such a strategy. The economic life of the product, or of the embedded technology, is also a determining factor. When the economic life of the product or the embodied technology is shorter, or when the competition is intense, the time to achieve positive cash flow should be shorter. In these situations, strategic alliances and leveraged growth strategies may be pursued to boost the operating leverage and shorten the time to achieve sustained positive cash flow (see chapter 7).

CHAPTER SEVEN

Is the Business Model Efficient and Sustainable? Reconfigure the Business Model

A business model should be capital efficient, cost efficient, risk mitigating, and sustainable. A venture's return on investment is the product of the operating leverage, the capital leverage, and the operating margin. The business model design can be reconfigured to enhance the operating margin, operating leverage, and capital leverage to provide a higher return on investment. An increase in the operating leverage widens the gap between the unit price and the unit cost of the product, enhancing competitive advantage and generating sustainable positive cash flow. The four attributes of the business model design—namely operating efficiency, supplier and customer lock-in, product market complementaries, and differential advantage—can enhance the operating leverage and provide sustainable scale economies. Several strategies are discussed regarding how to reconfigure the business model and value chain to enhance the competitive advantage and scale economies. Leveraging digital assets can provide high operating leverage and significant scale economies, enabling startups to compete more effectively with larger companies. With digital assets and high customer switching costs, a startup has strong incentive to be a first mover.

The business model is a strategic tool; thus, the business model design is a part of the strategy formulation process. But the business model design is the least understood and is often ill defined when formulating a business strategy. Often, the business model design is separated from the business strategy formulation. At times, the business model is confused with the revenue model. The value chain or the sequence of value-adding activities underlies the business model design. A business model innovation can be achieved by reconfiguring the underlying value chain; that is, how customer value can be created and delivered more efficiently and sustainably.

An innovative business model can offer a more efficient and sustainable way of making, delivering, and monetizing a product or service. Product innovation may enhance its market success, but a business model innovation in conjunction with product innovation can provide faster growth and greater profitability. For example, Apple introduced an innovative product (iPod) but offered it in conjunction with an innovative business model (iTunes platform), thereby achieving sustainable scale economies and enhanced profitability. A business model innovation can increase the investor's return by enhancing the operating leverage (i.e., the net sales divided by the operating expenses) and the capital leverage (i.e., the operating expenses divided by the investment) of the venture.

A business model creates, delivers, monetizes, and sustains customer value. The basis of the business model is the customer value definition. Redefining customer value necessitates a change in the business model design. In chapter 5, the business model design characteristics such as how the customer value is created, delivered, monetized, and sustained are considered. In chapter 6, a financial model is developed to finance the milestones associated with the business model implementation efficiently and adequately at each stage of the venture development. In chapter 8, we will consider how to prepare a risk mitigation plan at the time of investment. In this chapter, we discuss how the business model design can provide greater operating leverage, capital leverage, competitive advantage, and thus provide sustained positive cash flow and a higher return on investment.

Kim and Mauborgne (2000) offered a simple three-step process to design a business model: (1) decide a target price point; (2) determine the target cost structure; and (3) choose who you want as a partner(s). Skarzynski and Gibson (2008) further offered a checklist of questions to ask when refining a business model design: (1) whether the delivery and support activities can be made easier and more enjoyable for the customers, (2) whether the customer experience with the product can be enhanced to increase customer loyalty, (3) whether there are opportunities to improve the efficiency and effectiveness of the underlying value chain, (4) whether barriers to market entry can be created by reconfiguring the value chain, and (5) which partners can help the business to create and deliver customer value more efficiently and sustainably (see chapter 5).

In deciding with whom to partner, examine the venture's value chain activities and supply chain configuration. Note that a supply chain links the value chains of the partnering companies who together create and deliver the customer value. Raz (2008) suggested a checklist of questions to be addressed when designing a supply chain configuration and identifying key partners: (1) who provides the materials and component parts, and where they are located; (2) what distribution channels are used to deliver the product or service to the end users; (3) how relationships can be built with the suppliers, distributors, and other key partners; (4) how information flow is coordinated; and (5) how the incentives of all partners are aligned (see chapter 5). To achieve an efficient and effective supply chain design, information coordination and incentive alignment among the key partners are critical.

Stern and Sturdivant (1987) offered an approach to design a customer-driven distribution system: (1) find out what the customers want and desire; (2) identify all possible outlets and channels; (3) construct and assess the market clusters; (4) determine the channel costs, (5) compare the channel options and costs, and (6) choose the appropriate channel partners (see chapter 5). A startup's initial distribution strategy may be constrained by its limited financial resources. But the startup can enhance its distribution system as the consumers increasingly adopt its product and the startup enters the mainstream market. Thus, a stage-wise distribution system design is more appropriate for a startup.

Several revenue models are discussed in chapter 5, such as the freemium model, bait and hook model, insurance model, advertising model, affiliate revenue-sharing and cost-sharing models, long-tail model, inside-out and outside-in models, multisided platform models, and integrated models (also see Osterwalder and Pigneur, 2010). The revenue model must align with the customer value offering and the pricing structure. Each type of revenue model is appropriate under different market conditions and poses different implementation challenges. The business model is not the revenue model, but the revenue model is an integral part of the business model. The other decisions related to the business model design are the value chain configuration, the cost structure, and the customer relationship strategy (see chapter 5, figure 5.1). The revenue model choice must align with these other components of the business model design as well.

Kumar (2014), for example, to address the challenges associated with the implementation of a revenue model, proposed a checklist of questions a startup should ask before choosing the freemium revenue model: (1) what should be free, (2) whether the customers fully understand the premium offer or they need to be educated, (3) what is the target conversion rate, (4) whether the startup is prepared for the conversion life cycle, (5) whether the free users are becoming evangelists, and

(6) whether the startup is committed to an ongoing product innovation program (see chapter 5). Note that the goal of the freemium model is to attract new users; thus, incorrect choices would cause the freemium model not to work.

The activity-based costing model, as discussed in chapters 5 and 6, can be very useful when determining the unit cost of the product or service and in estimating the required resources for the startup. Traditional product-costing systems, such as absorption costing, do not account for all costs related to the product development, the business model implementation, and the underlying value chain activities. For example, absorption costing when determining the unit cost of the product does not include the marketing and sales costs or the product development costs (the two major costs of a startup), thus masking the level of resources needed for the startup to succeed. Product development and customer acquisition are the two key activities in a startup. Use the activity-based costing method to determine the unit cost of the product and to estimate the resources necessary for the venture (see chapter 6).

The activity-based costing model accounts for all relevant costs in creating and delivering a product or service, and thus provides a better estimate of the resources needed in a startup. The activity-based costing method uses the underlying cost drivers as the basis for cost projections. Thus, the cost projections are more accurate. A startup may first set a target price point (see chapter 4) and then determine a target cost of the product. The target product cost then may be compared with the product cost derived by the activity-costing model, and the startup's resource constraints can be thus identified. The resource shortages thus identified can be financed with additional funding or by forming strategic alliances.

The business model must enable a startup to overcome the barriers to market entry and sustain customer value. To develop a strategy to sustain customer value, determine the critical success factors and complete a SWOT analysis (i.e., strengths, weaknesses, opportunities, and threats) by analyzing the competition and industry (see chapter 5). Identify potential threats and opportunities as well as the strengths and weaknesses of the existing resources and capabilities. Then, alternative strategic options may be generated, such as leveraging the existing resources and capabilities to overcome the market barriers, establishing a market niche, reconfiguring the value chain and supply chain, or forming strategic alliances (see chapter 5). These strategies by themselves or in combination can lower the barriers to market entry and create new barriers to entry against the potential competition.

Reconfiguring the startup's value chain and supply chain design creates cost and operational efficiencies. Redefining the customer value targeting a niche customer segment lowers the barriers to market entry. A business model is sustainable when the business model design provides lock-in capabilities and market complementaries (Mishra and Zachary, 2014). The lock-in is achieved when the business model design creates strong incentives for customers, suppliers, and strategic partners. The complementaries are achieved when the business model supports complementary product offerings and adjacent markets. A sustainable business model design offers operating efficiency, differentiation, lock-in, and complementaries. A sustainable business model can achieve increasing returns to scale, thus greatly enhancing the investor's rate of return.

In chapter 5, the industry structure is analyzed to identify the critical success factors for a business opportunity to secure a path of least resistance when entering a new market. The critical success factors are derived from the positive and negative forces driving the venture profitability. Porter's five forces, and the current social and regulatory, and technological trends, can be used to analyze the industry structure in order to identify the critical success factors (Porter, 2008). The critical success factors are the key activities and capabilities that a business must employ and monitor regularly to succeed in the market. The five forces include the power of buyers, the power of suppliers, the threat of new entrants, the threat of substitutes, and the intensity of rivalry among the existing competitors (see chapter 5).

Analyzing the five forces can uncover the barriers to market entry. Barriers-to-entry are advantages the existing businesses have that are difficult for a new entrant to surmount. The barrier-to-entry advantages arise from scale economies, network effects, customer switching costs, capital requirements, proprietary technologies, preferential access to suppliers and channel partners, favorable geographic locations, established brand names, and favorable government regulations (Porter, 2008). Analyzing the sources of barrier-to-entry advantages not only helps one to identify where the barriers are the weakest to enable the startup enter the market with the least resistance, but also provides the startup the opportunities to erect new barriers to secure and protect its future market share and competitive position.

The power of suppliers and strategic partners can raise the barriers to market entry for the startup by increasing its operating costs and lowering the profitability. The startup's cost structure should be analyzed and the major costs and the related suppliers should be identified. The power of key suppliers and strategic partners then must be assessed. A supplier is more powerful when it is concentrated in the industry to which it sells, when its revenue does not heavily depend on one industry, when there is heavy switching cost to change the supplier, when the supplier offers a product that is highly differentiated, when there are no or few substitutes for the component or raw material provided by the supplier, and when the supplier can credibly threaten to vertically integrate to become a potential competitor (Porter, 2008).

The power of the buyers and market intermediaries also creates barriers to market entry and reduces the startup's profit margin. A buyer has greater power when there are a few large volume buyers, when the products are more standardized or commoditized, when the buyers have low switching costs, and when the large volume buyers can credibly threaten to backward integrate to become potential competitors (Porter, 2008). A buyer is powerful when the buyer is price-sensitive; that is, price-sensitive buyers pressure for a price reduction, lowering the profit margin of the startup. A buyer is more price-sensitive when the buyer's purchase amount represents a significant fraction of its cost structure, when the buyer's profit margin is low, when the buyer is strapped for cash, and when the product performance is less important to the buyer or its downstream customers (Porter, 2008).

The threat of substitutes can also raise the barriers to market entry for the startup and limit the price the customer is willing to pay for the product or service. The threat of a substitute product is high when the substitute offers an attractive price-performance tradeoff to the customer or when the customer switching costs are low. It is important to understand the structure of substitute industries. Also important is to monitor the technology and social trends as well as the changes in the customer tastes and preferences that might favor a substitute product. The customer's experience with the substitute products and the related customer pain points should be also examined to mitigate the threat of competition from the substitute products (see chapter 2).

The intensity of rivalry among the competitors can limit the profitability potential of a business. The intensity of rivalry is greater when the competitors are numerous and roughly equal in size, when the industry growth is mature and declining, when there is excess capacity in the industry, and when the industry is using highly specialized assets such that the barriers to exit for an existing business are high (Porter, 2008). The competition may be price-based or non-price-based. Price-based competition is more harmful to the startup's profit margin. Price-based competition is more likely when the products are nearly identical, when the customer switching costs are low, when the unit cost or the cost of goods of the product is low, when there is excess capacity in the industry, when the product is perishable, and when the technology embedded in the product can become rapidly obsolete (Porter, 2008). The startup should avoid competing on price and rather develop a relative advantage for the product based on non-price differentiators (see chapter 2).

Understanding the industry structure and critical success factors can help the entrepreneur to reconfigure the business model design. The venture strategy may be guided and the venture performance monitored using the critical success factors and key performance indicators (see chapter 6). The critical success factors are used as the basis for a SWOT analysis of the business model. The SWOT analysis then can be used to refine the business model design and formulate the venture strategy, to guide the venture development, and to determine the required resources and critical capabilities. The business model and venture strategy are refined such that the venture can leverage its strengths and capabilities to mitigate the potential threats and exploit the value-creating opportunities. The venture may reconfigure its value chain and find strategic partners to overcome its weaknesses and mitigate the potential threats.

Consider the case of Bright Horizons, a workplace childcare provider (Brown, 2001). The childcare industry is a mature industry suffering from low and declining operating margins. However, Bright Horizons, by redefining its customer and reconfiguring the business model design, was able to offer its investors an attractive rate of return on the investment, a return in excess of 50 percent per year.

The return on investment is the operating income divided by the invested capital. The return on investment (ROI) is driven by the following three drivers:

$$\text{ROI} = \text{Operating Margin} \times \text{Operating Leverage} \times \text{Capital Leverage}$$

The ROI can be enhanced by increasing any of the three drivers, namely the operating margin, the operating leverage, and the capital leverage. Note that the operating margin is the operating income divided by the net sales; the operating leverage is the net sales divided by the operating expenses; and the capital leverage is the operating expenses divided by the invested capital. A venture's ROI potential can be high when any of the above three drivers in the ROI equation is high. The greater the operating margin, the operating leverage, or the capital leverage, the greater is the return on investment. In a mature industry, although the operating margin may be low, the operating leverage or the capital leverage can be enhanced by using efficient and sustainable business model designs. A startup thus can offer an attractive rate of return to its investors by enhancing the operating leverage, even in a mature industry where the operating margin is low.

The degree of operating leverage can be measured by the percentage change in the net sales divided by the percentage change in the operating expenses. The degree of capital leverage can be measured by the percentage change in the operating expenses divided by the percentage change in the capital invested. The greater the degree of operating leverage or the greater the degree of capital leverage, the greater is the potential for increasing returns to scale (see the last section in this chapter), such that the operating margin increases at an increasing rate as the sales volume increases. With constant returns to scale, the operating margin does not vary with the sales volume. However, with increasing returns to scale, the success with a business model feeds back positively and brings greater success as the sales volume increases, resulting in increasing scale economies and a higher return on investment for the investor.

In the case of Bright Horizons, the operating margin potential was limited but the company enhanced its operating leverage and capital leverage, and was thus able to provide a higher rate of return to its investors. Bright Horizons enhanced the capital leverage by partnering with the employers who provided their workplace facilities so that Bright Horizons did not have to invest in its facilities, thus lowering the capital needs and boosting its capital leverage. Bright Horizons made its corporate partners invest more than $500 million in developing their on-site facilities, thereby boosting its capital leverage. Furthermore, the partnering corporations funded a part of Bright Horizons' operating expenses, thereby boosting its operating leverage. Note that the operating leverage is the net sales divided by the company's operating expenses. Bright Horizons was thus able to finance its growth without the need for much external capital and delivered an attractive rate of return to its investors.

Bright Horizons was also able to turn its industry's weaknesses to their advantage in entering new markets and securing the market share. The childcare industry has very low entry barriers; anyone can enter this market. But by partnering with and locking-in the corporations, Bright Horizons created formidable entry barriers so that its competitors couldn't offer childcare at those corporations' workplaces. Bright Horizons also exploited positive network externalities when the satisfied customers recommended the service to their networked corporations. The positive network externalities created enhanced returns-to-scale and sustainable profitability for Bright Horizons. With an efficient and sustainable business model design, Bright Horizons was thus able to offer an attractive rate of return to its investors.

The childcare industry is subject to heavy government and regulatory oversight, which becomes a high cost burden and a high entry-barrier for many childcare providers. However, Bright Horizons, by choosing to expand in those states where the regulatory standards were heavy, used the industry's weakness to its advantage by formulating its customer value concept with high quality childcare offering, and thus created another formidable entry barrier for the competitors. Furthermore, not only did Bright Horizons' client corporations invest financially in developing the onsite facilities but also they contributed to the development of Bright Horizons' state-of-the-art technology in providing childcare. The employees of the client corporations as well as the corporations wanted the best care for the children. The client-developed state-of-the-art technology used by Bright Horizons created a differentiation opportunity for its business model, creating further entry barriers for the competitors. Bright Horizons thus exploited the industry weaknesses to create competitive advantages and erect high entry barriers to secure and grow its market share.

A business model design should be risk mitigating and capital efficient. Risk mitigation is achieved by staging the financing of the business model into several stages, such that the outcome of each stage mitigates certain risks, which then refines the business model design in the subsequent stages. Capital efficiency is achieved when the capital required to finance each stage is minimized. A business model design is thus tested and validated though a series of low-cost stage experiments, with each stage consisting of a set of hypotheses and target milestones. Adequate funding should be available to finance the resources and activities necessary to achieve the stage milestones. A venture should mitigate the critical risks as early as possible (see chapter 8).

It is thus critical to prioritize the sequence of activities, such that the completion of certain activities results in information that refines the hypotheses and determines subsequent activities, thus progressively mitigating risks as the venture develops. It is the task of the entrepreneur to actively identify and manage key risks at the lowest cost possible (see chapter 8). Some of the key risks include product performance risk, customer demand risk, competitive risk, price risk, revenue model risk, funding risk, human resource risk, management and leadership risk, intellectual property risk, and so on. (see chapter 8 for how to develop a risk mitigation plan).

In the early stages, the scarce resources of a startup should be utilized to address the critical sources of uncertainties. All noncritical activities, if possible, should be outsourced in the early stages. In later stages, however, some of the outsourced activities may be internalized within the venture and the organizational capabilities may be built in-house to achieve scale economies, but only after the business model is stabilized. Scale economies and pursuing rapid expansion are goals for the later stages of the venture development, not for the early stages when the business model is still being refined. A venture should also not get locked into relationships with strategic partners too early, and the scarce resources of a startup also should not be invested in specialized, fixed assets before the business model is finalized.

Moreover, approaching investors too early for funding may lead to the loss of flexibility needed in the early stages. It is thus not appropriate to lock into relationships with investors in the very early stages, as the investors would have rigid expectations that might hamper flexibility in decision making. Thus, the early development stage is often bootstrapped by the entrepreneur; and the investors are not approached until the entrepreneur has proven the customer value concept. Furthermore, by approaching investors too early, the entrepreneur would give away the precious equity of the venture at a low valuation. Moreover, very early involvement of the investors with their rigid performance expectations may lead to the dismissal of the entrepreneur, which might result from potential disagreements or conflicts between the entrepreneur and the investors.

The venture development cycle consists of five stages, namely the early development stage, early operations stage, expansion stage, major expansion stage, and investment liquidity stage. During the expansion stages, the investors may also exit through a liquidity event such as an initial public offering or an acquisition by an established company. The early development stage is often bootstrapped by the entrepreneur, or may be financed by a seed round from angel investors, startup accelerators, crowdfunding platforms, or individual investors. Bhide (1992) proposed a set of rules for bootstrappers in the early development stage: (1) get operational quickly; (2) forget about an A+ team; (3) keep the growth in check; (4) focus on cash, not on profits or market share; (5) look for quick cash generating opportunities; (6) offer high-value products requiring direct personal selling; and (7) cultivate relationships early with potential investors and financiers (see chapter 6).

To determine the funding necessary to finance the resources required when implementing a business model, the following may be estimated (see chapter 6): (1) operating income, (2) capital expenditures, (3) operating working capital, and (4) net cash flow to equity. The operating income is derived using a pro-forma income statement. The sales projections are obtained from the startup's go-to-market plan. The operating expenses and capital expenditures are obtained from the startup's operating plan. The operating working capital needed is the accounts receivable estimate plus the inventory requirement minus the accounts payable. The net cash flow to equity is the operating income minus the sum of the capital expenditures, increase in the operating working capital, and priority payments (such as taxes payable, interest and royalty payments, debt repayment, etc.). The cumulative cash flow surplus or deficit determines the shape of the cash flow curve, which determines the timing and the amount of financing needed (see chapter 6). A scenario simulation can provide a probabilistic estimate of the financing needed under different scenarios, including high-growth and low-growth scenarios. A startup should raise enough capital to finance 12–18 months of the cash flow deficit.

As discussed earlier, the return on investment (ROI) is the product of the operating margin, the operating leverage, and the capital leverage. Below, we discuss several strategies to reconfigure the business model design in order to enhance the operating margin, the operating leverage, and the capital leverage, and thereby achieve a higher ROI. The greater the operating leverage or the capital leverage provided by the business model, the greater is the potential for scale economies. The strategies for a startup to achieve sustainable scale economies with an efficient and sustainable business model design are discussed in the following sections.

Can the Business Model Enhance Operating Leverage?

The operating leverage is measured by the net sales divided by the operating expenses. The degree of operating leverage is measured by the percentage change in the net sales divided by the percent change in the operating expenses. The lower the operating expenses, the greater is the operating leverage sustained by the business model design. The business model design is thus more operationally efficient. For example, with outsourcing noncritical activities, the operating expenses are lower, and the startup's operating leverage is greater. With negative working capital (see chapter 6), the startup's operating expenses are partially funded by the surplus in operating working capital, boosting its operating leverage.

Consider the case of Bright Horizons (discussed earlier), a workplace childcare provider. The company boosted its operating and capital leverage by partnering with employers to provide onsite child care to their employees, thus requiring less capital for the facilities and operations, which led to a higher return on investment for its investors. Bright Horizons achieved a return on investment on an average of 50 percent per year, even though the childcare industry suffers from a chronically low operating margin. The partnering corporations, the customers of Bright Horizons, invested their own capital in developing their on-site facilities; thus, Bright Horizons required less external capital from its investors. The low profitability of the childcare industry makes it more difficult to find external capital, and most companies operate at low operating margins. Because of the high operating leverage associated with its business model design, it was possible for Bright Horizons to deliver a high return on investment.

The leveraged growth strategy can boost a business model's operating leverage (Hagel III, 2002). When using the leveraged growth strategy, a company benefits from the growth and scale while avoiding the economic costs of owning and maintaining fixed assets. A leveraged growth strategy is thus less risky and the time to achieve positive cash flow is shorter. In the leveraged growth strategy, the role of the entrepreneur is as a knowledge broker and process coordinator. For example, consider Li & Fung, a Hong Kong-based apparel company (Hagel III, 2002). The company purchases yarn from Korea, which is woven and dyed in Taiwan, cut in Bangladesh and then shipped to Thailand for the final production, before the company ships out the finished product to retailers around the world. The entire production process is well coordinated and works according to a well-specified schedule. Li & Fung does not own most of the operating assets required to make and distribute the apparel, thus boosting its operating leverage and the return on investment. The company's business model, however, has the capability to orchestrate and coordinate a process network of several partnering companies.

Li & Fung, in the above example, did not own all the operating assets required to process the raw material into finished goods. The ratio of the company's fixed assets to its net sales was only 5 percent in 2002, but its return on investment was greater than 30 percent. Li & Fung generated $5 billion in sales in 2002 with less than $0.25 billion in assets. The company, however, had privileged access to the operating assets of 7,500 supply chain partners (Hagel III, 2002). The success of the leveraged growth strategy depends on having an in-depth knowledge of the industry and the customers, and the needs and incentives of the supply chain partners.

A more extensive knowledge of the partners' operating capabilities and limitations is thus necessary to align the partners' incentives and needs in order to effectively and efficiently coordinate the operating activities and resources. In the leveraged growth strategy, the role of the entrepreneur is to coordinate and manage a process network, instead of owning the operating assets. The operating costs and need for investment are reduced, but the need for operating knowledge and coordination is increased. The leveraged growth strategy speeds up the time to bring a product to market and the time to achieve positive cash flow, enhancing the investor return and the venture valuation. The leveraged growth strategy also provides greater strategic flexibility, such that the venture can quickly respond to changing market needs and technology shifts.

The development of information technology and the Internet can help enhance the operating leverage and facilitate the implementation of leveraged growth strategies by an effective coordination of the process network. Asset and resource sharing under the leveraged growth strategy requires a seamless operation of the activities spanning several companies along the supply chain (Hagel III, 2002). The development of the supply chain technologies makes the leveraged growth strategy viable for an array of business models. A typical supply chain spans two to three levels encompassing suppliers, distributors, and retailers. However, in the case of the leveraged growth strategy, it is necessary to coordinate the operating activities across several partnering companies and mobilize their resources efficiently along the supply chain.

In the case of a leveraged growth strategy, supply chain partnerships are not necessarily governed by rigid legal agreements, but by market-based economic incentives. The coordinating role of an orchestrator with a leveraged growth strategy necessitates defining the requirements of the partnering companies who must meet these requirements to participate in the process network. Thus, the orchestrator is thereby recruiting companies to participate, retaining them with proper economic incentives, structuring an information technology architecture for communication and coordination, tailoring the process to meet the customer needs, specifying the roles of all participants, creating performance feedback mechanisms so that the participants can improve their performance, and assuming the ultimate responsibility for the final product and the process outcome (Hagel III, 2002).

The entrepreneur or orchestrator here serves as the gatekeeper, certifying the operating resources and capabilities of the partners, and ensuring the performance of all participants. The number of partners in a network tends to expand over time, as each partner will specialize in a narrower set of activities. The orchestrator does not manage the operating activities of each partner, but manages the links and nodes along the supply chain and the relationships between the partners by defining and tracking the milestones that are critical to the performance of the overall process.

Two other leverage growth strategies, in addition to the orchestration strategy, namely the resource aggregation strategy and the platform strategy, can also boost the operating leverage (Hagel III, 2002). With the resource aggregation strategy, rather than coordinating the activities of the supply chain partners, the company may make third-party operating resources available to its customers. Consider Charles Schwab, a financial brokerage firm, which aggregates a rich array of specialized resources on its website and by doing so, offers its customers the ability to make better investment decisions. Charles Schwab does not own these operating resources, but the company carefully qualifies and monitors the performance of these resource partners. Schwab's reputation hinges on the performance of these partners. Microsoft also has a similar strategy, aggregating the resources of several vendors who are Microsoft-certified to serve its customer base.

With the resource aggregation strategy, Charles Schwab offers an operating platform for its resource partners to offer complementary products and services. Complementaries, a key business model attribute (discussed later in the chapter), can enhance the business model's operating leverage, providing sustainable scale economies and a higher return on investment. With complementary products and by serving adjacent markets, the company's brand name and reputation are enhanced; and a positive network effect is achieved as one company's operating performance feeds back positively to enhance the success of the partners, resulting in a greater return on investment.

The third strategy to achieve leveraged growth and thus enhance the operating leverage is for the company to place itself in the center of an economic web and actively shape that web. The participants enter the economic web voluntarily, guided by their own economic incentives (Hagel III, 2002). Microsoft, for example, created just such an operating platform with its Windows operating system. Intel's web centers on its microprocessor chip. Apple's web centers on its iTunes and App Store platforms. The web shapers pursuing a leveraged growth strategy do not choose who joins their operating platforms but they indirectly influence the economic incentives of the platform partners. The platform shapers play a more passive role than the resource aggregators or the process coordinators play, mostly exerting an indirect influence through the control of their operating platform.

Leveraged growth strategies—namely, the orchestration strategy, the resource aggregation strategy, and the platform strategy—enhance the operating leverage of a business model design by leveraging the operating resources and capabilities of the partnering companies, thus magnifying the investor's rate of return. By drawing on other companies' resources and assets, a new venture can meet the customer needs more precisely at a competitive price point, thereby boosting the company's market share, scale economies, and profit margin. Furthermore, the time to bring the product to market and the time to achieve sustained positive cash flow can become shorter, enhancing the venture's valuation and the investor's rate of return.

The strategic flexibility of the business model with greater operating leverage reduces the operational risk, such that the business model is risk mitigating and capital efficient. However, for a venture to employ a leveraged growth strategy, the venture must have a distinctive and durable competitive advantage as well as an in-depth knowledge of the operating capabilities and incentives of the potential partners. To implement a leveraged growth strategy, a company must decide which of the resources should be integrated within the venture and which resources can be outsourced from partnering companies. The company's in-house resources and capabilities should be such that they can create powerful economic incentives for the network partners to mobilize their operating assets and resources. The company with the most powerful assets or the differential advantage thus becomes the network orchestrator, the resource aggregator, or the platform operator (Hagel III, 2002).

Andrew and Sirkin (2003) further offered a framework to choose a leveraged strategy to bring the product to market such that the strategy enhances the operating leverage and is risk efficient. Here there are three strategic options, namely the orchestration strategy, the integration strategy, and the licensing strategy. The framework involves analyzing the venture's industry, the product market, and the risk factors. The industry analysis includes determining the operating assets needed, understanding the nature of the supply chain and the intensity of the competition, and assessing the importance of the brand. A brand may create a temporary advantage for the market entry or a more durable advantage to boost the market share. When the supplier base in an industry is sophisticated, the supply chain partners' operating resources and capabilities are well developed, the competition is intense, and the value attributed to developing a brand is high, the orchestration strategy is preferred. However, when the partner maturity levels are low, the integration strategy is preferred. With the integration strategy, the company builds in-house operating capabilities instead of leveraging the resources and capabilities of the partners.

The product characteristics, such as the embedded technology, the economic life of the product, and the need for complementary products and services to serve the customer needs, also determine when to pursue the integration strategy as opposed to the orchestration strategy. For example, when the economic life of the product is shorter or when the product requires complementary products and services, the orchestration strategy is preferred. With longer product life and strong intellectual property protection, a startup later on may switch from an orchestration strategy to an integration strategy by building in-house resources and operating capabilities at a later stage when the business model is stabilized and competitive threats are minimal.

An alternative to the integration strategy is to license the technology or brand to another company, such that the manufacturing and marketing expenses are borne by the licensee. A similar strategy is to franchise a proven business process or a well-known brand to a franchisee. The technology licensing strategy is generally preferred when there is strong intellectual property protection, when the product brand importance is low, and when a significant investment is required to manufacture and market the product. However, the franchising strategy is preferred when the business process can be proven and the brand value is high. With strong intellectual property protection, such as a technology or a brand, the company may license or franchise the intellectual property to another company, thus leveraging the licensee's (or the franchisee's) operating resources and assets to boost the operating leverage of the business model.

An alternative to the licensing strategy is the OEM strategy (where OEM stands for the original equipment manufacturer). With the OEM strategy, the company manufactures a part or component and sells it to an OEM partner who then integrates the component in the final product and markets the complete product to its customers. The startup is thus responsible for the product development, intellectual property protection, and manufacturing the component. Thus, in the OEM strategy, the OEM partner provides the operating resources and capabilities for the marketing and distribution of the final product and is responsible for manufacturing or outsourcing the remaining parts and services. The OEM partner is thus a network orchestrator or process coordinator.

When choosing among the integration strategy, the orchestration strategy, and the licensing strategy, a startup should evaluate the four risk factors, namely the product risk, the customer risk, the substitute risk, and the funding risk (Andrew and Sirkin, 2003). The product risk evaluation requires finding whether the new product can actually deliver the relative advantage and customer value propositions that it claims. The customer risk evaluation entails whether the customer will actually buy the product. The relative advantage of the product may not be superior enough for the customer to purchase the product (see chapter 4). The substitute risk arises from the availability of close substitutes with similar benefits, which can result in the company's shrinking profit margins. The funding risk arises from the lack of sufficient funding required to bring the product to market. The analysis of these four risk factors can help a startup decide which operating strategy it should choose in order to boost its return on investment.

In general, the integration strategy generates the greatest return on investment when the industry conditions are relatively stable, the customer needs and preferences are well understood, and the product life is relatively long (Andrew and Sirkin, 2003). The orchestration strategy is appropriate when the company has developed a breakthrough product, there are several partners available with well-developed operating resources and capabilities, and the time to bring the product to market is critical. The licensing or franchising strategy is preferred when the market is new to the company, the intellectual property protection is strong, and there is a need for complementary products and services. A combination strategy, such that initially licensing the product followed by the integration strategy after the company becomes more familiar with the market, may be pursued. With such a strategy, the loss of revenue from initially licensing the product can buy the venture an option to establish the manufacturing and distribution capabilities later if the product market outcomes are more favorable.

Can the Business Model Enhance Competitive Advantage?

A business cannot claim any value unless it adds some value in the marketplace relative to its competitors (Ghemawat and Rivkin, 1999). The underlying value chain of a business model can be reconfigured in such a way that the company can improve its competitive position in the industry. According to the transaction costs theory (Coase, 1937), a company has added value when the marketplace, including its suppliers, customers, and partners, is better off with the firm than without it. The wider the gap between the unit price and the unit cost of the product, the greater is the value added by the firm and the greater is the firm's competitive advantage. The unit price of the product is determined by the customer's willingness to pay (see chapter 4); and the unit cost of the product is determined by the value chain or the sequence of activities in making and selling the product (see chapter 5). The unit price is linked to the customer value concept; and the unit cost of the product is linked to the value chain configuration. The wider the gap between the unit price and the unit cost of the product, the more efficient and sustainable is the business model design.

The difference between the unit price and the unit cost is the operating margin, one of the three value drivers determining the investor's return on investment (ROI), as shown earlier. The three drivers of the investor's return (see the ROI equation discussed earlier) are the operating margin, the operating leverage, and the capital leverage. The operating margin is the operating income divided by the net sales; the operating leverage is the net sales divided by the operating expenses; and the capital leverage is the operating expenses divided by the capital invested. A venture can enhance its competitive advantage by widening the gap between the unit price and the unit cost, thus increasing the operating margin, which can be further enhanced by the operating leverage or capital leverage. We define the operating efficiency as the product of the operating margin and the operating leverage. The operative efficiency can be improved by reconfiguring the value chain underlying the business model design; that is, by choosing a sequence of value-added activities that delivers the customer value more efficiently and effectively than do the competitors. In the previous section, we showed how to enhance the operating leverage by employing leveraged growth strategies and reconfiguring the supply chain. In the next section, we will show that the operating margin can be further enhanced by the operating leverage and capital leverage. In this section, we show how the operating margin (i.e., the gap between the unit price and the unit cost) can be widened by reconfiguring the value chain and thus enhancing the startup's competitive advantage.

The operating margin, and thus the investor's return on investment, can be enhanced by widening the gap between the unit price and the unit cost of the product, by increasing the unit price or reducing the unit cost, or both, when compared to the competition. The operating margin increases with the product's relative value differential (see chapter 4). The product's relative value differential is the additional value added by the product in the marketplace when compared to the competition. The relative value differential is thus the difference between the product's benefit differential and cost differential relative to its closest competitors or substitutes (see chapter 4). The maximum value added by a product or service cannot exceed the relative value differential of the product or service. Note that a product's relative value differential in a marketplace can be negative.

The unit cost of the product, or the cost to serve (see chapter 4), includes the cost of goods and operating costs (i.e., the operating costs are allocated to the unit cost using the activity-based costing method). The greater the product's relative value differential when compared to the competition, the greater is the price the customer is willing to pay for the product (see chapter 4). Furthermore, the greater is the relative value differential, the greater is the operating margin, and the more sustainable is the business model design and the higher is the return on investment. The greater is the product's relative value differential, the more scalable is the venture and the greater is the investor's valuation of the venture.

By further widening the gap between the unit price of the product and the unit cost relative to the competition and thus enhancing the relative value differential of the product or service in the marketplace, the operating leverage enhances the operating margin and thus provides the venture a sustainable competitive advantage. Enhancing the operating leverage boosts the return on investment and the venture valuation. The greater the gap between the unit price and the unit cost of the product, the more sustainable is the business model design and the greater is the sustainable scale economies.

To enhance the operating leverage and therefore the competitive advantage, when reconfiguring the business model design, a number of strategic options can be generated with each option comprising of the value-added activities (determining the unit cost to serve) and the customer value propositions (determining the unit price). For a commodity product, when there is little difference between the competing products such that the customer's willingness to pay does not vary, the product's benefit differential is negligible. The relative value differential of a commodity product then accrues primarily from its cost differential relative to the competition.

Ghemawat and Rivkin (1999) offered a four-step approach to analyze the underlying value chain of the business model in order to enhance the product's relative value differential and the venture's competitive advantage: (1) catalog the value chain activities underlying the business model, (2) estimate the product's cost differential relative to the competition, (3) estimate the product's benefit differential relative to the competition, and (4) reconfigure the value chain to maximize the product's relative value differential. In the first step, catalog the value chain activities, namely the primary activities and supporting activities (see chapter 5 and Porter, 1985). Primary activities include the activities related to venture's inbound logistics, operations, outbound logistics, marketing and sales, and customer service. Supporting activities include the activities related to product development, human resources, accounting and legal support, information technology, and so on. Detail the key activities and required resources in each category.

In the second step, estimate the cost of each key activity by identifying the underlying cost drivers associated with each activity. The cost drivers are the factors that can make the cost of an activity rise or fall. Use the activity-based costing method (see chapter 5) to estimate the unit cost of your product and that of the competitor's product. To estimate the competitor's unit cost of the product, which is difficult to observe directly, determine the competitor's activities. Then, using the numerical relationships between your cost drivers and the unit cost of your product, estimate the competitor's unit cost from the competitor's activities. The product's unit cost is then compared with the competitor's unit cost, and the product's cost differential is the difference between the two unit costs.

In the third step, the revenue drivers are identified and they are linked to the activities in the value chain. The revenue drivers are the factors that make the customer's willingness to pay rise or fall. The differences in the willingness to pay for a product account for a greater variation in the operating margin than the differences in the cost structures. The revenue drivers can be determined from the customer pain points, which influence the customer's willingness to pay. Assess the relative success of the product's customer value propositions against the competitor's value propositions in satisfying the customer needs and meeting the customer's purchasing criteria. The value of customer benefits is determined for the product as well as for the competitive product. The opportunity scores, discussed in chapter 2, can be used to assess the product's benefit differential. It is difficult to estimate the value of the benefits of the competitive product. However, the price of a competitive product can be used to estimate the lower bounds on the value of benefits offered by the competitive product (see the competitive price equation in chapter 4).

Thus, the product's cost differential and benefit differential are estimated above. The product's relative value differential is then the difference between the benefit differential and the cost differential. In the final step, alternative strategies to widen the relative value differential, or the gap between the unit price and the unit cost relative to the competition, may be generated. These strategies are related to varying the revenue drivers and the cost drivers so that the product's relative value differential is maximized (note that the cost drivers and the revenue drivers are identified in the second and third steps above). A venture should eliminate those activities that incur costs without creating a commensurate willingness of the customer to pay. A venture should find inexpensive ways to generate an additional willingness of the customer to pay (see chapter 4). The relative strengths and weaknesses of these strategic options are evaluated using the critical success factors (determined in chapter 5; see figure 5.2). The final strategies are then chosen such that they can likely increase the relative value differential or the gap between the unit price and the unit cost of the product relative to the competition.

Can the Business Model Provide Sustainable Scale Economies?

Scale economies are achieved when the gap between the unit price and the unit cost of the product, or the operating margin, widens with an increase in the sales volume. With constant returns to scale, the gap or operating margin does not vary much with the sales volume; and with diminishing returns to scale, the gap declines after the sales reaches a certain volume. However, with increasing returns to scale, the operating margin widens at an increasing rate as the sales volume increases; and a startup can achieve a sustainable growth in scale economies. With the potential of the business model to achieve increasing returns to scale and thus a sustainable growth in scale economies, the startup may race to acquire and lock-in customers early on as long as the customer acquisition costs are less than the gain in scale economies. Thus, the startup may choose to be a first mover in a market and may invest heavily in the infrastructure capabilities in the early stages. Furthermore, the greater the operating leverage with a business model design, the greater is the rate at which the scale economies may grow. (See the multiplying effects of operating leverage on the operating margin in the ROI equation discussed earlier.)

The four elements of a business model design that have the potential for achieving a sustainable growth in scale economies include the operating efficiency, supplier and customer lock-in, differential advantage, and product market complementaries. Amit and Zott (2001) discussed these four elements of a business model design in the context of Internet companies. The business model lock-in is achieved with the customer and supplier lock-in. The product market complementaries are achieved when complementary products and adjacent markets can be supported by the business model design. The business model differentiation is the differential advantages the customer value concept and the business model design may have. The operating efficiency increases with the relative value differential (see the previous section).

The greater the business model efficiency, lock-in, complementaries, or differentiation, the greater is the business model's potential for achieving increasing returns to scale and a sustainable growth in scale economies (Mishra and Zachary, 2014). Each of these elements of a sustainable business model design can reinforce the other elements by feeding back positively to achieve sustainable scale economies. That is, sustainable scale economies are achieved when the success of one element of the business model design feeds back positively to reinforce the other elements of the business model, thus amplifying the value creation potential of the business model and enhancing the return on investment.

Business models of high-growth ventures provide the greatest potential for a sustainable growth in scale economies (or the potential for increasing returns to scale); while business models of lifestyle or low-growth ventures provide diminishing or constant returns to scale. Thus, the industries with high-growth potential and high customer switching costs have the greatest potential to achieve greater scale economies and a higher return on investment.

The business model lock-in is achieved when the business model is repeatable, in that the competitive advantage is sustainable, generating sustainable and recurring cash flows. With the customers and suppliers locked-in, their incentives are aligned with the venture's success, which creates a positive network effect and greater scale economies. The lower the lock-in, the less sustainable is the venture cash flow, and the more vulnerable is the venture to competitive threats and market uncertainties. The business model lock-in increases customer loyalty and customer retention, lowering the customer acquisition and retention costs. The lock-in also increases the customer switching costs, thus creating further entry barriers in the market. Customer switching costs are incurred by a customer when they switch from one product to another product. The customer switching costs include account termination fees, learning and opportunity costs, new investments in hardware and software, and so on. When the customer switching costs are high, as they are in certain industries, there is a greater potential for a business model to achieve sustainable scale economies by locking in customers, suppliers, and strategic partners early on. In these industries, the first mover advantage provides the business model lock-in, resulting in greater scale economies and a higher return on investment. Investors prefer to invest in these industries.

Sustainable scale economies can be thus achieved with first mover advantages when the business model lock-in potential is high because the customer switching costs are high. First movers in a market often can lock-in customers, suppliers, and strategic partners before the competitors and followers move in. Market entry barriers can be activated by first movers, which can generate increasing returns to scale and sustainable scale economies. When the business model design provides lock-in, differentiation, complementaries, and efficiency (i.e., the four elements to sustain increasing returns to scale), the startup would have a motivation to be a first mover in the market. The company then may set its profit margin below the level determined by the competitive price equation (see chapter 4), in a race to acquire and lock-in new customers. The company would thus set the unit price below the competitive level and may invest heavily early on in building and acquiring the infrastructure capabilities. The first movers can then lock-in scarce resources, secure patent protection, and acquire key technologies, preempting infrastructure capabilities to achieve increasing returns to scale and a sustainable growth in scale economies. Startups in certain industries are thus more likely to succeed as first movers when the potential for increasing returns to scale are present; that is, when the business model design in these industries offers lock-in, efficiency, complementaries, and differentiation.

The presence of an increasing returns-to-scale opportunity with a business model design and the level of market maturity (see chapter 3) can determine when the startup may enter the market (Eisenmann, 2007). Three scenarios are possible upon the startup's entry into the market: (1) the startup may not confront competition for some time; (2) the startup may enter simultaneously with several others; and (3) the startup may be a late mover when the market has one or two established leaders. In the first scenario, when the startup does not expect competition for some time, it can leverage the increasing returns opportunity with its business model design to lock-in customers and suppliers before the rivals move to enter the market. In the second scenario, when several companies enter the market simultaneously, the startup would invest heavily early on in infrastructure capabilities and secure key technologies and scarce resources in order to dominate the market. In this scenario, a few firms would succeed in dominating the market, earning sustainable scale economies, while the others would fall in the fringe positions. This scenario creates winners-take-all dynamics. In the third scenario, when a late mover with an increasing returns-to-scale potential faces the established market leaders, the best strategy for the late mover is to find an underserved niche market segment or leapfrog the competition with a superior technology or process (see chapter 5 for how to crack a well-guarded market).

A startup should not aggressively pursue increased scale economies until its customer value concept and the business model design are relatively stable. If a startup has to pivot its customer value definition and reconfigure its business model after it starts scaling, then all its investments in the infrastructure capabilities can be negated. However, when winner-take-all dynamics are present, as is true in certain industries (see the second scenario above), a startup has a strong incentive to scale early on and may race to acquire customers. With digital assets in the marketspace, the unit cost of production drops to a near-zero level and at the same time the customer's willingness to pay increases due to the positive network effects of the business model complementaries and lock-in; thus the startup's incentive to race to acquire customers is greater. With digital assets and high customer switching costs, a startup has a strong incentive to race to be a first mover in a market to achieve customer and supplier lock-in, enhancing its potential to achieve a sustainable growth in scale economies.

The complementaries within a business model are achieved when the business model can support existing and complementary products in existing and adjacent markets. The greater the number of complementary products offered in the same market, or the greater the number of markets served by the same product, or the greater the number of channels the business model can use to deliver the product, the greater are the complementaries within the business model. The greater the business model complementaries, the greater is the potential for sustainable scale economies provided by the business model design. The first mover advantages and the lock-in advantages with a business model are greater when the business model design includes the complementaries. Thus, when the business model complementaries are present, the success of one product in a market feeds back positively to the complementary products and their adjacent markets, creating a positive network externality and greater scale economies. The platform revenue model (see chapter 5), for example, provides a high level of product and market complementaries and sustainable scale economies.

Furthermore, with positive network effects, when a success with a customer group feeds back positively to bring about success with other customer groups, the customer's willingness to pay increases with the customer demand; that is, when a new customer remains affiliated with a proprietary platform, all other customers should be willing to pay slightly more to access that platform (Eisenmann, 2011). The increase in the willingness to pay may be very small, but when it is aggregated across the customer base, the demand-side scale economies (see the next section) can be substantial. As a result, with a greater potential for scale economies, the company can make additional investments in a race to acquire new customers as long as the customer acquisition costs are less than the gain in the demand-side scale economies.

Amit and Zott (2001) illustrated the four elements of a business model design, namely lock-in, efficiency, complementaries, and differentiation, using several case examples. Consider one of their cases, Autobytel.com, an online automobile dealer, which was founded in 1995 and went public in 1999. Autobytel used a platform revenue model. Autobytel achieved business model efficiency when the automobile buyers benefited from the value of the online content such as vehicle valuation and inspection reports; and the automobile dealerships benefited from the value of lower inventory costs and lower marketing and sales costs.

The business model achieved complementaries when Autobytel enabled strategic partners such as insurance providers and financing companies to offer complementary products to the company's customer base (i.e., a resource aggregation strategy). Autobytel achieved customer lock-in when its business model created customer loyalty with repeat purchases and through word-of-mouth customer relationships. The dealership lock-in was achieved when the dealerships had sunk investments in Autobytel's proprietary hardware and software platforms, thus increasing the dealership's vendor switching costs. The business model lock-in, efficiency, and complementaries were further reinforced by Autobytel's differential advantage, and the company could achieve increased returns-to-scale with its digital assets, generating a higher return on investment for its investors.

Internet and digital assets can be thus leveraged to achieve the business model lock-in, operating efficiency, complementaries, and differentiation, as in the case of Autobytel.com. The Internet facilitates a company's ability to move from a physical value chain to a virtual value chain (Rayport and Sviokla, 1995). Both the physical value chain and the virtual value chain (with digital assets) can be employed simultaneously to generate sustained scale economies. Information technology and digital assets can be leveraged by migrating certain activities from the physical value chain to the virtual value chain, to enhance the startup's operating leverage and generate the relative value differential when compared to the competition.

The product's relative value differential (i.e., the gap between the unit price and the unit cost of a product relative to the competition) is generated in a virtual value chain by a sequence of five activities, by gathering, organizing, selecting, synthesizing, and distributing information (Rayport and Sviokla, 1995). The raw information is processed and refined to generate the product's relative value differential that can be sustained. The business model innovation including the lock-in, differentiation, complementaries, and efficiency reinforce the product's relative value differential further. To form a parallel virtual value chain, a company applies the above five steps to the information collected at every stage of the physical value chain, creating additional relative value differential for the product when compared to the competition.

A startup can add value-adding information to its physical value chain to form a parallel virtual value chain in three stages (Rayport and Sviokla, 1995). In the first stage, the physical activities are monitored and their information is gathered, organized, selected, synthesized, and distributed. In the second stage, the company substitutes virtual activities for the physical ones, creating a parallel value chain in the digital space. In the third stage, the company uses both the physical value chain and the virtual value chain to enhance the relative value differential and a sustained growth in scale economies. Valuable digital assets are thus created, which further widens the product's relative value differential between the unit price and the unit cost when compared to the competition. The virtual value chain is leveraged to further enhance the business model's lock-in, efficiency, complementaries, and differentiation, reinforcing the product's relative value differential, enhancing the competitive advantage and operating leverage, and thus generating sustainable scale economies, as shown in the case of Autobytel.

Thus, by leveraging both the physical value chain and the virtual value chain, a company can generate additional relative value differential than the company would have done with the physical value chain alone (see the previous section). Rayport and Sviokla (1995) offered certain principles related to the creation of digital assets. First, the law of digital assets states that digital assets, unlike physical assets, are not depleted with their consumption, resulting in a near-zero unit cost of production, which thus maximizes the product's relative value differential (i.e., the gap between the unit price and the unit cost relative to the competition), and provides greater sustainable scale economies. Digital assets can create significant scale economies, allowing startups to compete more effectively with larger companies, lowering the entry barriers significantly and erecting new barriers (see chapter 5 for overcoming the barriers to market entry).

Second, digital assets also create significant product and market complementaries, creating new opportunities for the development of complementary products and services. Furthermore, digital assets enhance the supply chain efficiency and supplier lock-in, further enhancing the operating leverage. Digital assets also increase demand-side scale economies as customer lock-in is enhanced and the customer is then willing to pay a premium price, thus widening the relative value differential between the unit price and the unit cost. With digital assets and the virtual value chain, the unit cost can be lowered to a near-zero level and the unit price can be increased to a premium price point, thus maximizing the product's relative value differential, which can provide a greater competitive advantage and sustainable growth in scale economies.

The business model lock-in, efficiency, differentiation, and complementaries increase the business model's potential to achieve a sustained growth in scale economies, widening the value gap further between the unit price and the unit cost of the product relative to the competition. This relative value differential or the operating margin relative to the competition increases further as one element of the business model feeds back positively to reinforce the other three elements of the business model design. Enhancing the operating leverage and capital leverage, which has a multiplying effect on the operating margin and the investor's rate of return, provides increasing returns to scale and a sustainable growth in scale economies. The operating leverage and capital leverage can be enhanced by the supplier and customer lock-in, product market complementaries, business model differentiation, and value chain and supply chain efficiencies. Also, the greater the business model's operating margin, operating leverage, or capital leverage, the greater is the return on investment for the investor. Thus, the strategies that enhance and sustain the business model lock-in, efficiency, complementaries, and differentiation, can achieve a sustainable growth in scale economies and provide a higher return on investment.

PART IV

Is the Reward Worth the Risk and Effort?

CHAPTER EIGHT

Risk and Return

Effective risk management is a core competency of successful entrepreneurs. The entrepreneur should determine what the most important uncertainties are and how to test and mitigate those uncertainties at the lowest cost. A framework is provided to develop the risk profile of a venture and develop an efficient risk mitigation plan. Do not simply use a high hurdle rate or the worst-case and best-case scenarios when qualifying potential investment opportunities. The company-killer risks should be prioritized and sequenced such that the deal-killer and incentive risks are tackled first, the path-dependent and critical operational risks next, and the remaining operational risks as they occur. The insurable risks and the nuisance risks can be addressed easily. The risk profile of a venture is determined. A framework is provided to estimate the risk of investment loss and the maximum potential investment loss. A two-stage due diligence procedure is shown to yield the risk-consistent and return-efficient investment opportunities. The venture delta may be used to assess the relative riskiness of a venture and to estimate the investor's expected rate of return. The Venture Capital Asset Pricing Model (VCAPM) may be used to make venture investment and investor exit decisions.

Risk management is at the heart of the entrepreneurial process. The investor return is based on those risks that cannot be eliminated. Investors maximize their expected return at their acceptable level of risk (Mishra and Zachary, 2014). Investors stage the financing of a startup such that the greatest risks are tested and mitigated early. Successful entrepreneurs and investors are effective risk managers. Investors evaluate a startup, when considering funding, based on its underlying risks; thus, the investor criteria for funding a startup are risk-based. Investors use a two-stage due diligence process when evaluating a potential investment opportunity.

The selected investment opportunity is return efficient at the investor's acceptable level of risk. In the first stage of due diligence, investors screen available investment opportunities and select those opportunities with acceptable risks to investors. In the second stage, from the pool of investment opportunities short-listed in the previous stage, the investor might fund an investment opportunity that maximizes their expected return.

When evaluating potential investment opportunities, during the due diligence process, the investor evaluates the investment risks and the likelihood of investment loss. If the likelihood of investment loss is below the acceptable level of loss for the investor, the investment opportunity is included in the pool of opportunities in the first stage of due diligence. The investor then estimates the expected timing and return of their investment in the second stage of due diligence and selects the final opportunities, with expected returns that exceed the investor's target return. The investment risk is thus consistent with the investor's acceptable level of risk, and their expected return is maximized at their acceptable level of risk. The investment is then risk consistent and return efficient for the investor.

Macmillan et al. (1985) identified six categories of risks related to investing in a startup: the risk of failure to implement the business model (i.e., implementation risk), the risk of failure of the management (i.e., management risk), the risk of competition (i.e., competitive risk), the risk of failure of the entrepreneur to lead the team (i.e., leadership risk), the risk that the investor may not realize the expected return (i.e., liquidity risk), and the risk of failure to bail out the investment in adverse performance situations (i.e., bail-out risk). Kaplan and Stromberg (2004) further grouped investment risks into three broad categories, namely, internal risks, external risks, and execution risks. Internal risks are mainly due to unknown abilities of the entrepreneurial team and the performance of the product. External risks are external to the startup, such as market demand uncertainty, competitive threats, regulatory and legal uncertainties, investor exit uncertainty, financial market uncertainty, and so on. Execution risks are due to the failure of the business model and strategy, including the product development strategy and financing strategy. The internal risks of a venture are greatest in the early stages and gradually decline as the venture develops. The external risks and execution risks span the entire life cycle of the venture.

Investors show a risk preference consistent with the psychological theory of risk, in that an investor or investor group would have a preference to invest at their acceptable level of risk (Mishra and Zachary, 2014). Investors differ in their acceptable levels of risk. Some investors prefer to invest in the early stages of venture development and others prefer to invest in the later stages. In the early stages, the risks are the greatest. Those investors who prefer to take the greatest risks would invest in the early stages; and those investors who prefer to take lower risks would invest in the later stages. In the very early stage, however, the startup is not investor-ready, as no investor is willing to invest in a startup before the entrepreneur can demonstrate a working concept. The earliest stage of a venture, such as the early development stage, is often bootstrapped and self-funded by the entrepreneur and their family and friends (see chapter 6).

The venture life cycle consists of five stages: early development stage, early operations stage, expansion stage, major expansion stage, and investment liquidity stage (see chapter 6). Each stage of venture development is fraught with risks, and the greatest risks are in the early stages. Investors choose to fund a startup in stages, such that a stage or a part of a stage is funded to achieve certain milestones. If the outcomes of a funded stage are favorable, the subsequent stages may be funded. The risks vary across the five stages of venture development. In the early development stage, the risks may include a delay in the product development and inherent flaws in defining the product and market concepts. In the early operations stage, the major risks include unsatisfactory product performance, lukewarm consumer response, less than anticipated market demand, and the founding team unable to work together.

In the expansion stage, the major risks include an excessive burn rate (i.e., very high operating expenses) and the management's inability to respond to competitive threats. In the expansion stage, a promising high-growth venture may slip into a "living-dead" condition, in that the profitability of the venture is at best marginal. Investors may be able to recoup their original investment amount but they do not expect to earn a return on their investment. In the major expansion stage, the major risks include the inability of the business model to sustain scale economies and the failure of the management to retain key executives and strategic partners. In the investment liquidity stage, the startup may be ready for the investor exit. The major risks at the time of the investor exit (i.e., a liquidity event), include adverse financial market conditions and the absence of potential strategic acquirers.

Risk Mitigation Plan

Successful entrepreneurs and investors are relentless about managing risk, a core competency of entrepreneurs and investors (Gilbert and Eyring,

2010). Risks should be identified and mitigated in order of their importance. The costs of risk mitigation should be kept low. The greatest risks should be tested and mitigated first. For example, the customer demand risk should be tested first before the operational risks are mitigated. The prioritization and sequencing of risk mitigation is critical for the venture's success and growth. Before making significant financial investments and operational commitments, the entrepreneur should ensure that the greatest risks are mitigated and the business model is stabilized. The entrepreneur should continually identify the critical risks and challenges, and find creative solutions to mitigate them at the lowest cost. Successful entrepreneurs quickly identify and eliminate the risks in the right order using the right level of resources (Gilbert and Eyring, 2010). Successful entrepreneurs and investors are effective and efficient risk managers.

Gilbert and Eyring (2010) classified the venture risks into three broad categories. In order of their importance, the three risk categories are the deal-killer risks, the path-dependent risks, and the operational risks. Another important risk category is the incentive risks (i.e., see chapter 1; the risks associated with the ability and incentives of the entrepreneur and management). Thus, the incentive risks are the risks that the entrepreneur and management team may not have sufficient ability and incentives to execute the business model and lead the organization (also known as the adverse selection and moral hazard risks; see Mishra and Zachary, 2014). The incentive risks occur at all stages of the startup, in conjunction with the deal-killer risks, the path-dependent risks, and the operational risks (see the investment model in chapter 1).

The deal-killer risks and incentive risks are those uncertainties that, if left unresolved, could undermine the venture's success. Deal-killer risks are less obvious at first, but they appear in hindsight after the venture has failed. When there is a failure to spot a deal-killer risk, the venture is doomed; but the failure to hedge a path-dependent risk raises the odds that the startup will run out of funds; and the failure to address the operational risks in an orderly way may transform temporary setbacks into insurmountable obstacles (Gilbert and Eyring, 2010). Structuring the investment agreement to provide sufficient incentives to the management team and through the regular monitoring of the performance of the management team by serving on the startup's board of directors, the investors can lower the incentive risks (see chapter 10).

Deal-killer risks arise from the unexamined assumptions about the basic premise of the venture (i.e., the thesis underlying the business concept). The critical assumptions that underlie a venture's success and the customer value definition (i.e., the product market concept) should be tested very early before the product development even begins. The customer demand risk and the product performance risk fall under the deal-killer risks (see chapters 2, 3, and 4 for the customer value concept), which require testing the assumptions underlying the consumer acceptance of the new product, the relative advantage of the product, the unit cost of the product, the price-point, and the market size. The customer value concept may then be refined accordingly (see chapter 4).

Path-dependent risks are the strategic and financial risks; these risks are associated with the business model and venture investment strategy. The venture investment strategy includes a path-to-market strategy, a path-to-cash-flow strategy, and a path-to-investment-liquidity strategy. After the deal-killer risks associated with the customer value concept are addressed, the path-dependent risks should be addressed. Because the business model and venture strategy are built on the customer value definition, it would be appropriate to test and address the risks associated with the business model and venture strategy only after the risks associated with the customer value definition are addressed, since the business model design and venture investment strategy may change after the customer value concept is redefined.

The business model elements are based on the customer value definition and the critical success factors related to the market (see chapter 5, figure 5.1). The customer value concept is refined (i.e., the customer is redefined and the customer value propositions are reconstructed), after the deal-killer risks are tested and mitigated. The business model risks are then tested and the business model design is reconfigured. The business model and strategy risks, or the path-dependent risks, require testing the assumptions underlying the venture's go-to-market strategy, operating plan, financial model, and customer acquisition and retention strategy. The path-dependent risks should be tested early, but only after the deal-killer risks are tested; and the business model design should be stabilized before major financial and human resource commitments are to be made. The greater the customer retention, the operating efficiency, the differential advantage, or the product and market complementaries, the lower are the path-dependent risks (see chapter 7).

The operational risks are the remaining risks after the deal-killer risks and the path-dependent risks are tested and mitigated. The incentive risks associated with the entrepreneurial ability are addressed not only at the time of investment but also during the venture development. The operational risks should not be addressed before the deal-killer risks and path-dependent risks are addressed. A change in the customer value definition and a revised business model design may create different operational risks and challenges. Furthermore, the operational risks need not be addressed all at once. However, the more critical the operational risks, the faster these risks should be eliminated and the greater then are the odds of venture success.

Thus, it matters in what order a startup tackles its risks. The risk mitigation strategy is more efficient and effective by sequencing and prioritizing the risks. Consider an example of an e-commerce startup (Gilbert and Eyring, 2010). The risks in the order as they might occur are the development of a website, creation of warehouse capabilities, inventory and consignment, customer demand, operations, and product mix. If these risks are addressed as they occur, the venture might not survive and significant financial resources would have been wasted. Among the above risks identified, the deal-killer risk is the customer demand risk; unless customer demand is tested and the customer value concept is validated, it does not matter much how sophisticated is the e-commerce website, there simply would not be enough customers for the venture to survive. The path-dependent risk identified is the product mix strategy. It should be tested and the business model should be reconfigured accordingly, after the customer demand risk is mitigated and the customer value concept is redefined. The rest of the risks identified are the operational risks, which should be addressed at the lowest cost and at the appropriate time and stage of venture development.

By addressing the deal-killer risks, incentive risks, and path-dependent risks early, the scarce financial resources of the venture can be conserved, and the likelihood of the venture's survival and growth can be maximized. In each of these risk categories, a common mistake the entrepreneur makes is to focus on one key risk to the exclusion of the other risks (Gilbert and Eyring, 2010). Sometimes a partial resolution of one risk should not stop the entrepreneur from considering how to work in other risk areas. A major problem, however, the entrepreneur may have is a confirmation bias (Gilbert and Eyring, 2010), such that the entrepreneur, instead of testing the key assumptions underlying the venture's success, may become more invested in confirming their assumptions. Confirmation bias often arises due to the entrepreneur's excess passion and optimism. Instead, the entrepreneur should devise low-cost experiments to disprove their critical assumptions before it is too late. The entrepreneur should then accordingly redefine the customer value concept and reconfigure the business model design as early as possible.

The stage risk experiments addressing the critical assumptions underlying a venture's success may be either targeted experiments or integrated experiments (Gilbert and Eyring, 2010). The targeted experiments are used to test the assumptions underlying the deal-killer risks, whereas the integrated risk experiments are used to test the assumptions underlying the path-dependent risks and operational risks. For example, a marketing focus group or testing a product prototype is an example of a targeted risk experiment. A pilot operation or beta test is an integrated risk experiment. The targeted experiments are carried out in the very early stage, such that the deal-killer risks are mitigated efficiently and the customer value concept is refined (see chapter 4). The integrated experiments are carried out (after the customer value concept is well defined) in order to prove and stabilize the business model. The stage risk experiments are prioritized to conserve the scarce financial resources of a startup.

Sull (2004) suggested a disciplined approach to risk experimentation when managing the startup risks, such that the risk mitigation costs are minimized and the results are effective. It is the task of the entrepreneur and management to actively identify the key risks and mitigate them at the lowest cost possible. Investors expect the entrepreneur to have mitigated certain critical risks, namely the deal-killer risks, before the venture may qualify for funding. Furthermore, the investors expect the entrepreneur to use the money from a financing round to mitigate the stage risks most efficiently (see chapter 6).

Sull (2004) warned against experiment creep, when a risk experiment drags on too long, costs too much, or lacks clarity with regard to the source of uncertainty. Therefore, the critical sources of uncertainty at each stage of the startup should be identified early and tested before committing additional funds to continue the subsequent stages. Experiment creep may arise if the entrepreneur loses objectivity and become relentless in spite of the unfavorable results and poor performance. An entrepreneur can avoid the experiment creep and effectively mitigate the risks by getting timely feedback from the advisers and investors who regularly monitor the progress and performance of the startup. Investors have a direct incentive to minimize the cost of risk experiments and limit their investment loss; therefore, their advice can be more objective and can help strike a balance between entrepreneurial passion and real-world objectivity.

Furthermore, poorly designed risk experiments vary with too many risk factors occurring at the same time, increasing the cost of risk mitigation and making it difficult to understand what causes what (Gilbert and Eyring, 2010). It is thus better to limit the duration of a risk experiment, rather than analyzing the data to death and trying to be perfect. Even the deal-killer risks in the early stages should be tested quickly and efficiently.

The stage risk experiments should be devised such that each experiment is focused on resolving major uncertainties one by one. Moreover, the entrepreneur may miss the point of these risk experiments, in that these experiments are meant to refine the customer value concept and reconfigure the business model design, not to confirm whether the entrepreneur's initial ideas were correct. Furthermore, it is better to turn off a risk experiment when sufficient insight is obtained, and apply the lesson to refine the concept and the venture strategy, and then move forward.

Gilbert and Eyring (2010) defined "the curse of too much capital" as the case of having more capital than necessary at a given stage of venture development. Having too much capital, especially in the early stages of venture development, could undermine the venture success. For example, as is common in corporate ventures, a corporation funds the total capital needed for a venture all at once. Most corporate ventures and some failed venture-backed investments involve more resources and are financially inefficient. In comparison, venture capital provided in stages, known as stage financing (see chapter 6), is more successful, such that if a stage's outcomes are favorable, the subsequent stages may be funded. Sufficient funds, not too much or too little, and not too early or too late, should be raised to test and mitigate the deal-killer risks first and then the path-dependent risks as soon as possible. The operational risks are then tested and mitigated as they occur, such that scarce financial resources are used efficiently to learn the most one can and then apply these lessons quickly.

The critical risks should be identified early and regularly, and prioritized by examining the critical assumptions underlying these risks, and sufficient funding then should be provided to resolve these risks efficiently and in the right order. Gilbert and Eyring (2010) recommended a number of steps that can be taken to manage the risks more efficiently and effectively, such as limiting the duration of the risk experiments, testing one key risk at a time before addressing the subsequent risks, applying the lessons learned continuously by redefining the customer value concept and reconfiguring the business model design, and turning off the risk experiments and moving on to pivot the product market concept and redirect the venture strategy. Most successful new ventures, according to a study of *Inc.* 500 ventures (reported in Gilbert and Eyring, 2010), refined their business concept and venture strategy at least five times before they stabilize their strategy.

According to the Small Business Administration (reported in Hirai, 2013), about 60 percent of startups fail in the first four years. In a given year, the number of businesses that fail (i.e., either they close or go bankrupt) equals the number of new startups. Many startup failures could have been prevented if the entrepreneurs and their investors had given heed to the risk identification and mitigation. Most business plans fail to take risk analysis seriously and do not provide a risk mitigation plan.

According to modern financial theory, the greater the potential for reward, the greater is the risk; however, the converse is not true. That is, a greater risk is not always associated with a greater reward. Furthermore, a risk that can be efficiently managed and mitigated does not carry a reward. In the case of financial securities, the portfolio theory suggests that, by holding a diversified portfolio of financial assets, the unsystematic or firm-specific risks can be eliminated. In the case of venture capital investments, a proactive approach to risk identification, testing, and mitigation can eliminate or reduce the undesirable risks. The investor or the entrepreneur is not rewarded by taking the risks that can be mitigated. Thus, neither the investor has nor should the entrepreneur have the incentive to take such risks. Effective risk mitigation requires that the entrepreneur understands, at every stage of venture development, what could go wrong, which risks should be tested and mitigated then and in what order, and what should be done to manage these risks effectively and efficiently.

Hirai (2013) presented an approach to identify and mitigate venture risks efficiently to maximize the odds of venture survival. The venture risks fall into four broad groups, based on the likelihood of risk occurrence and the impact the risk has on the venture's success. The risks that have a low impact and have a low likelihood of occurring fall under the ignorable risks. The risks that have a low impact but may occur with a high likelihood are the nuisance risks. The nuisance risks can be mitigated by simple adjustments to the business operations or with built-in contingencies. The risks that have a high impact but occur with a low likelihood are the insurable risks. Insurance works by spreading the cost of a low-likelihood risk among a large group of insured businesses. Many business risks are insurable, such as product liability risks, property and casualty risks, errors and omissions, unexpected deaths of key executives, liability of directors and officers, among others.

However, the risks that have a high impact on venture survival and occur with a high likelihood are the company killers (Hirai, 2013). The company killer risks can sink a startup and waste significant financial resources. Thus, these risks should be tested and mitigated as early and as much as possible, and the lessons learned should be quickly used to redefine the customer value concept and redirect the business model and venture strategy. The key performance indicators should also be developed to continuously monitor these risks (see chapter 6). These company killer risks include the critical risks discussed earlier, namely deal-killer risks, path-dependent risks, and critical operational risks.

For example, consider a startup, for which ten risks are identified, and when each risk is reduced by 90 percent, there still remains a 65 percent chance that the startup might fail (Hirai, 2013). Specifically, there is a 90 percent chance that a genuine market need is identified, a 90 percent chance that the addressable market is large enough as estimated, a 90 percent chance that the business model is right, a 90 percent chance that the management team is right to execute the business strategy, a 90 percent chance that there would be no lawsuit, a 90 percent chance that the business would not get entangled in regulatory red tape, a 90 percent chance that the startup would not run out of cash, and a 90 percent chance that nothing else would go wrong. Even in this very optimistic situation, the chance of the startup's survival is 35 percent (i.e., 0.90^{10}), assuming these risks are independent. There still remains a 65 percent chance that the startup might fail. However, the chance of the startup's survival would have been greater and there would have been less waste of financial resources if these risks would have been prioritized and mitigated in the right order, as discussed earlier. That is, the deal-killer risks and incentive risks are mitigated first, the path-dependent risks next, and the operational risks as they occur.

Figure 8.1 develops a risk mitigation plan. The risk factors are listed in the first column. These risk factors vary by industry and can be different from one venture to another in the same industry. The risk factors associated with a venture and the underlying critical assumptions (or the hypotheses) should be identified in figure 8.1. These risks include product performance risk (including relative advantage and embedded technology risks), customer demand risk, price risk, market potential risk, competition risk, management risk, go-to-market risk, revenue model risk, cost structure risk, funding risk, regulatory and legal risks, and economic and social risks, among others. In the second column in figure 8.1, the underlying critical assumptions or the hypotheses related to each risk factor are identified. The next two columns in figure 8.1 rate each risk factor based on their likelihood of occurrence and the impact of the risk factor on the venture success. The likelihood of risk occurrence could be low or high; and the impact of the risk on the venture success could be low or high. The high-impact, high-likelihood risks are company killers. The high-impact, high-likelihood risks can be sequenced as the deal-killer risks, the path-dependent risks, and the critical operational risks, and should be addressed in the right order as described earlier. Although the low-impact, low-likelihood risks are ignorable risks, these

Risk Factors	Critical Assumptions	Risk Likelihood	Risk Impact	Risk Testing and Mitigation Strategy	Risk Mitigation Costs
Product Performance					
Customer Demand					
Competition					
Management					
Product Price					
Customer Acquisition					
Revenue Model					
Cost Structure					
Funding					
Regulatory and Legal Concerns					
Economic and Social Trends					

Figure 8.1 Risk mitigation plan.

risks should be monitored regularly since their importance may change as the market and competitive conditions change.

The last two columns in figure 8.1 detail how and when to test the critical assumptions or the underlying hypotheses related to the identified risk factors, as well as provide estimates of the resources and costs required for the risk experiments. The critical risk factors should be continually monitored and the risk mitigation plan should be reviewed and updated regularly. The lessons learned from the risk experiments should be applied as quickly as possible to reconfigure the business model and strategy. The risk experiments should be cost effective and efficient, and prioritized such that the greatest risks are tackled first. The deal-killer risks, and then the path-dependent risks and critical operational risks should be tackled early. The remaining operational risks are tackled as and when they occur. Among the remaining operational risks, the insurable risks should be insured by purchasing appropriate insurance policies. The nuisance risks should be tackled by factoring in contingencies.

It is difficult to gauge the likelihood of consumer response to a product until the product is sold in the market. Test marketing with an early version of the product may test the critical assumptions underlying the customer value design (see chapter 2). The customer feedback received during the test marketing experiment can also help to design a finished product that has an increased likelihood of market acceptance (see chapter 4). Proving that the customer need exists is not enough. Another risk factor is the size of the addressable market (see chapter 3). The addressable market size needs to be ascertained. Market research can indicate the market demand at proposed price points, given a certain marketing and sales budget. However, these assumptions should be tested as well. The early market response would indicate who is buying and whether the customer demand can be as large as estimated or the demand will be too small. If the demand is estimated to be too small, the product may need to be redesigned and the customer value may have to be redefined (see chapter 2).

It is also difficult to predict the competitive risks in advance. It is best not to initially target the competitors' best or most profitable customers so that the retaliation from the competitors can be minimized. Competitors may react in several ways (Hirai, 2013). For example, the competitors may replicate a business process if they find it working. The competitors may outspend the startup on marketing, or start a price war. The competitors may work around the product design or try to steal the trade secrets. They might steal the company's key employees. To minimize retaliation from the competitors, it is best to initially target a customer segment that is not most profitable for the competitors. In addition, the startup should stay ahead of the competitors by adding additional product features based on the feedback received from its customers.

A weak management team can cause the venture to fail. The management may be unable to lead the team or execute the business strategy. It is important to have the right people on the leadership team and to align their incentives with the venture success. It is also important to have a strong board of advisors and an experienced board of directors who can work together with the management team. The key strategic partners also should be carefully chosen. All team members and leadership should work together with one vision. A clear and unified vision is key to effective execution of the business strategy and the venture's survival. It is often the case that different entrepreneurs and board members have different visions and strategies. These visions and strategies must be reconciled as soon as possible; and a unified vision and strategy must be pursued. A divided team presages a sure failure.

The product development may take more time and resources than the business plan has anticipated. Furthermore, the early version of the product or the prototype may not perform as expected. Product development and testing can be costly, especially when the product requires a redesign after customer feedback has been received during a test market. A functionally viable product may be offered to the early customers in the test market. After customer feedback is received, the product features should be finalized.

Often the startup's go-to-market or customer acquisition strategy is flawed. The choice of the initial target market and the early customer acquisition strategy might fail. Thus, examine the assumptions underlying the startup's go-to-market plan. The go-to-market strategy for a product also depends on the market maturity and industry life cycle (see chapter 3); thus, the startup's customer acquisition strategy in a growth or mature market can be different from that for a new product category. Furthermore, examine the startup's channel strategy and the costs. Examine the assumptions underlying the startup's customer acquisition and retention strategy. Does the startup have enough money to fund its customer acquisition efforts and costs? Are the assumptions about the sales cycle and conversion rate realistic? The test market can provide vital data on the likelihood of customer acquisition and the go-to-market success of the startup.

Take a look at the assumptions underlying the business model, including the revenue model and revenue drivers, the cost structure and cost drivers, and the operating plan including the key activities, resources, and strategic partners. Many of these variables could go wrong. List the critical assumptions or the assumptions that are more likely to go wrong and devise low-cost and simple experiments to test these assumptions. Consider how the likelihood of these risks can be lowered and their adverse impact on the venture's success can be lessened. For example, during an early pilot operation, the critical assumptions underlying the business model can be evaluated to find out which elements of the business model are working and which ones are not working. Accordingly, the business model and strategy should be refined before making major investments and operational commitments.

Consider the assumptions underlying the financial model and funding needs. Investors fund a startup in stages. In each stage, some of the critical assumptions are tested and certain risks are mitigated before the venture may qualify for another round of financing. Funding is always scarce for a startup. There is always a likelihood that the startup may not receive the next round of funding or the funding may be delayed. Having two operating plans, one plan for low growth in case the funding is delayed, and another plan for high growth if the funding is sufficiently available, can mitigate the funding risk (Hirai, 2013). Prioritize the operating activities and operating expenses to correspond to the stage milestones (see chapter 6), or the deliverables expected in each financing round (see chapter 6 for financing deliverables). Keep the operations lean and efficient, and do not make major operational commitments before the business model is stabilized and until sufficient funding is available. Bootstrap the operations when funding is not available or delayed. Outsource all noncritical functions when possible. Restrain the venture's growth and consider some quick ways to generate cash (see chapter 6).

Most startups need more working capital than they have estimated. The startups may run out of cash and not have enough funds to finance the inventory and purchase orders. Moreover, the working capital assumptions such as the days' inventory, the days' accounts receivable, and the days' accounts payable are often wrong (see chapter 6). A pilot operation can test these assumptions. Furthermore, the operating working capital estimate should have a sufficient cushion to mitigate the excessive inventory risk or a delay in accounts receivable. Keep the growth in check in the early stage unless sufficient funding is available. Absent large funding, the startup growth should be restrained. Faster growth requires a greater amount of working capital (to finance the inventory and accounts receivable) in addition to the capital needed for fixed assets and operating expenses. Bootstrap with a low-growth operating plan when the funding is delayed. Flexibility in the early stage is key to the venture's survival.

Do not initially order large inventories of parts and materials, but wait to increase the production batch size after the product market concept is proven and the product design is finalized (after sufficient feedback is received from the test market customers).

Startups may fall victim to poorly structured legal agreements and inadvertent regulatory noncompliance. These events can drain a startup's scarce resources and time. Always retain a good attorney to help with structuring the contracts and maintaining regulatory compliance. Consult a good accountant to manage the accounting and tax records and maintain them in order. Finally, give attention to the current trends in the industry, including economic, social, and regulatory trends. These systematic risks can lower the revenues and increase the costs. Anticipate these trends and position the company to its advantage. Systemic risks are often ignored and can cause the venture to fail. For example, when the dot-com bubble burst in 2000, and as a result, the financial markets took a plunge, many startups could not find sufficient funding, and thus were forced to go bankrupt.

It is important to have the right investor on the team. The investor is a value-added strategic partner. The entrepreneur should evaluate the investor's ability to add value and meet the current needs of the startup. Pratch (2005) studied a leading venture capital firm, Vesbridge Partners, to understand how venture capital investors help their investees build and grow their business, besides supplying financial resources. Vesbridge Partners developed a unique framework focusing on six key value-added areas (called the value levers) to mitigate risk and create value in a startup. The six value levers are the venture strategy and business model, the management team, customer acquisition, future financings, industry positioning, and venture liquidity. Each time the investment firm finances a startup, it evaluates these six key potential value-added areas for its abilities to effectively mitigate the critical risks associated with the startup. Vesbridge's investment partners also use these six key areas to monitor the startup's performance and its risk mitigation effectiveness. The investor must have a working plan and financial resources for risk mitigation when investing in a new venture.

Risk mitigation is in the heart of the entrepreneurial process and is the core of the venture capital investment model (see chapter 1). It is important to prioritize and sequence the critical risks for efficient and effective risk mitigation. Efficient risk mitigation is key to the success of the venture capital investment model (see chapter 1). An entrepreneur or investor should develop a risk mitigation plan based on figure 8.1 and regularly monitor the company killer risks and regularly update their risk mitigation plan. Prioritize the risks and develop low-cost and effective risk testing and mitigation strategies. Address the deal-killer risks and incentive risks very early and then as soon as possible address the path-dependent and critical operational risks. Address the remaining operational risks as soon as they occur. Furthermore, develop an early warning system and choose critical performance indicators (see chapter 6) to lower the likelihood of a risk occurrence and lessen its adverse impact on the venture performance. Mitigate the incentive risks by aligning the interests of the entrepreneur and management with those of the investor such that the management will proactively identify and manage the critical risks (see chapter 10).

Risk of Investment Loss

The risk of investment loss and the maximum potential investment loss are two important indicators investors may consider when evaluating the risk profile of an investment opportunity. The risk of investment loss is highest in the early development stage of a venture and lowest in the investment liquidity stage. The likelihood of investment loss is on average about 66.2 percent in the early development stage and 20.9 percent in the major expansion stage (Ruhnka and Young, 1991). In each round of funding, to mitigate the risk of investment loss, investors may use a two-stage due diligence process. In the first stage, a pool of opportunities is chosen such that the risk of loss corresponds to the investor's risk preference. For example, some investors may invest in certain industries or at a certain stage of venture development. In the second stage of due diligence, from the pool of investment opportunities chosen in the previous stage, an investment opportunity is chosen that maximizes the investor's expected rate of return. Thus, with two-stage due diligence, the investment opportunities chosen are risk-consistent and return efficient for the investor.

The risk of investment loss is defined as the likelihood that the return on investment is less than or equal to zero. For example, if the risk of investment loss of a venture is 66 percent, then there is a 66 percent likelihood that the expected return on investment will be zero or less. According to modern financial theory, the greater the expected rate of return, the greater is the risk of investment loss; but a greater risk does not mean the investor return would be greater. The distribution of investment losses can vary significantly from one venture to another. Investor returns also show an asymmetry in their distribution; that is, more ventures provide lower-to-average returns, and few ventures provide very high returns. A two-stage due diligence process is more efficient because one investment opportunity may not always dominate another opportunity for an investor in terms of their risk preference and return expectation. The greater investment risk does not always mean there is a greater return. However, the greater return often means there is a greater risk.

Consider the risk-reward structure of the two investment opportunities, Investments X and Y, in figure 8.2. In each case, the greater the reward, the greater is the risk of investment loss. However, one investment opportunity does not always dominate the other. An investor with a lower risk preference would choose Investment X over Investment Y, because Investment X has a higher reward relative to Investment Y at a lower level of risk. However, if the investor's risk preference were high, the investor would choose Investment Y over Investment X, as shown in figure 8.2. *P** is the indifference point, such that if an investor's risk preference is above *P**, they would choose Investment Y, and if their risk preference is below *P**, they would choose Investment X. Thus, with two-stage due diligence, a risk-reward efficient investment opportunity can be chosen by the investor, such that the first stage selects the investment opportunities consistent with the investors' risk preference, and

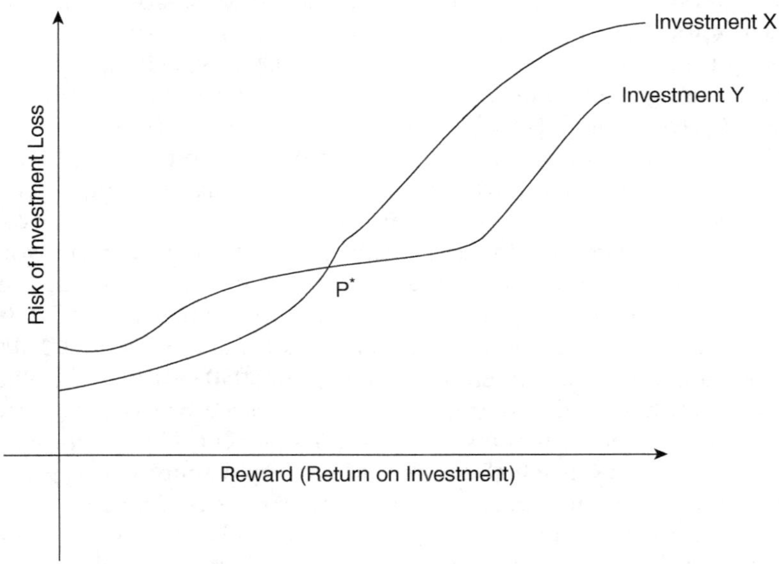

Figure 8.2 Two-stage due diligence.

the second stage maximizes the investor's expected return at their given level of risk preference.

Hertz (1979) offered a simple framework to develop and evaluate the risk profile of an investment. A risk simulation tool such as Oracle's Crystal Ball (www.oracle.com) can be used to develop the risk profile of a venture and estimate the risk of investment loss. Most investors, instead of estimating the risk of loss, simply use a high hurdle rate to screen the ventures. But a higher hurdle rate does not always provide a risk-return efficient choice for the investor. For example, in figure 8.2, Investment Y would be always chosen over Investment X when a high hurdle rate is used. But as shown in figure 8.2, for some investors, based on their risk preference, Investment X is preferred to Investment Y (e.g., when their acceptable risk of loss is below *P**).

Hertz (1979) thus cautioned investors against simply using a high hurdle rate for evaluating all investment opportunities. Consider the following investment opportunity (Hertz, 1979). The unit price of the product is $5 and the expected total sales are 200,000 units per year. The estimated operating costs and expenses are $800,000 per year. The investment amount required is $1 million. Accordingly, the expected return on investment (i.e., the revenues minus the total costs, divided by the investment amount) equals 20 percent (i.e., $5 per unit times 200,000 units, minus $800,000 costs, and then divide the difference by $1 million). Thus, when the investor uses a hurdle rate above 20 percent (e.g., a 40% hurdle rate), then this investment opportunity would not be acceptable to the investor. (By using a 40% hurdle rate to evaluate this investment opportunity, the net present value [NPV] of the investment is negative.)

Furthermore, investors also commonly use the best-case and worst-case scenarios. Hertz (1979) cautioned investors against using best-case and worst-case scenarios, as these might not lead to the right choice of an investment opportunity. In the preceding example, consider the worst-case and best-case scenarios. Suppose the unit price of the product can range from $5 to $5.50 per unit; the operating costs range from $700,000 to $875,000; the number of units sold range from 175,000 to 225,000; and the amount of investment may range from $950,000 to $1.1 million. Using these figures, the return on investment in the worst-case scenario is zero and in the best-case scenario is 56.5 percent. Thus, there would be some scenarios in which the investment opportunity would provide a return on investment greater than 40 percent (i.e., the investor's target rate of return as considered above); but there are other scenarios in which the investor's return would be much less than 40 percent. Thus, simply using the worst-case and best-case scenarios, as commonly employed in practice, would not help the investor in making the right investment decision. It is therefore important to have a sense of likelihood that the venture can achieve the investor's target rate of return. The investor may decide to pursue the investment opportunity if the estimated likelihood of achieving the target rate of return, and the estimated likelihood of loss, are acceptable.

The risk of investment loss can be determined from a simulation of the risk profile of an investment opportunity. To construct the risk profile of an investment opportunity, follow a three-step procedure: (1) identify the key determining variables that contribute to the uncertainty of the return on investment, (2) estimate a range of values for each of these input variables, and (3) run a simulation to generate the risk profile of the investment opportunity. The key input variables may be market-related (such as unit price, sales units, sales growth), cost-related (such as unit cost, operating expenses, working capital, capital expenses), and investment-related (such as the amount and timing of the investment needed). Some of these determining variables could be correlated; that is, they move in the same direction when they are positively correlated, and move in the opposite direction when they are negatively correlated. The simulation software generally allows the user to input which variables are positively correlated and which ones are negatively correlated.

Thus, when using a simulation program to construct the risk profile of an investment opportunity, determine the key input variables and assign each one a probability distribution. The simulation software comes with a library of probability distributions from which a distribution may be chosen for each input variable. The simulation software can also estimate the distribution of an input variable if a range of values and their likelihood are provided by the user. Next, the outcome variable is chosen and the simulation is run using the software. In the simulation step, the software chooses the input values according to their pre-assigned probability distributions, and the outcome variable is computed. The range and the likelihood of the outcome variable (in this case, the output variable is the return on investment), is the output of the simulation. Thus, a probabilistic estimate of the return on investment (see figure 8.3) determines the risk profile of the investment opportunity and provides the odds of the expected return to be zero or negative (or the risk of investment loss).

Several simulation programs are available on the market. The same three steps are used with any simulation software to determine the risk profile of an investment opportunity: that is, choosing the key input and output variables, assigning probability distributions to the input variables, and running the simulation to generate a probability estimate of the output

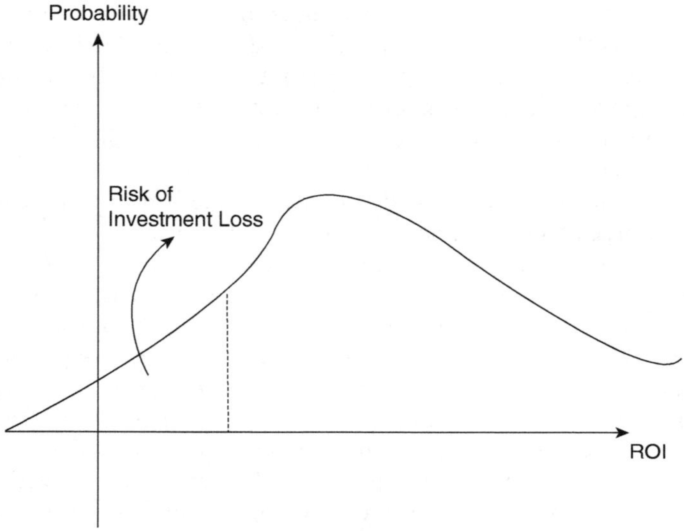

Figure 8.3 Risk of investment loss.

variables. Crystal Ball is a simulation tool offered by Oracle Corporation (www.oracle.com), as an add-in to Microsoft Excel. Figure 8.3 shows the risk profile of a new venture, drawn from the output values generated with Crystal Ball. In this example, the number of units sold, the unit price of the product, the operating costs and expenses, and the investment amount were chosen as the key input variables; and a triangular distribution was assigned to each input variable. A triangular distribution requires only three parameters, the minimum value, the maximum value, and the most likely value. The simulation chooses a random value for each input variable according to the assigned distribution. Other probability distributions can be chosen from the available library of distributions in the simulation software; or customized distributions can be fitted to the user-provided values and likelihood of the input variables.

The simulation results in figure 8.3 show that there is a 24.23 percent chance that the return on investment can be zero or negative. That is, the risk of investment loss in the above example is 24.23 percent. Analyzing the simulation results further, we find that the return on investment in this case can vary from −28 percent to 50 percent. Thus, in some scenarios, the return on investment can be as low as −28 percent. Moreover, the maximum return achievable is 50 percent. The average return on investment is estimated to be 8 percent, much smaller than the investor's target return of 40 percent. The average return estimated using the simulation is also much lower than the return estimated using the single point estimates of the input variables. Thus, a probabilistic estimate of the return on investment provides information that is more meaningful to the investor when evaluating a potential investment opportunity. The maximum potential investment loss can be calculated from the minimum return estimated with the simulation. In the above example, the minimum return is −28 percent; that is, the investor could lose 28 percent of their original investment amount. The maximum potential investment loss is then 28 percent of the original investment amount. The risk of investment loss and the maximum potential investment loss are two important considerations for investors when evaluating an investment opportunity.

Venture Delta and the VCAPM

Venture delta is a measure of the relative riskiness of the venture compared to the industry to which the venture belongs. Venture delta is estimated by (Mishra and Zachary, 2014):

$$\delta = \frac{1 + rT}{1 - \pi}$$

In the above equation, δ = venture delta; π = the estimated risk of loss; T = the expected time to investor exit; and r = the industry cost of capital. For example, if the estimated risk of loss (π) with a venture investment is 25 percent, the industry cost of capital (r) is 20 percent, and the expected time to investor exit (T) is 4 years, then the venture delta (δ) is 2.40. That is, the venture is 2.4 times riskier than an average established company in the industry to which the venture belongs. Venture delta increases with the industry risk and the venture risk. The greater the industry risk or the earlier the venture stage, the higher is the venture delta.

The proof for the above equation was not provided in Mishra and Zachary (2014) but the proof is very simple. Consider an investor who has two choices, either to invest "I" dollars or not to invest in a venture. If she chooses not to invest, her payoff is zero. If she chooses to invest, she would borrow "I" dollars at a cost of capital rate of "r" percent (i.e., her opportunity cost is "r" percent). She would invest for T periods. There are two potential outcomes; that is, either the venture succeeds the likelihood of which is $1 - \pi$; or the venture fails the likelihood of which is π and the investor loses her investment plus the opportunity cost of capital. See figure 8.4 on next page.

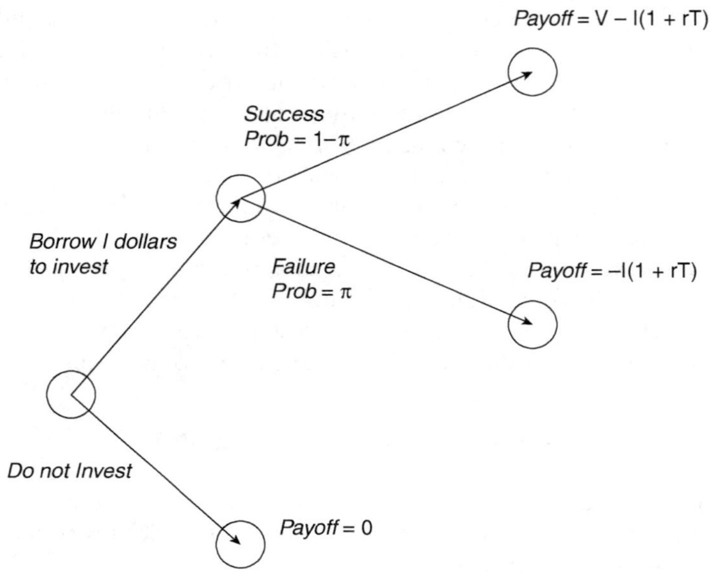

Figure 8.4 Venture Delta.

The venture may fail and the likelihood of which is "π", in which case the investor's payoff will be "$-I(1 + rT)$". If the venture succeeds and the likelihood of which is "$(1 - \pi)$", then the investor's payoff is "$V - I(1 + rT)$", where "V" is the investor's share of the venture's exit value or the final wealth of the investor accruing from the investment in the venture after T periods. The investor will be indifferent between investing and not investing in the venture when her two corresponding payoffs are equal. That is: E (Payoff when investing) = E (Payoff when not investing); or, $(1 - \pi)(V\text{-}I(1 + rT)) + \pi(\text{-}I(1 + rT)) = 0$. After simplifying the preceding equation, we obtain: $\delta = (V/I) = (1 + rT)/(1 - \pi)$. Thus, the venture delta (δ), or the investment multiplier (V/I), equals $(1 + rT)/(1 - \pi)$. The venture delta is thus the expected investment multiplier. For example, if the venture delta is 4x, the investor expects her final payoff to be four times the investment amount. Thus, the venture delta is a function of the time to investor exit, the investor's opportunity cost of capital, and the risk of investment loss.

Note that the risk of investment loss is always less than one, and thus the venture delta is always greater than one. As a new venture is always riskier than an average established company in the industry is, the venture delta is always significantly greater than one in the earlier stages of venture development. To estimate the venture delta using the above equation, the investor needs to determine the risk of investment loss, the expected time to investment liquidity (i.e., investor exit), and the industry cost of capital (or the investor's opportunity cost of capital). The investor may determine the risk of investment loss using the risk profile approach (see the previous section), or estimate it intuitively from their prior experience with similar ventures in the same industry. Furthermore, industry costs of capital (i.e., potentially the investor's opportunity costs) are widely reported by stock analysts and readily available. In lieu of the industry cost of capital, the investor may use their opportunity cost of capital. The investor exit is typically in four to six years following the investment.

In the absence of publicly available data, the industry cost of capital can be estimated by using the Capital Asset Pricing Model (CAPM). The industry cost of capital is a function of the industry beta, which in turn depends on the financial market and the industry conditions. Note that the beta in the CAPM measures the riskiness of an asset relative to the stock market as a whole. Thus, the beta is a measure of the systematic risk of a real or financial asset relative to the stock market. Therefore, the systematic risk implied in the industry beta determines the industry cost of capital. An industry with a lower industry beta or lower systematic risk (i.e., the risk relative to the financial market), would have a lower cost of capital. A high-risk industry with a higher industry beta (e.g., high technology industries) would have a higher industry cost of capital. Thus, the industry beta measures the relative riskiness of the industry to the stock market. In a more favorable market condition, the industry cost of capital would be lower. The riskiness of the industry and the financial market uncertainty determine the industry cost of capital. The venture delta increases with the industry cost of capital.

Venture capital investors show a preference for high returns (also known as "home runs"), as the investors often desire a multiple of 5x to 10x of the amount of their investment. Venture delta is thus consistent with the investor's preference for high investment multiples when investing in a new venture. Furthermore, according to the Entrepreneurial Value Creation Theory (Mishra and Zachary, 2014), the asymmetry in investor returns is consistent with the skewness (or the asymmetry) in investor risk preferences. In the early stages of venture development, when the risk of investment loss is higher, the venture delta is higher. In the later stage of the venture, when the risk of loss is lower, the venture delta is lower. At the time of investor exit, during the investment liquidity stage, when the venture valuation is more certain, the venture delta is closer to one when the expected return is slightly above the industry cost of capital.

The investor's expected return is implied in her venture delta. By rearranging the venture delta equation, the investor's expected return, E(R), equals to:

$$E(R) = e^{(\text{Ln } \delta)/T} - 1$$

In the above equation, "δ" is the venture delta; "T" is the time to investor exit; and "e" is the exponential function. For example, if the venture delta is 4x and the time to exit is 4 years, the investor's expected return is 41 percent per annum. Similarly, if the venture delta is 10x and the investor's time to exit is 5 years, then their expected return is 58 percent per annum. The Venture Capital Asset Pricing Model (VCAPM), developed by Mishra and Zachary (2014), can be used to estimate the implied venture beta. Thus, the Security Market Line (SML) as shown in figure 8.5 can be used to make venture portfolio investment and investor exit decisions.

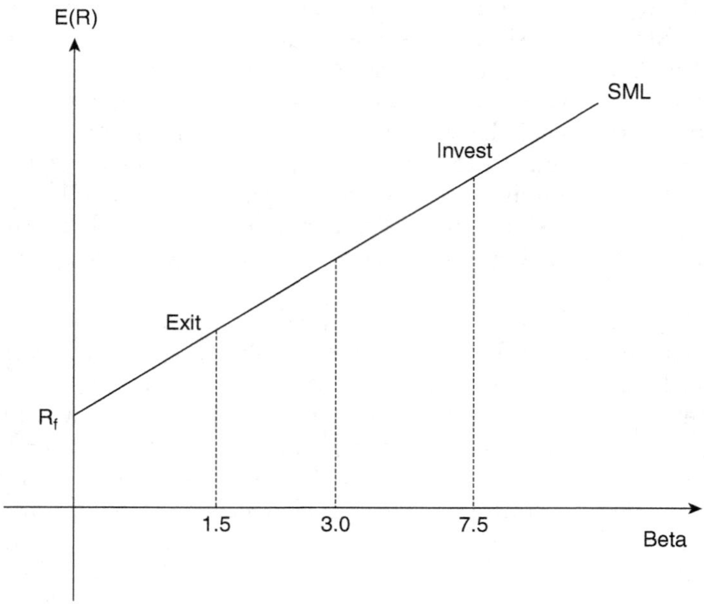

Figure 8.5 The Venture Capital Asset Pricing Model (VCAPM).

Mishra and Zachary (2014) developed the VCAPM, or the relation between the investor's expected rate of return and the venture beta. The VCAPM is specified as:

$$E(R) = R_f + \beta_v (R_m - R_f)$$

In the above model, $E(R)$ = the investor's expected rate of return; R_f = risk-free rate; β_v = venture beta; and R_m = stock market return (such as the return on a stock market index). For example, suppose the risk-free rate is 5 percent and the stock market return is 15 percent; and using the venture delta equation, the investor's expected return (based on the venture delta of 10x and the time to exit of 5 years) is 58 percent per annum. Then, using the VCAPM equation, the implied venture beta is 5.35.

Figure 8.5 shows the VCAPM. The VCAPM, similar to the CAPM, uses the Security Market Line (SML) to estimate the expected rate of return given the beta. The expected return is on the vertical axis, and the venture beta is on the horizontal axis. When the beta is zero (for a risk-free asset), the expected return is the risk-free rate (R_f); and when the beta is 1.0 (i.e., the market beta), the expected return is the market return (R_m). In the above example, the market return is 15 percent and the risk-free rate is 5 percent. Given the industry beta is 1.5, the expected return from the industry is 20 percent (using the CAPM). When the venture beta is 3.0, the expected rate of return from the venture is 35 percent. However, when the venture beta is 7.5, then the expected rate of return from the venture is 80 percent (see figure 8.5). As shown here, the venture beta and the expected rate of return can be calculated using the venture delta and VCAPM equations.

In the above example, the investor may invest in the early stage of the venture (i.e., when the venture beta is 7.5 and their expected rate of return is 80%) or they may invest in the later stage of the venture (i.e., when the venture beta is 3.0 and their expected rate of return is 35%); and they may exit when the expected return from the venture is close to the industry average rate of return of 20 percent. Note that the investor's expected rate of return and the venture valuation are inversely related; that is, the greater the expected rate of return, the lower is the venture valuation. Thus, the investor invests at a lower valuation when the valuation is more uncertain and their expected return is high, and exits at a higher valuation when the valuation is more certain and the expected return is closer to the industry average.

In figure 8.5, the venture delta and the venture beta decrease as the venture develops and matures. The venture may move down the SML, as shown in figure 8.5, from a higher point on the SML (where the venture risk is high and the valuation is more uncertain) to a lower point (where the venture risk is lower and the valuation is less uncertain), as the venture moves from the early stage to the investment liquidity stage. The investor invests at a higher point on the SML and exits at a lower point on the SML (see figure 8.5).

As discussed earlier, the venture delta is a function of the risk of investment loss, the time to investor exit, and the industry cost of capital (or the investor's opportunity cost of capital). The greater the risk of investment loss, the longer is the time to investor exit, or the greater the investor's opportunity cost of capital, the greater is the venture delta and thus the greater is the investor's expected rate of return. The expected rate of return, estimated using the venture delta equation, determines the venture valuation. The VCAPM is used to make venture investment and exit decisions. In the next chapter, we will discuss the investor's exit options and several venture valuation methods.

CHAPTER NINE

Investment Liquidity and Valuation

Investors value the venture based on the risks and challenges they foresee. The venture valuation depends on the likelihood of investor exit at the investor's anticipated exit valuation. Investors would like to see a clear path to liquidity prior to investing in a venture. Successful investors are proactive in planning an exit strategy at the time of investment. Most investors are very good at conducting due diligence and managing their investments, but they are not so good at exiting their investments. A framework is presented to develop an investor exit plan, including selecting potential strategic acquirers and developing an investment thesis for the acquirers that would then guide the venture development. Valuing a venture too high or too low may foreclose future financing options for the venture. Several venture valuation methods are presented, including the venture capital method, prior-round-plus method, milestone-based valuation method, valuation multiples method, risk-adjusted investor equity method, and simulation method. The simulation method determines the maximum investment available to a startup and the minimum percentage of equity required by the investor. The venture valuation may be based on the economic value of the startup's intellectual property.

Wall and Smith (1997) reported the results of a survey by the Price Waterhouse Corporate Finance Group, commissioned by the Exits Committee of the European Venture Capital Association (EVCA). The survey was undertaken to offer guidance on how to improve the investor exit performance. The main finding of the survey was that there was a significant overhang of venture-backed companies waiting to exit but they were unable to exit. The survey also found that there was a clear problem in achieving the investor exit within an acceptable time period, when the acceptable time period was within seven years after the initial investment was made.

The EVCA survey found that 70 percent of the investors interviewed had some difficulty in exiting their investments. The main reasons for the difficulty with investor exit are the lack of strategic or financial buyers at the time of exit, uncooperative management, uncooperative co-shareholders, unfavorable financial market conditions, and the poor performance of the venture. Many of these problems can be avoided by having an investor exit plan in place during the due diligence at the time of investment. Given that the exit preparation takes two to three years and the investment horizon is often five years or less, it would make more sense for an investor to prepare an exit plan at the time of investment.

Successful investors are proactive in planning an exit strategy at the time of the investment in a venture. Investors have a limited time between investing in a venture and realizing the return from the investment. Venture capitalists, known as institutional investors, manage venture capital funds structured as limited partnerships with a seven to ten-year life. In the first three to four years, the investments are made; and in the last four years, the fund realizes the return when the investments are liquidated and the gains realized are distributed to the limited partners of the fund.

Investors are reluctant to invest in a venture when they sense that the entrepreneur may not be willing to cooperate with their exit. For example, investors are reluctant to invest in lifestyle ventures where not only is the growth limited, but so too are the investor exit options. An entrepreneur who pitches that the investor would make a lot of money by investing in their venture better have an investor exit plan and show how much money the investor can realistically make upon exit. Investors would like to see a clear path to liquidity or investor exit. The path to liquidity is as important as the path to bring the product to market and the path to achieve positive cash flow.

The venture investment cycle consists of three stages: (1) invest, (2) build, and (3) exit. The investors invest in a venture when it is investor ready and exit when it is acquisition ready. The invest stage is when the investor conducts the due diligence. Prior to the invest stage, the deal-killer risks should have been removed and the entrepreneur can demonstrate a working concept. In the build stage, the venture may receive multiple rounds of financing as the investors fund a venture in stages (see chapter 6). In the build stage, the path-dependent risks are removed and the business model is stabilized. The operational risks are also identified and removed as they occur. The incentive risks are mitigating by aligning the interests of the management team with those of the investors. Risk management is in the heart of the entrepreneurial process. In the build stage, the venture achieves scale economies and sustained positive cash flow. Sustainable growth is achieved. The venture valuation increases significantly in the build stage. In the exit stage, the investor exits at a higher valuation and realizes the investment return.

A venture may not be investable when it is in the early development stage and the deal-killer risks are still present (see chapter 8). The deal-killer risks include the customer demand risk and the product performance risk. An entrepreneur should approach the investors after the deal-killer risks are removed. During the early development stage, the entrepreneur often funds the venture with money from their personal savings or money from their family and friends. In the early development stage, the business concept is still uncertain and the product development is in progress. Sometimes the venture may receive seed funding in the early development stage. As the venture transitions into the early operations stage, the venture begins to attract investors. A venture becomes investable when the deal-killer risks are removed. Investors finance a venture in stages. Each stage of financing provides sufficient capital to achieve the stage milestones (see chapter 6). Furthermore, within each stage of venture development, there may be a need for multiple rounds of financing to achieve the stage milestones.

At the time of considering an investment, the investor, especially a proactive investor, wants to be relatively certain of the venture's potential for investor exit or investment liquidity. Having an investor exit plan in place can certainly improve the entrepreneur's chance of getting funded. The investor exit plan, including a list of potential strategic acquirers and a realistic exit valuation, can convince an investor to invest in the venture. Furthermore, the investor exit plan and the investor's expected exit valuation determine how much equity the investor may seek from the venture in exchange for their investment. The investor exit plan identifies potential exit options, such as strategic or financial acquisition of the venture, initial public offering, share buyback by co-shareholders, management buyout option, and so on. The exit plan also determines the timing of the investor exit and the expected exit valuation.

The venture valuation at the time of investment can be determined by several methods as will be shown in this chapter. The venture valuation depends on the investor's anticipated exit valuation and their expected rate of return. The expected rate of return may be estimated with the venture delta equation (see chapter 8). To use the venture delta, the investor estimates the risk of investment loss and the time to investor exit. The risk of investment loss may be intuitively determined by the investor or derived from the risk profile of the venture. The risk of investment loss can be estimated from the investor's prior experience with similar ventures, or from a simulation using software such as Crystal Ball (see chapter 8). Most investors, however, have an intuitive sense of investment loss based on the investor's determination of the venture risks and challenges at the time of investment consideration.

The investor's expected exit valuation is discounted relative to the time to investor exit. Most investors exit in four to six years, if not earlier. The longer the investor waits to exit, the greater is the valuation uncertainty and the higher is the discount rate. With the longer time to investor exit, the venture delta would be also higher (see the venture delta equation in chapter 8). Thus, the discount rate or the investor's expected rate of return would be higher. The greater the discount rate or the longer the time to investor exit, the lower is the venture's valuation at the time of investment and the greater is the investor equity in the venture. The investor exit plan thus determines the venture's valuation and the percentage of equity the investor seeks at the time of investment.

Investor Exit Plan

The investor exit survey by the European Venture Capital Association (EVCA) spanned several industries and countries (Wall and Smith, 1997). The survey found a clear distinction between two types of investors: proactive investors who plan an exit strategy at the time of investment, and passive investors with no specific exit route in mind at the time of investment. In the case of passive investors, it was found that most often the investor exit was achieved by means of a share buyback by the management or co-shareholders. The EVCA survey covered the investor exit issues related to venture-backed companies, such as the record of investors who achieved exits, the significance of the venture valuation compared to other factors when deciding to exit, the advantages and disadvantages of available exit options, whether the investors were proactive in planning the exit at the time of investment, the steps the investors took when preparing for the exit, the use of intermediaries and advisors in achieving the exit, and the role of the management and their cooperation with the investor exit.

A finding of the EVCA survey was that most investor exits take place by acquisitions, not by initial public offerings (IPOs). Occasionally, when the stock market has strong years, there may a surge in IPOs. However,

IPOs are much fewer than acquisitions in any given year. For example, in 2003, the number of acquisition exits of venture-backed companies in the United States was 284, but the number of IPO exits was 29. In 2008, the number of acquisition exits in the United States was 342, whereas the number of IPO exits was only six. IPO exits are thus few and rare. The investor exit plan should not assume an IPO exit and should instead identify a list of potential strategic acquirers.

As IPO exits are rare, most investors should plan their exit through the acquisition route. That means the investor and the entrepreneur should identify a list of potential strategic and financial acquirers at the time of investment. Strategic acquirers are preferred to financial acquirers, as strategic acquirers offer a higher valuation. The greater the exit valuation and the greater the certainty of exit, the greater is the valuation of the venture at the time of investment, and the less is the equity share the entrepreneur must give up to the investors.

It is better to have more than one exit option in the plan. A venture that has planned an investor exit by means of acquisition is more prepared for an IPO than a venture that does not have an exit plan at all or a venture that is planning an IPO option only. Most proactive investors, who have an investor exit plan at the time of investment, earn a higher return on investment than passive investors would. Moreover, ventures with an investment from proactive investors achieve stronger venture performance. Poor performance of the ventures at the time of exit can be prevented by having an exit plan at the time of investment, by timing the investor exit and by adequately preparing the venture in advance for the exit. However, the preparation of the venture for investor exit needs management support, which can be obtained by properly incentivizing the management team (see chapter 10).

An entrepreneur should have an investor exit plan when seeking venture funding. However, often the management team, which has a vested interest in protecting their jobs, is reluctant to support the investor exit. At the time of due diligence, prior to investing in a venture, the investor should ensure the support of the management team for the exit plan. But passive investors, who know that investor exit through the acquisition route may not be welcomed by the management, are reluctant to discuss the investor exit options, so as not to risk management dissatisfaction. Managements generally prefer the IPO exit route; but since IPOs are rare and few, it is a risky exit route to plan. Furthermore, a venture with an acquisition exit plan is more likely to achieve an IPO.

The Entrepreneurial Value Creation Theory postulates that investors wait to exit until after a higher valuation offer comes along (Mishra and

Zachary, 2014). A higher valuation is possible when the valuation uncertainty is reduced. The optimal time for investor exit is when the venture valuation exceeds the investor's expected valuation. Moreover, the venture valuation is a function of the uncertainty of the venture cash flow. The more predictable and sustainable the venture cash flow, the greater is the cash flow valuation multiple and the higher is the valuation offered. Thus the more sustainable and predictable the venture cash flow, the less is the uncertainty with the venture valuation and therefore the greater is the exit valuation.

The investor invests at a lower cash flow valuation multiple and exits at a higher cash flow valuation multiple. In addition, the investor invests in a venture at the higher end of the Security Market Line (SML) and exits at the lower end of the SML, as discussed in chapter 8. The investor invests when the venture delta is greater than one and exits when the venture delta is closer to one. For example, the investor may invest when the venture delta is 5x, and may wait to exit when the venture delta is closer to 1x. Note that the venture delta increases with the risk of investment loss. The more predictable and sustainable the cash flow, the lower is the risk of investment loss, the lower are the venture delta and investor's expected rate of return, and the higher is the exit valuation. At some level of the venture delta, often closer to 1x, the venture valuation exceeds the investor's anticipated level, and the investor will accept the exit valuation offer.

Thus, the investor's expected exit valuation is a key determinant in deciding when and under what conditions the investor would exit. The IPO route generally provides a higher valuation to the investor; however, since IPOs are more uncertain, the investor exit would be thus more uncertain. The greater uncertainty in an IPO thus offsets a potential higher valuation advantage with the IPO option. However, one advantage with the IPO option is that the management team favors the IPO route more than the acquisition route. But IPOs are rare and generally not an option for many venture capital investors. IPOs are also costly relative to acquisitions. Furthermore, lock-up agreements that the investor cannot exit for a certain period after the IPO, creates even further uncertainty for the investor. Thus, the investor's realized return can be less than that which is implied in the IPO valuation. The success of IPOs also depends on the financial market and economic conditions. When the stock market is weak, the IPO valuation may be low or the IPO may not occur at all.

With the acquisition exit route, there is relatively more certainty with regard to the timing of investor exit and the potential valuation offers the investors may receive. The acquisition route is also less costly than the IPO route. Often the acquisition route is the only option for many startups. Strategic buyers who want to protect or increase their market share, or enter a new market, may be willing to offer a higher valuation at the time of investor exit. In an acquisition, the investors can also exit immediately rather than being stuck in a lock-up agreement as in the case of IPOs. However, the biggest disadvantage with the acquisition exit is the opposition from the management team who may lose their jobs or independence. Another big problem is finding potential acquirers at the time of investor exit unless the potential acquirers are identified very early and the startup cultivates the relationships early. A startup contemplating an acquisition exit for its investors should identify the potential acquirers early and then pursue strategic and operational partnerships with them, thus cultivating strong relationships with the potential acquirers prior to approaching them for a possible merger.

In addition to potential strategic acquirers, the investor exit plan should include potential financial acquirers such as private equity firms. Private equity firms are limited partnerships with funds managed by general partners who buy a company when its performance is poor or it is in financial distress. Private equity firms buy a financially distressed company at a lower valuation, turn it around to improve its financial and operating performance, and then sell the company at a higher valuation to a strategic acquirer or take the company public through an IPO. Private equity investors also invest in management buyouts; that is, these investors provide capital sponsoring a management team to buy out the shares of their current investors. Management buyouts are attractive to private equity investors when the venture's growth potential is limited, but its cash flow is sustainable such that the buyout can be financed with high debt. Thus, most management buyouts are leveraged buyouts, where the private equity investors provide one-third capital and the other two-third is financed with debt. The high cash flow of the venture pays for the interest expenses and debt repayments associated with the debt financing.

However, financial acquisition as an exit option is not very lucrative for venture capital investors. Financial buyers offer lower valuation. Often a financial buyout is the option of last resort for the investors to exit. Financial buyout is effectively an interim exit option to keep the venture afloat, such that the existing investors are replaced by a group of new investors who would then prepare the company for an eventual exit, possibly in another three to five years. When the startup is not ready for the investor exit in six or seven years after the investment is made, when the startup has a poor performance, or when the startup fails to find strategic buyers, then the only option left for the current investors to exit is to seek financial buyers. A sale to a financial buyer often means less success and a lower venture valuation.

Institutional venture capital investors whose limited partnerships are about to expire are under pressure to exit their investments. Furthermore, passive investors, without having an exit plan at the time of investment, end up with financial buyers. Managements favor a management buyout sponsored by a financial buyer to a strategic acquisition, as the new investors may retain the current management team when the venture performance is good and the cash flow is strong. Furthermore, when there is a breakdown in the relationship between the current investors and the management team, such that it becomes difficult to find strategic buyers, a financial buyout may be the only option left for the investors.

Many investment agreements contain a share buyback clause or an investor's redemption provision in case all exit options fail (see chapter 10). The main disadvantage with the investor's redemption provision is that it effectively caps the return the investor may receive. In case the venture value is worth more but there is difficulty in finding potential strategic or financial buyers, the investor's redemption option might kick in but the return received by the investors is capped by a predetermined redemption price. Share buyback or redemption provisions are the least desirable exit options for investors; but for a bad investment, it is the only way out for the investor, short of bankruptcy. Furthermore, passive investors, compared to proactive investors, are more likely to exit through a share buyback or redemption provision.

Investors as well as entrepreneurs should consider the investor exit options at the time of investment. The exit-related issues the investor must consider are the potential exit options, the timing of investor exit, the expected value and certainty of exit valuation, potential strategic and financial acquirers, whether the venture strategy is appropriate to achieve the desired exit within the expected time period, and whether the management team will be cooperative and can they be incentivized to support the investor exit. If the management will not be supportive of the investor exit under any circumstances, it is best for the investor not to invest in the venture. Furthermore, if the management is in agreement with the investor exit, they may be further incentivized with stock options and pay-for-performance bonuses such that the venture strategy is in alignment with the investor's timing for the exit. The incentives should be structured such that it is in the best interests of the management to create a high-quality business that can be sold at a higher valuation at the time of investor exit, and the management would thus share the wealth with the investors. However, the incentives would not be very effective unless the management agreed in principle for the investor exit.

The investors should evaluate possible exit options at the time of investment and put an exit plan in place during or immediately after the due diligence stage. Notwithstanding the preference for an IPO exit, the investor must consider the acquisition exit options and identify a list of potential strategic acquirers, including developing a plausible investment thesis for each potential acquirer. A venture when positioned for a strategic acquisition is also attractive to financial buyers. Financial buyers should be identified early in the event that a strategic buyer cannot be found but the investors are pressured to exit. Many investors look for strategic buyers within the same industry to which the venture belongs. However, strategic buyers from outside the industry should be also considered who might even pay a premium valuation for the venture to enter a new market.

The investment thesis for a strategic acquisition may state how a strategic acquirer can leverage the venture's capabilities to enhance the acquirer's strengths, overcome its weaknesses, enable the market opportunities, and eliminate the potential threats. Thus, an understanding of the strengths, weaknesses, opportunities, and threats (SWOT) of the potential acquirers is required in order to qualify them and to develop an investment thesis for the potential acquirers selected. A venture that can show how its capabilities, such as products, processes, and people capabilities, can be leveraged by a potential acquirer is an attractive acquisition target. The most promising strategic buyer is the one that can best utilize the venture's assets and capabilities. The investor exit plan and therein the investment thesis for a strategic acquisition should thus determine the venture's assets and capabilities that the potential acquirers would value; and the venture's strategy is then to build and develop these assets and capabilities, which would increase the likelihood of an acquisition at the time of investor exit. It is important to know the acquisition criteria of potential acquirers well before the entrepreneur approaches the investors for funding.

Unlike an IPO exit, in which the venture's revenues and cash flow are key to a successful IPO, a strategic acquisition requires a strategic fit between the acquirer's assets and capabilities and the venture's assets and capabilities. One may use a set of screening criteria to identify and qualify potential strategic acquirers. An entrepreneur may use the following screening criteria to identify potential acquirers (McKaskill, 2009): (1) who makes money when the venture makes money; (2) who does not make money when the venture makes money; (3) who can make more money than the venture can with its product, process, or people capabilities; (4) who can remove the venture's resource constraints; (5) who has a problem the venture can fix; (6) who sells to the same customers as the venture does; (7) who uses either similar or complementary technologies or products; and (8) who needs the venture's customer base. Asking such questions will generate a list of potential strategic acquirers. From that list, the entrepreneur may then choose four or five potential acquirers whose acquisition criteria the venture can meet in a reasonable time frame as determined by the expected time to investor exit. Furthermore, the selected acquirers should have preferably completed successful acquisition deals in the past and have paid a premium valuation for their acquisitions.

The most common acquirer candidate is a complementor, such as strategic partners, suppliers, and channel partners. The complementors make money when the venture makes money. The other common candidates are the competitors who do not make money when the venture makes money. A competitor may wish to upgrade its technology, add new products to its product mix, acquire a new customer base and increase its market share, reduce pressure on price by eliminating a competitor, acquire a new process, or enhance its human resources (McKaskill, 2009). Established companies with assets and complementary capabilities, which can remove the venture's resource constraints and scale its business more rapidly, are the potential acquirers who can make more money with the venture's product and capabilities than the venture can do on its own. These strategic acquirers may be from within or outside the industry; when from outside the industry, they may want to enter a new market by leveraging their distribution and supply chain capabilities.

A candidate strategic acquirer may have a weakness in its processes, technology, or people, which can be overcome by the venture's processes and capabilities. Alternatively, a candidate acquirer may be facing declining revenues and need the venture's product or technology to restore its competitive position and market share. A candidate acquirer may be selling to the same customer base to which the venture sells, such that the acquirer can further enhance its brand intensity in that market segment. Furthermore, a potential acquirer might be interested in the venture's intellectual property to protect itself from potential patent infringement lawsuits. Besides, many corporations have limited research and development capabilities, so they are constantly acquiring new technologies from outside to enhance their technology portfolio (i.e., the open innovation business model; see chapter 5). Furthermore, in the technology sector, the strategic acquirers may be short of specialized knowledge workers that the venture can provide.

A candidate acquirer must have certain complementary assets and capabilities to leverage the product, process, or people capabilities of the venture, such that the acquirer can increase its revenues or lower its costs, and thereby enhance its competitive position. It is important for the entrepreneur to know the acquisition criteria of potential acquirers of the venture. Thus, when generating a shortlist of potential acquirers and qualifying them, it is important to develop a plausible investment thesis for each selected potential strategic acquirer. The investment thesis should enhance the acquirer's competitive position, by increasing its revenues or lowering the costs. The strategic fit between a potential acquirer's capabilities and the venture's capabilities is paramount.

The investor exit plan should thus develop an investment thesis for potential acquirers based on their acquisition criteria. The startup may then use the investment thesis to develop an exit checklist to guide the venture's strategy to position itself to become an attractive acquisition target at the time of investor exit. Wall and Smith (1997) proposed a checklist that investors and entrepreneurs may use to guide their business strategy and processes to better prepare for the investor exit. Note that the exit checklist should be developed after the investment thesis for strategic acquisition is formulated. The checklist includes guidelines on developing processes and timing related to business strategy, public relations, financial reporting, the legal structure, and hiring key executives. The business strategy should achieve a consistent and sustainable growth and deliver the proposed investment thesis for the potential acquirer within the limited time frame. The acquisition criteria of potential acquirers should be paramount in guiding the venture's business strategy. It is thus imperative to review the past acquisitions of the potential acquirers and understand their acquisition criteria. The investor's goal of the venture strategy is for the venture to develop to become an attractive acquisition target, to grow the venture to the point where it is acquisition ready.

All achievements by the venture, especially the large purchase orders received and the key executives hired, should be reported in the public media and business press. Note that the marketing and advertising function of the venture is not only to sell the product but also to sell the business by attracting potential strategic buyers (Wall and Smith, 1997). All accounting records, company records, and financial statements should look professional and be consistent from year to year. It is important to keep the company's legal structure simple and to avoid minority stakes unless there is a strategic purpose in selling a minority ownership to a key partner. Note that a minority shareholder can potentially block the acquisition. The management team should be balanced, experienced, and of high caliber, and each member of the management team should be able to individually demonstrate success and a track record of achievement. Do not allow management gaps to develop during the growth phase of the venture; a management succession plan should be in place prior to the acquisition. From the outset, follow a company policy that is consistent with professional business practices. The legal and regulatory practices should be also appropriate for the business.

The investor exit plan should also include the investor's expected exit valuation—a reservation valuation above which the investors would be willing to exit. Mishra and Zachary (2014) proposed that the investors would exit when the venture valuation exceeds their reservation valuation. Review the past acquisitions of the potential acquirers and determine the valuation multiples the acquirers had offered in the past. Consider comparable exits of similar startups in the industry and determine the valuation multiples they received. When reviewing similar startups, determine the time frame between their initial investment received and the time of their investor exit; and know the size of the startup at the time of exit in terms of the number of employees or the sales. Several merger and acquisition databases are available that report the details of public and private comparable acquisition transactions.

Venture Valuation and Investor Equity

Venture valuation is inherently subjective. Valuation in general is in the eye of the beholder. The valuation is negotiated between a willing buyer (i.e., the investor) and a willing seller (i.e., the entrepreneur). The venture valuation is thus determined in the negotiation between the investor and the entrepreneur. Furthermore, the entrepreneur's valuation is based on several assumptions that can be challenged by the investors. In the case of established companies, the valuation is based on historical data of operations and cash flows. But in the case of a new venture, historical data do not exist. Common valuation methods used to value established companies, such as the discounted cash flow method (DCF method), which discounts the projected future cash flows, are not reliable when valuing a new venture.

In this section, we discuss six valuation methods for a startup, namely the venture capital method, prior-round-plus method, milestone-based method, valuation multiples method, risk-adjusted investor equity method, and simulation method. More than one valuation method should be used to justify the venture's valuation, and the assumptions made with each method should be examined using a sensitivity analysis.

An entrepreneur's valuation is often a reason why the venture may not receive funding. That is, when the entrepreneur's valuation is too high, the investors will not invest in the venture. Investors are willing to pay for the current value of the venture, not for the potential future value of the venture. Investors buy equity in a venture at a lower valuation when the venture valuation is more uncertain and the venture risk is high, and sell their equity at a higher valuation at the time of exit when the venture valuation is less uncertain and the venture risk is low. Investors share the upside potential with the entrepreneur by purchasing an equity share in the venture. Investors also value their time and effort in addition to their capital invested in the venture. The investors thus require an equity share greater than the financial valuation alone justifies.

The venture valuation increases as the venture develops and the more risk is mitigated. Often in a very early stage of the venture (e.g., in the early development stage), if a venture is able to secure external funding prior to the customer value concept is proven, the venture valuation should be postponed until the next financing round after the customer value concept is established. It is difficult to value a venture when the concept is yet to be proven. These early investors may receive a step-up percentage in their equity share when the venture valuation is established. When the venture is valued too high in the early financing rounds, the venture may be unable to raise future financings or may raise financing in a "down" round. A down round is when the venture's valuation is less than the valuation it received in the previous financing round. Thus, when the early valuations are high, there is a funding risk associated with the venture, foreclosing the chance of getting funded in the future. Thus, it is important not to place too high a valuation on the venture in the early stages, and if possible, the venture valuation should be postponed to a future financing round until after the customer value concept is proven.

At the same time, by valuing the venture too low, the entrepreneur is also giving up more equity of the venture to the investor in the current round. That can increase the venture's funding risk as well (unless the venture valuation increases substantially), as it would be difficult to attract future investors with less equity remaining for the entrepreneur to stay motivated. In either case, valuing a venture too high or too low in the current round may foreclose the future financing options for the venture.

Furthermore, when the entrepreneurial competence is unproven, the entrepreneur will accept any valuation offered by the investor. However, when the entrepreneurial competence is more certain, the investor's valuation offer may be rejected by the entrepreneur (Mishra and Zachary, 2014). Thus, with higher entrepreneurial competence, the entrepreneur should not approach the investor until after the venture is sufficiently developed, so that the entrepreneur may receive a valuation greater than their reservation valuation. However, entrepreneurs with less proven ability may approach investors prior to their venture concept is well established.

The pre-money value of the venture is the valuation of the venture before it receives the investment, whereas the post-money value of the venture is the valuation of the venture with the investment capital. The pre-money value is thus the current value of the venture without the investment. The new investment enables the venture to pursue a higher growth strategy, and thus the investors would like to share the upside potential of the growth with the entrepreneur. The post-money value with the investment minus the investment amount is the pre-money value of the venture. For example, suppose the investment amount is $500,000 and the post-money value of the venture is $2 million; then the pre-money value of the venture is $1.5 million. However, as discussed earlier, the investors would negotiate a value to obtain a share of the upside potential of the venture with their investment, and to justify a return for their time and effort of active involvement with the venture. The final value of the venture is decided in the negotiation between the investor and the entrepreneur.

The pre-money value of the venture is not the same as the prior-round valuation of the venture. In the above example, the prior-round valuation may be $0.5 million. Nevertheless, in the current round the negotiated pre-money value is $1.5 million. Between the prior round and the current round, the venture value has increased by as much as $1 million (i.e., $1.5 million minus $0.5 million), as the venture risk was mitigated, and the likelihood of venture failure and the risk of investment loss has decreased.

In the prior-round-plus valuation method, the venture valuation is simply the prior-round post-money value plus a reasonable amount of additional value based on the progress the startup has made since the previous financing round. For example, suppose the prior-round post-money value was $500,000. Since then the startup has completed the product development and a successful beta test. If the new investors are willing to give an additional $1 million value for the progress the startup has achieved since the previous financing round, then the pre-money value of the startup in the current round is $1.5 million. The prior-round-plus valuation is subjective, as different investors will assign different additional value for the progress the startup has made.

If the new investors place a pre-money value of \$1.5 million on the startup, assuming the investors are investing \$0.5 million of new money, the post-money value of the venture is then \$2 million. The equity share of the investors is determined by the amount of investment divided by the post-money value of the venture. In the preceding example, the amount of investment is \$0.5 million and the post-money value is \$2 million; thus, the investors' equity share in the venture is 20 percent (i.e., \$0.5 million divided by \$2 million).

The additional value that can be assigned to the progress made by the startup since the previous financing round is subjective. The entrepreneur needs to justify the additional valuation, the assumptions of which may be challenged by the investors. The final valuation is an outcome of the negotiation between the entrepreneur and the investors. The entrepreneur may justify their valuation based on comparable startups in the industry at the current time and at the same stage of development. Investors, however, determine the venture's valuation based on the risks and challenges they foresee in the venture and the time and effort they need to put into the venture.

Another venture valuation method, namely the milestone-based valuation method, is also a subjective valuation method, often used by angel investors. For example, an investor may assign a venture a \$100,000 valuation for the working concept and a strong founding team; a \$250,000 valuation when the prototype testing is successful and the early product development is complete; a \$500,000 valuation after the product is finalized and a couple of major customer accounts are received, and so on. The valuations assigned to the stage milestones can vary significantly from one industry to another and from one investor to another. For example, in the Internet sector, the milestone-based valuations are generally higher as the time-to-market is shorter and the product development risk and the market risk are lower. The investors assign milestone-based valuations based on their prior experience, the likelihood of investment loss, and the comparable valuations of similar startups in the same industry.

A third method to value ventures is to use valuation multiples. The valuation multiple is the ratio of the venture value to a financial variable. For example, the financial variables may be the sales, the operating cash flow, or the number of employees. The valuation multiples can be drawn from comparable exit transactions in the same industry; or the industry standard valuation multiples or the public company trading multiples with appropriate illiquidity discounts may be used. Furthermore, the sales and cash flow valuation multiples can be estimated by using the following formulas, given the investor's expected rate of return, the venture's growth rate, and the product's gross margin. The valuation multiples based on the venture's sales and cash flow are estimated as:

$$\text{Value-to-Sales Multiple} < \frac{\text{Gross Margin}}{E(R) - \text{Growth Rate}}$$

$$\text{Value-to-Cash Flow Multiple} = \frac{1 + \text{Growth Rate}}{E(R) - \text{Growth Rate}}$$

In the above formulas, the gross margin is the gross profit divided by the sales; $E(R)$ is the investor's expected rate of return, either derived from the venture delta equation (see chapter 8) or simply the investor's target rate of return; and the growth rate is the venture's expected sales growth rate. Note that $E(R)$ exceeds the growth rate in the above equation. Consider an example of an early stage venture. The product's gross margin is 60 percent, the investor's expected rate of return is 80 percent, and the expected sales growth rate is 50 percent per year after the infusion of new capital. The value-to-sales multiple using the above formula is less than 2x. If the current net sales are $200,000, then the venture's post-money valuation cannot exceed $400,000. The industry standard valuation multiples and the public company trading multiples with illiquidity discounts can be used in conjunction with the above formulas to estimate the venture valuation.

In the preceding example, suppose the investor invested $100,000 for 25 percent equity of the venture (i.e., the post-money valuation at the time of investment was $400,000). At the time of investor exit, suppose the venture acquisition exit valuation is $8 million. Then, the investor's share of 25 percent equity (assuming no follow-on financing and thus no dilution of the investor's equity) is worth $2 million. Thus, the investor invested $100,000 and receives $2 million at the exit, making a 20x return on the investment or a "homerun" indeed. Several exit options (as discussed earlier) may be available to the investor. The exit valuation depends on the exit available. For example, the investor can exit when the venture is acquired by an established company or goes public (through an initial public offering); or the management may refinance the venture and buy back the investor's shares.

When estimating the valuation multiples, the investor's expected rate of return can be estimated using the venture delta equation (see chapter 8); or the expected rate of return may equal the investor's target rate of return based on the industry and the stage of venture development. The expected growth rate depends on the stage of venture development and the business model design. The gross margin can also vary with the business model design and the industry. The higher the gross margin, the higher is the value-to-sales multiple and the higher is the venture valuation. Investors invest in high-growth, high-margin ventures. Furthermore, the greater the operating leverage (see chapter 7), the greater is the value-to-sales multiple and the higher is the venture valuation.

For example, suppose the expected growth rate is 25 percent per year and the investor's expected rate of return is 55 percent; then, using the above formula for the value-to-cash flow multiple, the valuation multiple is 4.16x. Suppose the venture has an operating cash flow of $200,000; then, the estimated post-money value of the venture is $832,000 (i.e., 4.16 times $200,000). If the venture has a negative cash flow, the value-to-sales multiple may be used instead, and the venture valuation is then based on the multiple of the sales. In the above example, suppose the gross margin is 50 percent; then, using the value-to-sales formula, the valuation multiple is less than 1.67x. Suppose the venture's net sales are $500,000, then the post-money value is less than $833,333 (i.e., 1.67 times $500,000). The cash flow valuation multiple and the sales valuation multiple may yield different post-money valuation estimates; if so, then the average of the two valuation estimates is used to compute the post-money value of the venture. When the venture has no sales, one of the earlier methods, namely the milestone-based valuation method or the prior-round-plus valuation method, may be used.

Investors invest at a lower valuation multiple (when the venture valuation is less certain), and exit at a higher multiple (when the valuation is more certain). Investors thus buy a venture security at a low valuation and sell at a high valuation. For example, an investor may offer a valuation of $1 million for a venture when its sales are $500,000, at a value-to-sales multiple of 2x; and the investor may exit when the venture's sales are $2.5 million and the value-to-sales multiple reaches 4x, such that the exit valuation of the venture is $10 million. The investor thus invested at a valuation of $1 million when the sales were $500,000, and exited at a valuation of $10 million when the sales are $2.5 million. The investor thus earned an investment return of 10x on their investment, out of which 5x came from the growth in the venture's sales and another 2x came from the growth in the value-to-sales multiple (as the venture's valuation became more certain).

Venture capital investors are strategic growth partners and they thus invest in high-growth, high-margin businesses. The greater the venture's growth potential or scalability (measured by the operating leverage, see chapter 7) or the greater the product's gross margin, the greater is the value-to-sales multiple and the greater is the venture valuation. Thus, the more sustainable and efficient is the business model design (see chapter 7), the greater would be the venture valuation multiples. That is, the greater the venture's potential for sustainable scale economies (see the ROI equation chapter 7), the greater are the valuation multiples and the greater is the venture valuation. Furthermore, the greater the investor's expected rate of return (see the venture delta equation in chapter 8), the lower are the valuation multiples.

Valuation multiples can be also derived from comparable transactions in a given industry. However, it is tricky to find comparable transactions as the ventures and their business models may differ within the same industry; also, although the ventures are in the same industry and in similar stages, their success rates and the risks of investment loss may differ. Investors may consider their prior experience with similar ventures in the industry. Transaction databases such as PrivCo (www.privco.com) and Venture Source (www.venturesource.com) provide comparable venture financing transactions by industry. Post-money valuations of the ventures with their financing rounds are reported in these databases. These comparable transactions with appropriate adjustments may be used to derive the valuation multiples that can then be applied to estimate the venture valuation.

Another source for valuation multiples is the industry standard multiples, which are the averages of valuation multiples used in mergers and acquisitions in the industry. These standard valuation multiples should be adjusted for the venture's stage of development and the investor's risk of investment loss. Yet another source for valuation multiples is the trading multiples of public companies in the same industry. The standard valuation multiples and public company trading multiples should be adjusted downward for transaction illiquidity. Industry standard valuation multiples are drawn from the mergers and acquisitions transactions (i.e., acquisition valuation multiples) completed in an industry. For example, *Inc.* (www.inc.com) reports the valuation multiples by industry each year. For example, in 2008, for the commercial printing industry several valuation multiples were reported in *Inc.* magazine (www.inc.com): 0.64x of net sales; 0.99x of gross profit; 4.83x of EBIT (i.e., Earnings before Interest and Taxes); 5.40x of EBITDA (i.e., Earnings before Interest, Taxes, Depreciation and Amortization); 2.70x of discretionary earnings (i.e., operating profit + owners' compensation + noncash expenses such as depreciation and amortization); or 2.05x of the book value of invested capital (i.e., total assets minusshort-term liabilities). Several industry standard valuation multiples and public company trading multiples are available that can be adjusted further for the stage of venture development and the risk of investment loss as well as for the trading illiquidity, which can then be applied to estimate the venture's post-money value.

Note that the venture valuation is always net of current debt. Thus, if a venture is valued at $2 million but it has $0.5 million in current debt, then its post-money value is $1.5 million. If the investors want to invest $300,000, then the pre-money value of the startup is $1.2 million (i.e., $1.5 million minus $300,000). The percentage of equity for investors is based on the post-money value. In this example, if the post-money value is $1.5 million and the investment amount is $300,000, the minimum percentage of equity the investors receive is 20 percent (i.e., $300,000 divided by $1.5 million). The current debt, if any (including long-term and short-term notes), is subtracted from the total value of the venture to give the post-money value.

Another method to value the venture is the venture capital method. In the venture capital method, the venture value is the discounted value of the expected exit valuation of the venture. The venture capital method consists of three steps: (1) estimate the expected exit valuation and the time to investor exit, (2) determine a risk-adjusted discount rate or estimate the venture delta (see chapter 8), and (3) estimate the post-money value of the venture. The expected exit valuation can be estimated using the valuation multiples, such as the value-to-sales multiple or the value-to-cash flow multiple, or the industry standard valuation or the public company trading multiples with illiquidity adjustments. These valuation multiples are then applied to the expected sales or cash flow at the time of investor exit. However, the entrepreneur should be careful when using the projected cash flow or sales as the basis of venture valuation. Investors would typically discount as much as 50 percent of the entrepreneur's estimates of the future sales and operating cash flow. To estimate the expected exit valuation, the investor should prepare an investor exit plan, identifying the potential strategic acquirers and developing an investment theses based on the acquisition criteria (see the previous section).

A probabilistic estimate of the exit valuation can be determined using a software program such as Crystal Ball (www.oracle.com). Figure 9.1 is based on the data provided in the example in chapter 8 (see the section on the risk of investment loss). The expected exit is in the fourth year, but the exit could be as early as the third year or as late as the sixth year. The base-case scenario assumes the exit valuation multiple is five times the revenues and the exit year revenues is expected to be $5.28 million.

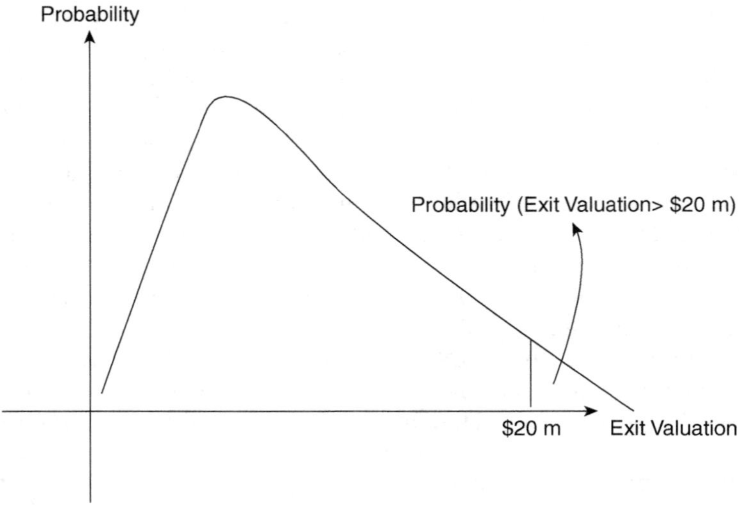

Figure 9.1 Exit valuation scenarios.

A single-point estimate of the exit valuation is thus $26.4 million (i.e., 5 times $5.28 million). However, simulation results in figure 9.1 show that the probability of achieving an exit valuation greater than $20 million is only 5.54 percent, which provides a very low level of confidence to the investors. The median value of the exit valuation is estimated to be $11 million. The expected exit valuation with a 90 percent confidence level is $6 million, with a 70 percent confidence level is $9 million, and with a 50 percent confidence level is $11 million. The investor's confidence level when estimating the exit valuation may depend on the stage of venture development and the risk of investment loss. The probabilistic exit valuation estimate is thus more meaningful to the investor than the base-case, single-point estimate of $26.4 million. Crystal Ball simulation is explained in chapter 8. It provides probabilistic estimates that are superior to the single-point estimates most investors use.

After the expected exit valuation and the time to investor exit are determined, the next step in the venture capital method is to estimate a risk-adjusted discount rate. The discount rate is the investor's expected rate of return given the risk of investment loss and the stage of venture development. The expected rate of return may be estimated using the venture delta equation (see chapter 8). On the other hand, the investor may simply use their desired rate of return as the discount rate. The investor's discount rate also varies with the expected time to investor exit.

The time to investor exit is typically four to six years. The longer the time to exit or the earlier the stage of venture development, the greater is the risk of investment loss and the higher is the discount rate.

In the final step of the venture capital method, the expected exit valuation is discounted at the risk-adjusted rate of return relative to the expected time to investor exit to determine the post-money value of the venture. Then the estimated post-money value minus the investment amount gives the pre-money value. The final pre-money and post-money values are determined in a negotiation between the entrepreneur and the investor. For example, suppose the expected exit valuation of a venture is \$12 million, the risk-adjusted discount rate is 50 percent or the estimated venture delta is 5x, and the expected time to investor exit is four years. Assuming no current debt, the estimated post-money value of the venture is \$2.37 million. When the venture has current debt, the debt is subtracted from the discounted present value to determine the post-money value. Thus:

$$\text{Post-money Value} = \frac{\text{Exit Valution}}{(1 + \text{Discount Rate})^T} - \text{Current Debt or,}$$

$$\text{Post-money Value} = \left(\frac{\text{Exit Valution}}{\text{Venture Delta}}\right) - \text{Current Debt}$$

In the preceding example, there was no current debt. Thus, as the post-money value is \$2.37 million, and suppose the investment amount is \$500,000, the investor would ask for at least a 21 percent equity share in the venture (i.e., \$500,000 divided by \$2.37 million). The actual equity share required by the investor, however, would be greater than 21 percent to compensate for the investor's time of involvement with the venture and to adjust for potential dilution of their equity in the subsequent financing rounds. For example, the investor determines that the startup needs at least two more financing rounds selling 30 percent and 20 percent equity shares respectively. The investor would then adjust their equity share to account for these future dilutions. The dilution-adjusted investor equity is the equity without dilution (e.g., 21% in the above example) divided by one minus the future equity shares to be sold (i.e., one minus 30%, times one minus 20%, etc.).

$$\text{Dilution-adjusted Investor Equity} = \frac{\%\ \text{Equity}}{(1-\alpha 1)(1-\alpha 2)(1-\alpha 3)\ldots}$$

In the above equation, % Equity is the investor's equity desired without dilution; and α_1, α_2, α_3, and so on, are the equity percentages to be sold in future financing rounds. In the above example, the investor's equity without dilution is 21 percent, and the additional equity shares expected to be sold in two subsequent financing rounds are 30 percent and 20 percent, respectively. Then, using the above formula, the investor's dilution-adjusted equity share is 37.5 percent. However, as discussed earlier, the investor would require more than 37.5 percent equity to compensate for their time of involvement with the venture. A venture capital investor is not a passive financial investor. The venture investor's equity reflects the financial risk-adjusted equity plus an added equity share for their time of involvement and effort for added value to the venture. For example, in the preceding example, the investor may ask for a 45 percent equity share in the venture (i.e., in this case, 37.5% equity share that is risk-adjusted and dilution-adjusted for two future rounds, plus an additional 7.5% equity for the investor's time of involvement and value-added effort).

The fifth method to estimate the venture valuation is to use a real-options method. The risk-adjusted investor equity method provides a minimum equity share the investor requires to invest in the venture, which would then provide an implied valuation of the venture. The premise of the method is that the investor holds an exchange real-option that gives the investor the right to exchange a low-valued security for a potentially higher-valued security in each subsequent financing round. It can be shown that (using the Black-Scholes Option Pricing Model, and then expanding and simplifying the probability terms):

$$\text{Investor Equity} = 0.4\sigma\sqrt{\tau}$$

In the above equation, τ is the expected time to investor exit and σ is the venture volatility. The venture volatility can be estimated from the industry volatility (reported in the financial press) and the venture delta (see venture delta equation in chapter 8). The venture volatility thus can be estimated using the following equation:

$$\text{Venture Volatility} = \sqrt{(\text{Industry Volatility}^2 \times \text{Venture Delta})}$$

Industry volatilities (i.e., the standard deviation of industry stock returns) are reported by stock option analysts and publicly available. For an example of the risk-adjusted investor equity method, consider a venture whose industry volatility is 40 percent per annum, and the venture's delta is 2x (see chapter 8 for how to estimate the venture delta). Thus, using the venture volatility equation, the venture volatility (σ) is 56.6 percent per annum. The venture delta adjusts for the stage of venture development, the risk of investment loss, and the expected time to investor exit (see chapter 8). Suppose the expected time to investor exit (τ) is four years; then the minimum equity share the investor would require, using the above risk-adjusted investor equity equation, is 45 percent. The risk-adjusted investor equity method thus determines the minimum percentage of investor equity required by the investor to compensate for the venture risk. The investor would ask for a higher equity percentage to compensate for their time of involvement and the potential dilutions due to future financing rounds, as discussed earlier. In the risk-adjusted investor equity equation, the greater the venture volatility or the greater the time to investor exit, the greater is the risk-adjusted percentage of equity required by the investor.

The sixth method to determine the venture's valuation and the percentage of equity share for the investor is the simulation method. One such simulation software explained in chapter 8 is Oracle's Crystal Ball (www.oracle.com). When using simulation software such as Crystal Ball, first determine the key input variables. Next, select and assign probability distributions to the input variables. A probability distribution commonly used is the triangular distribution, which requires three parameters, namely the minimum value, the maximum value, and the most likely value. The simulation draws the input values according to the assigned probability distributions and then generates a probabilistic estimate of the output variable. In chapter 8, an example is provided to determine the risk of investment loss using the simulation method. (The risk of investment loss is the probability that the return on investment is zero or negative.) When estimating the risk of investment loss using the simulation method, a minimum percentage of investor equity can be also determined given the investor's target rate of return.

Crystal Ball comes with a decision table tool, by which one can estimate a minimum percentage of investor equity. In addition to the input variables and the output variables, one can also define the decision variables when using Crystal Ball. In simulation, a decision variable is a controlled input variable. To estimate the minimum percentage of investor equity, one chooses the percentage of investor equity as a decision variable. For example, the input variables are the number of units sold, the unit price of the product, the investment amount, and the operating costs (see chapters 6 and 8). The investor equity is the decision variable; and the return on investment is the output variable. The decision table output

Minimum Investor Equity	Expected ROI
30%	1%
40%	8%
50%	15%
60%	20%

Figure 9.2 Minimum percentage of investor equity.

from Crystal Ball provides the minimum percentage of investor equity and the corresponding expected return on investment. Figure 9.2 shows the results obtained with Crystal Ball.

Note that if the investor were to ask for a 30 percent equity share in the venture, the results shown in figure 9.2 suggest that the investor's expected return on investment would be only 1 percent, which would not be acceptable to the investor. If the investor's desired rate of return is 20 percent, then the investor should require a 60 percent equity share in the venture. The venture delta may be used to determine the investor's expected rate of return (see chapter 8), or the investor may use a target rate of return. The decision table tool in Crystal Ball thus can be used by the investor when negotiating a minimum percentage of equity with the entrepreneur.

The decision table tool in Crystal ball also can be used with the venture capital method (discussed earlier) to determine the maximum investment amount available to a startup at a given stage of development. Consider an example. The expected time to investor exit varies from three to six years. The value-to-sales multiple at the time of investor exit may vary between 2x and 6x. The investor's expected rate of return based on the risk of investment loss varies from 30 percent to 60 percent per annum. The number of units sold and the unit price of the product are allowed to vary. In this example, the venture is seeking $3 million financing. However, the decision table results (see figure 9.3) clearly suggest that a $3 million financing is not currently feasible, as the investor would then require a 146 percent equity share in the venture (not possible). More likely, in this round, a financing of $1 million to $1.5 million may be possible at the current stage of the venture given the risk of investment loss. Most likely a $1 million financing may be offered, as the entrepreneur may not be willing to give up more than 48 percent equity in the venture. Thus the entrepreneur must wait to raise the rest of $2 million financing in the subsequent financing rounds. The investor would then provide the

Maximum Investment Amount	Minimum Investor equity
$1 million	48%
$1.5 million	78%
$2 million	97%
$2.5 million	121%
$ 3 million	146%

Figure 9.3 Maximum investment amount.

funding needed in multiple rounds to limit the risk of investment loss. The simulation method thus determines the maximum investment available to a startup and a minimum percentage of investor equity.

In this section, we discussed six methods illustrating how to value a startup and determine a minimum percentage of investor equity. More than one method should be employed to justify the valuation to the investor. However, the discounted cash flow methods that use the projected cash flows to value an established company should not be used to value a startup. A startup does not have the historical operating data to make the discounted cash flow (DCF) valuation method reliable. The final venture valuation and the percentage of investor equity are determined in the negotiation between the entrepreneur and the investor; that is, the final valuation is the value that the investor is willing to offer and the entrepreneur is willing to accept.

Intellectual Property and Intangible Asset Valuation

A startup may have an intellectual property such as a patent, trademark, copyrights, or trade secrets. Intellectual property is an intangible asset and has economic value similar to tangible assets. Intellectual property also includes other intangible assets such as customer lists and databases, regulatory approvals, packaging design, and so on. Intellectual property may be the only valuable asset a startup may have in the early stages. When valuing a venture for financing, the valuation of its intellectual property is relevant. However, an intellectual property to be valued must be readily identifiable and separable from the other assets of the venture, capable of producing economic benefits, and can be protected legally or through a de facto right (Bertolotti, 1995).

There are three primary methods to value an intellectual property or intangible asset, namely cost-based methods, market-based methods, and income-based methods. Cost-based methods value an intellectual property based on the historical cost of its development. Market-based methods are based on the royalty rates for comparable intellectual property in the market, whereas income-based methods are based on the income generation potential of the intellectual property. However, these valuation methods may overlap. For example, an income-based method may use the market-determined royalty rates to determine the economic value of the intellectual property. Cost-based methods use the historical cost of development or the replacement cost to value the intellectual property, which can be used as a reference value to compare with the economic value obtained using the other valuation methods. Instead of using the historical cost of development, the use of the replacement cost, or the cost of recreating the intellectual property is more appropriate.

In the context of the venture valuation, two methods to estimate the economic value of intellectual property and intangible assets are discussed, namely the excess earnings methods and the relief from royalty method. The economic value of an intellectual property is the potential income it can generate, net of its cost of development. The economic value of an asset is based on three parameters, namely the cash flow the asset generates, the risk of the cash flow, and the timing of the cash flow. The relevant cash flow for the valuation purpose is the incremental cash flow with the use of the intellectual property; that is, the differential cash flow accrued to the venture with or without the use of the intellectual property. The risk of the cash flow determines an appropriate discount rate for the valuation. These economic valuation methods consist of three steps. First, the incremental cash flows with the use of the intellectual property are determined. Second, the risk of the incremental cash flows is assessed and an appropriate risk-adjusted discount rate is determined. Finally, the incremental cash flows are discounted at the risk-adjusted discount rate over the useful life of the intellectual property to determine the value of the intellectual property.

In the first method, the excess earnings method, the relevant cash flow is the incremental earnings with the use of the intellectual property. For example, the use of an intellectual property may command a price premium in the market, increase the venture's market share, or generate a cost saving for the venture. The venture may achieve increased sales or lowered costs, generating additional earnings or an incremental cash flow. These additional earnings due to the intellectual property are estimated over its useful life. Similar to tangible assets, an intellectual property may depreciate in value over time. For example, a technology may become obsolete over time or be replaced by a superior technology.

A trademark may lose its brand value and the business may lose its market share to a superior brand. The shorter the useful life of an intellectual property embedded in a product, the sooner the product should be brought to the market.

To determine a risk-adjusted discount rate for valuing the intellectual property, consider the risks associated with the commercial application of the intellectual property. Four key risks should be considered (see figure 9.4): (1) technology risk (i.e., the technology capability); (2) product risk (i.e., the product performance); (3) competitive risk (i.e., the presence of alternative solutions); and (4) customer demand risk (i.e., the customer demand for the product). These four risks are assessed to determine the commercial potential of an intellectual property. A weighted scoring method may be employed to determine the commercial potential of the product with the embedded intellectual property, such that the risks of greater importance may be assigned a greater weight. The four risks are then scored and a weighted score is determined. The greater the weighted score, the greater is the likelihood of the commercial success of the product with the embedded technology, and the lower is the investment risk premium required by the investor. The risk-adjusted discount rate is then the investor's expected rate of return plus an estimated risk

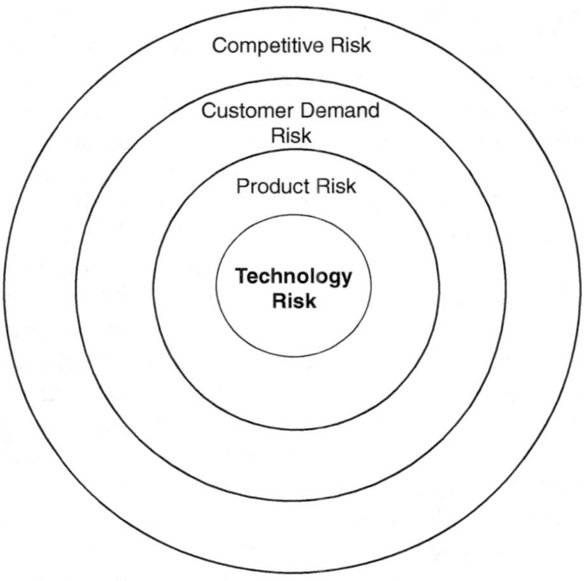

Figure 9.4 Evaluating commercial potential.

premium to adjust for the likelihood of commercial success with the intellectual property.

In the final step of the excess earnings method, the incremental cash flows due to the use of the intellectual property are discounted at the risk-adjusted discount rate over the useful life of the intellectual property. Consider an example. A software venture owns the computer software that is protected by a business process patent and can be licensed to end users. An end user can generate a cost savings of $10,000 per year. The software has an economic life of six years. The expected time to launch the software in the market is two years. Thus, the remaining useful life of the software is four years. Following the product launch, the number of end users is forecasted to be 100 in year 1, 200 in year 2, 500 in year 3, and 1,000 in year 4. After the fourth year, there is no certainty that the software will retain its economic advantage. The investor's expected rate of return is 40 percent, but based on the likelihood of high commercial potential of the software, it is determined that the risk-adjusted discount rate is 35 percent.

By multiplying the cost savings per user times the number of users in each period, the cash flow per period is determined over the four-year economic life of the software. Thus, for the users, the software generates a total cost savings of $1 million in year 1; $2 million in year 2; $5 million in year 3; and $10 million in year 4, respectively. When these incremental cash flows are discounted at the rate of 35 percent, the discounted present value of the software at the time of product launch is $6.88 million. Nevertheless, the investor has to commit $2 million now to invest in the product development and the expected time to launch the software is two years. Thus, the economic value of the software is the net present value (NPV) at the time of investment in the software. Therefore, discounting $6.88 million over the time to product launch (i.e., two years), at the discount rate of 35 percent, the NPV of the software, or the economic value of the intellectual property, is $1.78 million (i.e., the present value net of $2 million investment in the product development). The pre-money value of the venture, based on the intellectual property owned, is thus $1.78 million. The greater the risk of the commercial potential of the product with the intellectual property, the lower is the economic value of the intellectual property, and thus the lower would be the pre-money value of the venture.

In the above example, we used single-point estimates of the number of end users, the cost savings per user, the discount rate, and the investment amount. We can also use the simulation method to determine a probabilistic estimate of the economic value of the intellectual property.

For example, we consider the above values as the most likely values of the input variables, and further provide the minimum value and the maximum value for each input variable. Suppose the number of end users in year 1 can vary from 0 to 200, whereas the most likely value is 100. Similarly, the number of users in year 2 varies between 100 and 300, in year 3 between 200 and 600, and in year 4 between 200 and 1,200. The average cost savings per user can vary between $6,000 and $20,000 per year, the most likely value being $10,000. The expected time to launch the product can also vary from 1.5 to 3 years. The simulation results estimate the median value of the software, net of the investment cost of $2 million, is $1.5 million. The likelihood that the economic value of the software would exceed the investment cost of $2 million is 97 percent, a reasonable certainty for the investor. Knowing this, the investor may have greater confidence in investing in the venture. Using a probabilistic estimate of the value of the intellectual property is thus more meaningful to the investor than a single-point estimate.

Another method to estimate the economic value of the intellectual property is the relief from royalty method. A market-based royalty rate is determined first. The economic value of the intellectual property is then the discounted present value of a stream of royalty payments that the venture would have paid if it did not own the intellectual property and had to license the property from a third party. The premise of the relief from royalty method is that, if the venture does not own the intellectual property, it can license the property from another party. Industry-standard and market-based royalty rates for various intellectual property categories are widely available from several sources.

Most royalty rates for technology licensing vary between 3 and 7 percent of the net sales, and rarely does a royalty rate exceed 10 percent except in the case of software and digital technologies. The basis upon which the royalty rate is applied is often the net sales or the number of units sold. For example, if the net sales in a year are $1 million and the royalty rate is 5 percent, then the royalty payment in that year is $50,000. In addition to the royalty payments, an upfront fee may be required by the licensor. License agreements may also require other terms, such as a minimum royalty payment and other annual payments. Royalty rates can also vary for exclusive versus nonexclusive licenses. For relief from royalty method of valuation, the royalty rate should be based on an exclusive license.

The greater the gross margin on the product, the higher is the royalty rate. Intellectual properties such as software use a higher royalty rate because of their greater gross margin. For example, consider that the gross margin on a product that has an embedded intellectual property is

80 percent. Assuming a standard 25–75 benefit splitting rule (i.e., a 25% benefit for the licensor and a 75% benefit for the licensee), the royalty rate on the net sales basis then comes to a 20 percent (i.e., 25% times 80% gross margin).

Consider the preceding example where the software startup forecasted the number of end users to be 100 in year 1; 200 in year 2; 500 in year 3; and 1,000 in year 4. The time to launch the product is two years, and the remaining useful life of the intellectual property is four years. Suppose the software is sold at a price of $5,000 per end user; thus, the expected net sales of the startup are $0.5 million in year 1; $1 million in year 2; $2.5 million in year 3; and $5 million in year 4. Suppose the market-based royalty rate for a comparable intellectual property is 20 percent on the net sales, the royalty payments saved by the startup by owning the intellectual property are then $0.1 million in year 1; $0.2 million in year 2; $0.5 million in year 3; and $1 million in year 4. Then the economic value of the intellectual property or the present value of the royalty savings discounted at the discount rate of 35 percent is $0.69 million. The pre-money value of the venture is thus $0.69 million.

The value of the software using the excess earnings valuation method is $1.78 million and the value using the relief from royalty valuation method is $0.69 million. Note that the excess earnings valuation method may overestimate the economic value of the intellectual property. Therefore, the value of the software is estimated to be in the range of $0.69 million to $1.78 million, although it may be closer to $0.69 million. The value of the intellectual property is finally determined by the negotiation between the investor and the entrepreneur in the context of venture financing, or by a negotiation between a potential acquirer and the target company in the context of a merger or an acquisition. In the context of licensing of a technology or brand, the value of the intellectual property is determined by the negotiation between the licensor and the licensee. Based on the valuation of the software, in the above example, the venture's pre-money value can be between $0.69 million and $1.78 million. The investor may offer a valuation closer to $0.69 million. The investor may compare the value of the software with the cost of recreating it when the software is not legally protected by a patent. The cost of recreating the intellectual property may vary from one investor to another depending on the investor's cost of product development. The replacement cost or the cost of recreating an intellectual property is relevant when the intellectual property is not protected by a legal right such as a patent or trademark.

CHAPTER TEN

Is the Reward Worth the Risk and Effort? Realign the Incentive Structure

Investors invest in a venture when the venture is investor ready, and then grow the venture to a point where it is acquisition ready, at which time the investors may exit. An entrepreneur with a creative deal structure that minimizes the risk of investment loss and maximizes the investor's rate of return has a greater chance of getting funded. Investors, when structuring an investment in a new venture, consider whether the investment structure protects the investor in adverse performance conditions, whether the structure provides sufficient incentives to motivate the entrepreneur, and whether the structure enhances the likelihood of investment liquidity. The investment loss can be minimized using stage financing, anti-dilution protection, liquidation preference, protective provisions, and board representation. Investors ensure a minimum rate of return by using priority-claim securities such as convertible notes and preferred stocks, securing a minimum percentage of equity in the venture, and structuring the investment return using priority payments such as dividends, interests, and royalties. Incentive mechanisms to motivate the entrepreneur and management and align their economic interests with those of the investors, include stock option plans, share buyback rights, time and performance vesting, and the threat of the investor's ability to replace the management team.

Venture capital investors are business builders and growth partners. Investors not only provide investment capital, but are also actively involved with the venture in helping build and grow the business. Investors consider the risk of investment loss and their expected return when qualifying an investment. Investors can alter the risk-reward structure of an investment by actively participating in the venture and shaping its business strategy. Investors value their time of involvement with the venture, in addition to valuing the capital they provide to the venture. The investor's time and capital are scarce and valuable. It is important to consider whether the investment reward is worth the investment risk and the investor's time and effort. Investors structure the investment to mitigate their investment risks and at the same time incentivize the entrepreneur, such that the investment structure protects the investor in adverse performance conditions, provides sufficient incentives to the entrepreneur to provide sustained effort, and enhances the likelihood of investment liquidity (see figure 10.1). The success of a new venture is highly uncertain; thus, there is a substantial risk for the investors to lose their capital. Investors ensure a clear path to liquidity prior to investing in a new venture.

Venture capital investors are value-added investors who become actively involved in building and growing the venture, unlike financial market investors who are passive investors and do not actively participate in their investees' strategy and operations. Venture capital investors provide their company-building expertise and industry knowledge to a new venture. Investors also provide credibility and legitimacy to a new venture. Investors spend considerable time and effort in helping the entrepreneur build the venture, and grow the venture to a point where it is ready for the investors

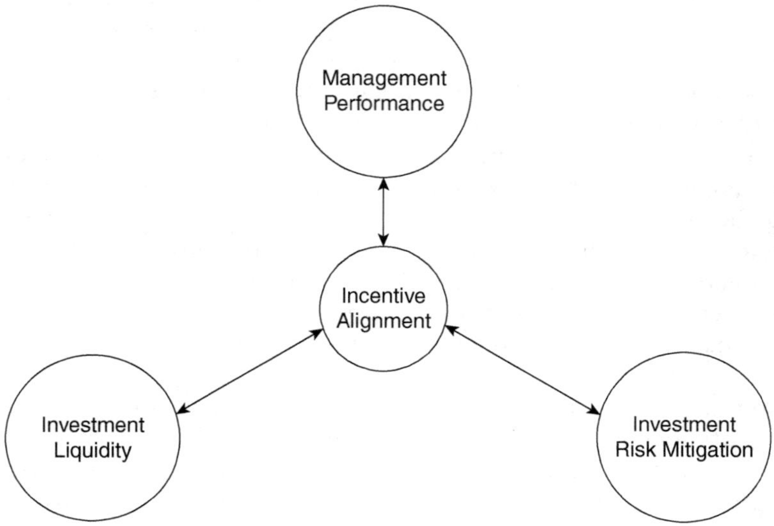

Figure 10.1 Investment structure.

to exit. The investor's reward must be adequate to compensate not only for the financial risk of the venture, but also for the time and effort of their involvement with the venture.

Venture capital investors, like all investors, are also value arbitrageurs. They invest in a startup at a lower valuation (i.e., buy low) and exit at a higher valuation (i.e., sell high), and they hedge their investment by actively participating in building the venture. Investors use a lower valuation multiple at the time of investment in a startup, and receive a higher valuation multiple at the time of their exit (see chapter 9). Investors receive most of their return at the time of exit. Thus, the likelihood of a liquidity event for the investor exit and potential exit options are important considerations for the investor when investing in a startup. However, most investors are good at conducting due diligence and structuring and managing their investments, but they often fail to exit their investments. The valuation of a startup is based on the likelihood of investor exit, the investor's anticipated exit valuation, and the time to exit.

It is important for the investor to consider the exit options when making an investment and valuing a startup. Entrepreneurs are generally optimistic and overconfident about the success of their venture. However, the entrepreneur may not be supportive of the investor exit. The investor should ensure the support of the entrepreneur and management team for the investor exit before investing in the venture. Furthermore, most ventures, even after they are successful, may fail to achieve an IPO (initial public offering). The entrepreneur should know that IPOs are rare and few. One in ten successful ventures might go public (IPO). Most ventures, when successful, are acquired by established companies. Acquisition exit valuations may not be as high as IPO exit valuations, but entrepreneurs should be realistic about the potential exit options for investors. Investors should be also realistic about their expected exit valuations. Investors should prepare an exit plan at the time of investment. The investor exit plan should identify potential strategic acquirers and develop an investment thesis for the acquirers. The investment thesis should subsequently guide the venture's strategy.

New ventures are fraught with uncertainties. Many new ventures fail to survive the first two years. As the startup failure rates are very high, there is a high likelihood that the investor might lose money. Investors estimate the risk of investment loss prior to investing in a venture. In a portfolio of ten investments that an investor makes after careful screening and due diligence, only one or two may achieve high returns (also called "homeruns"); three or four investments may fail; and the rest are the "living dead" with zero or marginal returns.

Venture risks are mitigated as the venture progresses from the early development stage to the investment liquidity stage. Investors invest in startups in multiple financing rounds, each round preparing the startup for the next financing round. Stage financing mitigates the investment risk and limits investment loss. A startup may receive three to five rounds of financing before the investors exit through a liquidity event such as an IPO or acquisition. In each financing round, the investor should consider the funding risk of whether the startup will be able to obtain additional financing in the future. In addition, in each financing round, the investor should consider whether the amount of investment is sufficient to achieve the milestones required to be qualified for the next financing round.

If a startup runs out of cash before it qualifies for the next financing round, the startup may not receive the next round of funding or it might get funding but at a lower valuation (called a "down round"). In a down round, the earlier investors suffer an investment value loss, as the pre-money value of the current round is less than the post-money value of the prior round. Venture capital investors manage stage risks and milestones, such that they invest sufficient funds in each financing round to mitigate the stage risks in order to attract and qualify for a follow-on financing round. When the investor cannot provide a sufficient amount of funding in a financing round to achieve the expected milestones, the investor is better off not investing at all in the venture.

Venture capital investors show a risk preference, in that different investors consider different levels of acceptable loss when investing in a venture. Early stage investors invest at a higher level of acceptable loss, whereas later stage investors prefer a lower level of loss. Consistent with their risk preference, investors choose to focus on different industries and stages of venture development. The stages of venture development include the early development stage, early operations stage, expansion stage, major expansion stage, and investment liquidity stage (see chapter 6). Investors have a stage preference when considering an investment.

Investor criteria when qualifying a venture for investment are based on the characteristics of venture risks. For example, Macmillan et al. (1985) characterized venture risks into several broad categories, such as implementation risks (associated with the execution of the business model and venture strategy), management risks (associated with the management performance), competitive risks (arising from existing and potential competition), leadership risks (from the failure of the entrepreneur to lead the team), and investor liquidity risks (with the uncertainty of investor exit).

Investors use a two-step due diligence process when qualifying a startup for investment (see chapter 8). In the first step, the risk of investment loss is assessed and if the loss is within the acceptable limit, the venture qualifies for the next step. In the second step, the investor chooses an investment from the pool of ventures selected in the previous step, such that the investor maximizes their expected return. Venture capital investments are thus risk-consistent and return-efficient for the investor.

A risk mitigation plan that identifies and prioritizes the critical risks of the venture and considers a strategy to test and mitigate the risks efficiently should be part of the investor's due diligence. A company-killer risk is one that has a high impact on the venture success and a high likelihood of occurrence. Company-killer risks include deal-killer risks, path-dependent risks, incentive-alignment risks, and critical operational risks (see chapter 8). The risks that are of low likelihood of occurrence and have a low impact on venture success may be ignored but should be regularly monitored. The risks that are of low likelihood of occurrence and have a high impact on the venture success are often insurable. The risks that are of high likelihood of occurrence but have a low impact on the venture success can be mitigated by making simple adjustments to the startup's operations. The deal-killer risks are associated with the customer value design; for example, the customer demand, market potential, and product performance risks. The path-dependent risks are the risks associated with the assumptions underlying the business model and venture strategy. The incentive-alignment risks are the uncertainties with the abilities and incentives of the entrepreneurial team. The operational risks are the remaining risks and are mitigated as they occur, but only after the deal-killer and path-dependent risks are addressed. The venture risks should be identified and prioritized such that the deal-killer risks, path-dependent risks, and incentive-alignment risks are tested and mitigated as early and as much as possible (see chapters 1 and 8).

A startup is not a small business but simply a temporary organization, which may evolve into a small business or a large business. Small businesses are low-growth, low-risk businesses, such as lifestyle businesses like franchisees, gas stations, restaurants, and dry cleaners. High-growth, high-risk startups may evolve into large businesses when successful. Venture capital investors often invest in high-growth, high-risk startups that have the potential to grow to become large businesses. Low-growth startups are self-funded by the entrepreneur or may be bank-financed.

A venture with a high reward potential always carries high risk; however, a high-risk venture may not always provide a high reward. Investors should assess the risk profile of the venture and the risk of investment loss when qualifying a venture for investment (see chapter 8). The risk of investment loss is the likelihood that the investment return is zero or negative. When the return is zero, the investor may get the principal back; but when the return is negative, the investment amount is at risk of loss. The risk of loss is highest at the early development stage and decreases as the risks are mitigated through the venture development cycle. The investor exits when the investor's risk of loss is lower and the venture valuation is more certain.

Simulation using Crystal Ball (www.oracle.com) may be used to generate the risk profile of a venture and estimate the risk of investment loss (see chapter 8). To determine the risk profile, the risk-determining variables are identified and more data are gathered to understand the range of their variation. The return on investment is the output variable. Simulation software picks the values of the risk-determining variables at random from their specified distributions, and after several runs, the simulation generates a distribution of the output variable (e.g., the return on investment). Several distribution choices are available for risk-determining input variables. Customized distributions can also be generated by providing a range of likely values for an input variable. The greater the risk of investment loss, the greater is the equity share the investor requires to invest in the venture. The risk profile of the venture and the risk of investment loss should be determined prior to investing in the venture.

The venture delta, a function of the risk of investment loss and the investor's opportunity cost, determines the relative riskiness of the venture (i.e., relative to the risk of investing in a diversified portfolio of the industry assets to which the venture belongs). Venture delta is always greater than one. The longer the time to investor exit, the greater the risk of investment loss, orthe greater the investor's opportunity cost of capital, the higher is the venture delta and the greater is the investor's risk premium. The venture beta, which is implied in the venture delta, measures the venture's risk relative to the financial market (see chapter 8). The venture beta can be determined using the Venture Capital Asset Pricing Model (VCAPM). The VCAPM is similar to the CAPM (Capital Asset Pricing Model), in that both models predict the expected return from an asset on the Security Market Line (SML). The investor may invest in a venture when the venture delta is high, such that their expected rate of return is high. The investor exits when the venture delta is close to one; that is, the expected rate of return is close to the industry rate of return.

Investors prefer to invest in high-growth, high-margin businesses. They invest at a lower valuation multiple when the venture valuation is more uncertain and exit at a higher valuation multiple when the venture valuation is more certain. The venture valuation multiples increase as the venture risks are mitigated and the venture progresses from the early development stage to the investment liquidity stage. Venture valuation multiples, such as the value-to-sales and value-to-cash flow multiples, can be estimated with the investor's expected rate of return, the venture's expected growth rate, and the product's gross margin (see chapter 9). The greater the venture's expected growth rate or the lower the investor's expected rate of return, the greater is the value-to-cash flow multiple and the greater is the venture valuation. In the absence of operating profits, the value-to-sales multiple may be used. The greater the product's gross margin, the greater the expected growth rate, or the lower the investor's expected rate of return, the greater is the value-to-sales multiple and the greater is the venture valuation.

Proactive investors consider potential exit options and plan an exit strategy when evaluating a venture for investment. When the investor exit options are limited, such as in lifestyle ventures, or when the management team does not seem to be cooperative with the investor's exit plan, the investors will be reluctant to invest in the venture. The investor's exit plan identifies potential exit options, an expected time to exit, and an expected exit valuation. The exit plan should include a list of potential strategic and financial acquirers, their acquisition criteria, and an investment thesis for the potential acquirers. Exit options include an acquisition by a strategic or financial buyer, management buyout, share buyback by management or co-shareholders, or an initial public offering (IPO). However, most exits take place through strategic acquisitions and share buybacks, not by IPOs.

Proactive investors plan their exit at the time of investment. In contrast, passive investors have no specific exit plan at the time of investment. In the case of passive investors, the investor exit is often achieved by means of a share buyback by co-shareholders or through a management buyout. Most exit preparations take two to three years. As the investment time frame for most investors is four to six years, an investor should be proactive in planning an exit at the time of investment. Passive investors think that an acquisition exit option may not be favored by management and thus are reluctant to plan an exit at the time of investment so as not to risk management dissatisfaction. In comparison, proactive investors who plan an exit at the time of investment earn a higher rate of return and their investees have a higher rate of success.

An investor exit plan must consider the acquisition exit option and thus identify potential strategic acquirers. A startup positioned for a strategic acquisition also has a greater likelihood of going public (i.e., IPO).

A startup positioned for strategic acquirers is also attractive to financial buyers in case strategic buyers cannot be found at the time of investor exit. Strategic buyers can be found both within and outside the industry. From outside the industry, a strategic acquirer may be willing to offer a premium valuation to acquire the startup in order to enter a new market.

Common exit candidates include competitors, strategic partners, and complementors. Competitors are the ones who do not make money when the venture makes money. In contrast, complementors and strategic partners are the ones who make money when the venture makes money. Potential exit candidates should also include the companies who sell to the same customer base to whom the venture sells. Potential acquirers also may be interested in the key assets of the venture, such as a proprietary technology, or the people with specialized expertise.

The investor exit plan should include an investment thesis for the potential acquirers. The investment thesis should explain how a strategic acquirer could utilize the venture's capabilities (i.e., product, process, or people capabilities) to leverage the acquirer's strengths, overcome its weaknesses, enable the market opportunities, and mitigate the major threats. An understanding of the threats, opportunities, strengths, and weaknesses of the potential acquirers can improve the likelihood of investor exit. The investment thesis developed for the potential acquirers should determine the key assets and capabilities the venture should build, which the potential acquirers can leverage, thus preparing the venture early on to become an attractive acquisition target.

Screening criteria may be used to generate and qualify potential strategic acquirers. Three to five acquirers may be selected whose acquisition criteria can be met in a reasonable time frame. Potential acquirers who have completed successful deals in the past and who have paid a premium price for their acquisitions should be the preferred exit candidates. Understanding the acquisition criteria of potential acquirers is critical to the success of investor exit and to guide the development of the venture's growth strategy.

The growth strategy of a startup should be to grow the business to a point where the potential acquirers find the business to be an attractive acquisition target at a valuation that exceeds the investor's anticipated exit valuation. The investor exit plan should also include a checklist to guide the growth strategy of the startup. The checklist should include the key milestones and strategic goals in areas such as operations, financial and legal structure, public relations, and human resources. It is important to review the past acquisitions of the potential acquirers, and then align the startup's growth strategy and business processes with the acquisition criteria of these acquirers. Public relations, legal structure, and financial reporting should be managed carefully from the outset. Also, do not allow management gaps to develop during the growth phase of the startup.

The investor exit plan should also include an anticipated exit valuation that is achievable. The investor's anticipated exit valuation and the time to investor exit are critical to the determination of the venture valuation. Reviewing the past transactions of potential acquirers provides the valuation multiples that the acquirers have offered in the past. Consider comparable exits of similar startups in the industry to determine exit valuation multiples and a reasonable time frame for the investor exit. Reviewing comparable exits in the industry also helps to identify potential strategic acquirers and understand their acquisition criteria. Investors should consider the likelihood of exit at their anticipated valuation, and a more meaningful, probabilistic estimate of the exit valuation using a simulation program such as Crystal Ball (see chapter 8).

The investor ensures that they earn a rate of return sufficient to compensate not only for the investment risk, but also for their time and effort of involvement in the venture. Venture capital investors are not passive investors like financial market investors. Venture capital investors are actively involved along with the entrepreneur in building the business and mitigating the risks. Investors invest in a venture when the venture's valuation is uncertain and the valuation multiple is low; the investors exit when the valuation is more certain and the venture valuation multiple is high. Investors expect to earn an adequate rate of return for their time and capital by securing a minimum percentage of equity in the venture (see chapter 9).

Investors often do not earn an investment return until they exit through a liquidity event such as an acquisition of the startup by an established company or through an initial public offering. The valuation of a startup is therefore based on the likelihood of investor exit, the anticipated exit valuation, and the time to exit. A startup often earns a negative cash flow in the early stages; thus, it is difficult to project the future cash flows. The discounted cash flow method based on the projected cash flows is thus not appropriate for the startup valuation. Six valuation methods appropriate in valuing a startup for determining a minimum percentage of equity for the investors are provided in chapter 9, namely the venture capital method, prior-round-plus method, milestone-based valuation method, valuation multiples method, risk-adjusted equity method, and simulation method. Each valuation method requires several assumptions and input values; thus, more than one method should be used by the entrepreneur to justify the venture's valuation.

The venture's final valuation is an outcome of the negotiation between the investor and the entrepreneur; that is, the valuation that the investor is willing to pay and the entrepreneur is willing to accept. The venture's valuation is therefore determined by the investor-entrepreneur negotiation. Often a venture's valuation in a very early stage is postponed until a financing round when there is more market data available to value the venture, such as the evidence for a working customer-value concept. When the valuation is postponed in the early stages of the startup, the investors are given a step-up in their equity shares to compensate for their earlier participation.

The venture valuation is based on the likelihood of investor exit in a reasonable time frame at their anticipated exit valuation. It is thus important to have an investor exit plan prepared before valuing the venture. Furthermore, common valuation methods, such as discounted cash flow methods, employed to value established companies are not appropriate for valuing startups. The valuation of an established company may be determined by a discounted cash flow method that values future cash flows based on the company's historical data. However, in the case of startups, very little established historical data are available to use in projecting the cash flows and using them as the basis for valuation.

The pre-money value of the venture is the current valuation of the venture without the infusion of a new investment, whereas the post-money value is the valuation of the venture with the new investment. The infusion of a new investment enables the venture to pursue a higher growth strategy, the value of which is reflected in the post-money value. The pre-money value the investor is willing to pay is the difference between the post-money value and the investment amount. The investor may offer a value less than the post-money value derived with the venture valuation method, as the investor would want a share of the future value generated with the infusion of their investment.

The valuation increases as the venture risks are mitigated and the startup progresses through the venture development cycle. However, if the venture is valued too high in the early stage, it will be difficult to obtain future financings; thus, there is a risk of a "down round" in the subsequent rounds. In a down round, the valuation of the current round is less than the valuation obtained in the prior round; as a result, the early investors suffer an investment value loss. The early investors demand an increased share of equity to compensate for the value loss, which might lower the likelihood of receiving new financing. Thus, when the venture is valued too high in an earlier round, the venture may be denied funding. Moreover, when the venture is valued too high in the current round, the entrepreneur may also be denied funding. A high valuation is often a reason for an entrepreneur not getting funded, especially when the venture's valuation is based on the projected future cash flows.

With the prior-round-plus valuation method, the startup's value is the post-money value in the previous financing round plus a reasonable valuation premium based on the progress the startup has made. In the milestone-based valuation method, the startup's value depends on the milestones it has achieved to date. The prior-round-plus valuation premiums and the milestone-based valuations are based on the prior experience of the investor with similar startups in the industry; and these valuations may vary from one industry to another and from one investor to another. Valuation multiples such as the value-to-sales and value-to-cash flow multiples can be obtained from past comparable transactions, or can be estimated using the formulas provided in chapter 9. Furthermore, the industry standard valuation multiples and public company trading multiples with appropriate discounts for trading illiquidity and the risk of investment loss can be used to determine the venture valuation. However, the industry standards and comparable transactions are sometimes not appropriate as the venture success rates, which depend on the entrepreneurial ability and the business model design, can vary significantly within the same industry. The lower the investor's expected rate of return, the higher the gross margin, or the greater the expected growth rate, the greater are the valuation multiples and the greater is the venture valuation. Investors therefore offer a higher valuation for high-growth, high-margin businesses.

The venture capital method provides a valuation based on the likelihood of investor exit at their anticipated exit valuation. To use the venture capital method, the investor must have an exit plan, such that the potential acquirers are identified and their acquisition criteria are determined. The expected exit value is discounted by the investor's risk-adjusted rate of return. The risk-adjusted rate of return of the investor can be estimated using the venture delta. The expected exit value is discounted relative to the time to investor exit. The investor typically anticipates the exit in four to six years. Furthermore, the longer the time to investor exit, the greater is the valuation uncertainty and the lower is the venture's valuation. The venture capital valuation method is more appropriate when investing in later stage ventures.

The risk-adjusted investor equity method determines the investor's minimum percentage of equity commensurate with the risk of investment loss. The premise of this valuation method is that the investor holds an exchange option to exchange a lower-valued security obtained at the time of investment for a potentially higher-valued security expected by the investor in the future financing rounds. The investor's exchange option is worth more when the investor expects the venture valuation to increase. The formula to determine the minimum percentage of investor equity is based on the options pricing model (see chapter 9). The longer the time to investor exit, or the greater the venture volatility, the greater is the percentage of equity the investor requires. The venture volatility can be estimated using the values of the industry volatility and the venture delta (see chapter 9). Industry volatilities are readily available and publicly reported by stock option analysts. The venture delta can be estimated from the risk profile of the venture and the risk of investment loss.

Often a startup's only valuable asset for the collateral for the investment is its intellectual property such a patent, trademark, customer list, copyright, trade secret, or another intangible asset. An entrepreneur has a better chance of getting funded and the investor may even offer a higher valuation when the startup has a valuable intellectual property. Intangible assets, similar to tangible assets, have economic value. An intellectual property to be valuable must be readily identifiable and separate from the other assets of the startup. The intellectual property must be capable of generating economic benefits and should be protected by a legal right or a de facto right. Two primary methods are offered in chapter 9 for estimating the economic value of an intellectual property, namely the excess earnings method and the relief from royalty method.

The excess earnings method simply discounts the incremental cash flows generated with the use of the intellectual property over the useful life of the property. The discount rate can be determined by examining the risk of the commercial potential of the intellectual property. The value of the intellectual property is then the net present value of the excess earnings; that is, the net of the investment cost to develop the commercial application (see chapter 9). Estimating the cost of recreating an intellectual property is another alternative to determine its value when the intellectual property is not legally protected.

The relief from royalty method uses market-based royalty rates and discounts a stream of royalty savings resulting from the startup's ownership of the intellectual property. The premise underlying this method is that, if the startup does not own the intellectual property, it could license the property from a third party by paying a royalty. The value of the intellectual property is thus the present value of the royalty savings when the business owns the intellectual property. Industry standard royalty rates are readily available and reported widely. The royalty rate is commonly applied to the product's net sales or the number of units sold. The royalty savings are discounted over the useful life of the intellectual property, using the investor's expected rate of return to determine the value of the intellectual property (see chapter 9). However, the economic value of the intellectual property based on projected excess earnings or royalty savings may provide a higher value than the cost of the investor's recreating the intellectual property.

Does the Deal Structure Enhance the Likelihood of Investment Liquidity?

Investors ensure a minimum rate of return and reduce the uncertainty of investment liquidity through certain rights and privileges in the investment agreement. The return to the investor can be structured in several ways, depending on the characteristics of the business. In high-growth ventures, the investor receives their return at the time of investor exit. In high-margin but low-growth businesses, the investor may insist on a royalty payment based on the net sales or the number of units sold, possibly in addition to an equity share in the venture, as the high-margin business can afford the payment of a royalty to the investor and the low-growth nature of the business does not justify the cash generated to be all reinvested in the venture. When investing in high-risk ventures, investors may structure the investment using convertible notes and preferred stocks, to ensure receiving a minimum rate of return in the event the venture is not as successful as anticipated. Moreover, the conversion feature of these securities provides the investor a share of the upside potential when the venture is successful.

Venture capital investors require priority-claim securities such as convertible preferred stocks or convertible notes when investing in a startup. A convertible note is a loan convertible to equity at the option of the investor. Investors hold the right to convert if the gain from the conversion is favorable to the investor. Otherwise, the note provides a downside protection to the investor providing a predetermined minimum return. Similarly, a convertible preferred security is a preferred stock that is convertible to common stock at the option of the investor. A preferred stock has a priority claim over the common stock. The entrepreneur holds the common stock. The investors thus have a priority claim over the entrepreneur in the event of liquidation. The conversion feature with these securities provides the investor the ability to share the upside potential with the entrepreneur, whereas the priority claim with the securities provides a downside protection and limits the investor's loss. Furthermore, preferred stocks and notes provide the investors with certain rights and privileges that the common stockholders do not have.

Convertible preferred securities also carry a dividend that has a priority over the common dividend. Unlike common dividends, the preferred dividends may accrue over time when a cash-strapped startup may not have funds to pay these dividends. Convertible notes also carry an interest payment, which ensures a minimum return for the investor. Furthermore, with the liquidation preference provided by a convertible preferred stock (see the next section), the investor can earn a minimum rate of return in a liquidity event under adverse performance conditions.

Preferred dividends enhance the investor return. In high-growth ventures, the dividends on the preferred stocks are not typically paid out, as the cash is needed to fund the venture's growth opportunities. Unlike common dividends, however, the unpaid preferred dividends to investors are accrued. Preferred dividends to investors, like interest payments to debtholders, are an obligation and mandatory irrespective of the company's cash position, and are not at the discretion of the board of directors. When the cash is not available, the preferred dividends are accrued and paid out when the investor exits. However, the accrued dividends may be waived if the preferred stock is converted to common stock at the discretion of the investor.

Preferred dividends are generally between 6 and 10 percent per annum. For example, on an investment of $1 million and with the expected time to investor exit of four years, the total accrued dividends at a rate of 8 percent per annum will be $320,000 (i.e., $80,000 × 4); that is a substantial amount of return to the investor on an $1 million investment, especially in adverse performance conditions when the venture is not as successful as expected. Along with the participating liquidation preference (see the next section), the accrued dividends enhance the investor's minimum rate of return. Sometimes, in high-risk ventures, the investors may require a preferred dividend rate of 12 percent. Preferred dividends can be higher in the early financing rounds when the venture valuation is more uncertain. Preferred dividends may be paid in cash, restricted stock, or warrants. The warrants are simply stock options attached to a stock or a note. At the time of exit, the investor may exercise the warrants to obtain additional shares in the venture.

The investment agreement may also include an auto-conversion feature such that the investor's convertible preferred stock may be converted to common stock at a predetermined conversion rate under certain liquidity conditions. For example, at the time of a liquidity event such as an IPO or a merger, the convertible preferred security is converted into common stock at a predetermined rate of 5x or 10x of the original purchase price paid by the investor, or of the prevailing conversion price of the convertible preferred security, whichever is higher. The auto-conversion feature is included so that a single investor will not block a potential acquisition, when the valuation offer received may not be sufficiently high for that investor. The investment bankers may be reluctant in the future to underwrite the IPO without an auto-conversion feature included in the investment agreement. Moreover, in a merger, a potential acquirer may be dissuaded from acquiring the venture in the absence of the auto-conversion feature, as the investors holding the preferred shares may block the merger or try to extract a higher premium that the acquirer is not willing to give. The auto-conversion feature thus ensures an adequate rate of return for the investor, but at the same time, the provision facilitates a liquidity event helping the co-investors to exit.

Typically, the auto-conversion feature is triggered at a predetermined conversion price. The auto-conversion price is set at a very high price relative to the original purchase price of the security at the time of investment. Auto-conversion provides a sufficiently high rate of return to the investor; at the same time, it protects the entrepreneur and co-investors, allowing them to pursue a liquidity event when the venture valuation is sufficiently high, even though some investors may disagree with the valuation offer received and would like to wait longer to receive a higher valuation. As discussed earlier (see chapter 9), investors expect a minimum exit valuation at the time of investment, and thus would support a liquidity event, such as an acquisition or IPO, when the exit valuation offer received is higher than their reservation valuation.

Investors include a redemption provision in the investment agreement. The redemption provision enables the investor to force the company to buy back the investor's shares at a certain price after a specified time period. The redemption provision ensures that the investor earns a minimum rate of return when the likelihood of investor exit through a liquidity event is low or a liquidity event is unlikely. The redemption feature thus reduces the uncertainty of investor exit. The redemption price set by the investor is a little higher than the original purchase price paid by the investor. At the time of redemption, the investor receives the redemption value of their shares plus the accrued dividends. In some high-risk conditions, investors may ask for 2x to 3x of the original purchase price plus the accrued dividends. However, a high redemption price can become a roadblock to receiving future financings, as the new investors would be reluctant to see their money being used to pay for the redemption of the shares of the early investors.

A high-growth venture with a shortage of cash to fund the growth opportunities would be forced to find cash to redeem the shares of early investors under a redemption provision, a situation that would make the venture less attractive to new investors. However, when an investor is granted the redemption right, it is generally constrained by requiring the investor to exit after a certain time period (typically five to six years following the investment), and the redemption of the investor's shares is spread over a time period, such that a portion of their shares is redeemed each year after the specified period following the investment.

The investment agreement also includes a preemptive right or the right of first refusal for the investor to participate in a follow-on financing round. The preemptive right or the right of first refusal protects the investor's percentage of equity from dilution; that is, the investor can participate in a follow-on round and purchase additional equity to preserve their original percentage of equity in the venture. Otherwise, a follow-on financing dilutes the investor's current equity percentage. The investor may choose not to invest additional money in the venture and thus would not exercise the preemptive right. However, in successful ventures, the investors often participate in more than one financing round. The right of first refusal also gives the investor the right to purchase shares from a co-shareholder in case the co-shareholder would want to sell their shares.

The investment agreement also includes a co-sale right for the investor. The co-sale right forces the company or an existing shareholder wanting to sell their share of equity to include the other shareholders in the sale. However, if the company issues new shares to strategic partners, employees, directors, or consultants, the right of first refusal and co-sale rights can be a problem. Thus, it is a common practice to include certain exceptions to these rights.

The investor agreement also includes the registration rights for the investors. At the time of a liquidation event such as an IPO or a merger, the investor's registration rights require the company to include the investor's securities when filing a registration with the Securities and Exchange Commission (SEC), and pay for the registration costs of the investor's securities. The federal laws require that, before selling the company or an interest in the company, the company must file a registration statement with the SEC. The investor's registration rights include unlimited piggyback rights and at least two demand rights. Piggyback rights require the company to include the investor's securities when filing a registration statement with the SEC; thus, under the piggyback rights, the investors' securities are included in the registration statement if the company chooses to file. With demand registration rights, however, the investors can force the company to file a registration statement with the SEC, thus forcing the company to achieve liquidity facilitating the investor exit. The registration process, and the federal and state reporting requirements associated with the registration process, can be very costly and prohibitively expensive.

The lock-up period, or the time the investors have to wait after the initial public offering (IPO) before they can sell their securities, is also specified in the investment agreement, so that the investment bankers and underwriters do not have to negotiate a lock-up period at the time of an IPO. The lock-up period in the United States is between 90 and 180 days. The lock-up period following an IPO can cause a share price uncertainty, and the investor return thus may be uncertain when they sell their shares in the post-lockup period. It is a reason why an IPO share is underpriced (i.e., the IPO price is set below the estimated value of the share) at the time the company goes public, to lower the likelihood of a fall in the share price during the lock-up period.

Does the Deal Structure Protect the Investor in an Adverse Performance?

The risk of investment loss with new ventures is very high, especially in the early stages of venture development. Investors use a high hurdle rate to qualify a venture for investment, but using a high hurdle rate does not help improve the investor's odds for success. As discussed earlier, of ten investments the investor makes, only one or two achieve high returns, the rest either fail or provide marginal returns. Investors therefore use several strategies to mitigate the investment risk and limit the investment loss. Investors employ certain provisions in the investment agreement to mitigate the investment risk. These investment terms and conditions include an anti-dilution provision, protective provisions, board seats, and liquidation preference, among others.

Convertible preferred securities include a liquidation preference that may be participating or nonparticipating. The investor obtains the liquidation preference that is specified in the investment agreement. A liquidity event in this case can be an acquisition, a merger, or the sale of the company's assets. Following a liquidity event, with a nonparticipating liquidation preference, the investor receives the amount specified in the liquidation preference; or they convert the convertible stock to the common stock and receive their pro rata share of the liquidation proceeds. With the participating liquidation preference, however, the investor can receive both; that is, the investor claims the amount specified in the liquidation preference plus a pro rata share of the balance of the liquidation proceeds.

Generally, the liquidation preference specified is the amount of the original investment plus the accrued dividends. However, in high-risk situations, the liquidation preference may be set as twice the original investment amount plus the accrued dividends. It is very rare to see liquidation preferences exceeding three times the original investment. Usually the participation feature is capped, such that if the liquidation proceeds exceed certain value, the participation feature is nullified, and the investor receives only their pro rata share based on the conversion rate as specified in the convertible security. Furthermore, the liquidation preference, especially a participating liquidation preference, provides a minimum rate of return to the investor in adverse performance conditions. In the earlier stages, the participation feature can be a roadblock for future financing rounds; but in the later stages, a capped participation feature is more common as the venture valuation is relatively more certain.

Consider an example of an investment in exchange for a convertible preferred security with a nonparticipating liquidation preference. An investor invests $1 million, and obtains a liquidation preference of 1x plus the accrued dividends (i.e., the liquidation preference specified is the original investment amount plus the accrued dividends). Suppose the preferred dividend rate is 10 percent per year. The post-money value at the time of investment is $3 million; so the investor gets 33 percent equity shares upon conversion (i.e., $1 million investment divided by $3 million post-money). Suppose after one year, the venture is sold to a financial buyer for $2 million. The investor may receive either the liquidation preference amount (i.e., $1 million plus $100,000 in accrued dividends; a total of $1.1 million) or a pro rata share of the proceeds if the investor chooses to exercise the conversion option (i.e., 33% share of $2 million proceeds; or $670,000). In this case, the investor is better off collecting the amount specified in the liquidation preference (i.e., $1.1 million) rather than the pro rata share upon conversion (i.e., $670,000). Thus, the investor would not convert their preferred stock to the common stock.

Consider the above example but with an alternative scenario. Suppose after one year the venture is sold to a strategic buyer for $5 million. The liquidation preference as above is still nonparticipating, such that the investor can collect either the amount specified in the liquidation preference or a pro rata share upon conversion to common equity. From the $5 million proceeds from the sale of the company, the investor may receive either the liquidation preference amount (i.e., $1 million plus $100,000 in accrued dividends; a total of $1.1 million) or a pro rata share of the proceeds if the investor chooses to exercise the conversion option (i.e., 33% share of the $5 million proceeds; or $1.67 million). In this case, the investor is better off choosing to convert to common stock and collect the pro rata share upon conversion (i.e., $1.67 million).

Consider the same two scenarios in the above example but this time the liquidation preference is participating but capped at $5 million. With the participation feature included in the liquidation preference, the investor now receives both the amount specified in the liquidation preference and a pro rata share of the remaining proceeds, until the company's sale price reaches $5 million (i.e., the cap amount). In the first scenario, the venture is sold to a financial buyer for $2 million. The liquidation preference specified is 1x times the original investment amount (i.e., $1 million) plus the accrued dividends (i.e., $100,000 for one year); a total of $1.1 million. The remaining proceeds are $0.9 million (i.e., $2 million sale price minus $1.1 million already paid to the investor). Of this remaining balance, the investor receives a pro rata share based on their equity percentage (i.e., 33% equity). That is an additional return of $0.3 million (i.e., 33% of $0.9 million) for the investor. Thus, the investor receives a total of $1.4 million (i.e., $1.1 million plus $0.3 million). The entrepreneur keeps $0.6 million (i.e., $ 2 million sale proceeds minus $1.4 million to the investor). With the participation feature, the investor thus received an additional $0.3 million from the company's sale proceeds, when the sale proceeds are less than the participation cap (e.g., in an adverse performance condition).

Consider the second scenario in the above example; in this scenario the company is sold to a strategic buyer for $5 million. The participation feature included in the liquidation preference is capped at $5 million. Thus, the investor has one of two options: either to collect the amount specified in the liquidation preference or the pro rata share amount as per the percentage equity share upon conversion of the convertible preferred security to the common stock. The liquidation preference amount, as shown above, is $1.1 million, which includes the original investment amount and the accrued dividends. The pro rata share of $5 million sale proceeds, based on the investor's 33 percent equity share upon conversion, is $1.67 million. Thus, the investor chooses to receive their pro rata share valued at $1.67 million. With the participation capped at $5 million, the investor cannot claim both the amount specified in the liquidation preference and the pro rata share of the remaining balance when the liquidation proceeds is greater than or equal to the cap amount. Most participation features are capped at the investor's anticipated level of exit valuation (or at a certain multiple of the original investment amount). For example, if the investment amount is $1 million and the participation is capped at 5x of the original purchase price of the convertible preferred stock, then the participation cap is $5 million.

Another provision in the investment agreement is the anti-dilution provision that protects the investor in a down round; that is, when the venture's valuation in a financing round is lower than the valuation received in the previous round. The venture may have to sell equity in a down round if the venture's performance has been poor, if the previous round's valuation was too high, or when the funding available is scarce due to an economic downturn. The anti-dilution provision preserves the original equity percentage of the investor; that is, the provision protects the investor's equity percentage by minimizing the value loss in adverse performance conditions.

Consider an example. An investor group invested $2 million in the previous financing round in exchange for a 50 percent equity share in a venture; thus, the post-money value in the previous round was $4 million. The investor group received 1 million shares at the original purchase price of $2 per share. In the current financing round, due to adverse economic conditions and scarce venture capital, the venture has received an offer of $1 million new investment at the share price of $1 per share. Thus, the share price in the previous round was $2 per share but the best offer in the current round is $1 per share. The new investors require 33 percent equity in exchange for their $1 million investment; that is, the post-money value of the venture in the current round is $3 million. This is a down round. The old investors may be protected by the anti-dilution provision, in that their shares will be re-priced and they will be issued additional shares that will come from the founders' equity.

The anti-dilution protection may use a full-ratchet or a weighted average adjustment. With the full-ratchet anti-dilution, the previous investors will be fully compensated for the value loss. However, with the weighted average anti-dilution, they will be partially compensated for the value loss. In the above example, the previous-round share price was $2 per share but the current round share price is $1 per share. With the full-ratchet anti-dilution protection, the shares of the previous investors are re-priced at $1 per share, and the investors will be issued additional shares that come from the founders' equity. With the weighted-average anti-dilution protection, the new conversion price of the shares of the previous investors will be somewhere between the old share price of $2 per share and the current share price of $1 per share. The following formula may be used, with the weighted average anti-dilution, to determine the conversion price of the shares held by the previous investors:

$$\text{Conversion Price} = \frac{(\text{Old Share Price} \times \text{Outstanding Shares}) + (\text{New Share Price} \times \text{New Shares})}{\text{Outstanding Shares} + \text{New Shares}}$$

In the preceding example, the old share price is $2 per share. The number of outstanding shares is 2 million before the current round. The new share price is $1 per share and the number of new shares issued is 1 million. The conversion price can be then calculated with the above weighted average anti-dilution formula. The conversion price is thus $1.67 per share, which is between the old share price of $2 per share and the current share price of $1 per share. In the current round, the new investors receive a 33 percent equity share based on their investment of $1 million and the post-money value of $3 million. Thus, after the current round is closed, the new investors will hold 1 million shares (or 33% equity), the previous investors 1.67 million shares (or 56% equity), and the founders 0.33 million shares (or 11% equity). Thus, the founders' equity share dropped from 50 percent to 11 percent. If the founders have no other alternative to raise the money to fund the operations, they may not have a choice but to accept the offer from the new investors. Note that the founders now own only 11 percent equity; the investors, the old and the new together, own 89 percent equity of the company. The investors together have now full control of the company and can replace the founder CEO or the entire management, if necessary.

Note that in the above example, if the anti-dilution protection were a full ratchet, the old share's conversion price would equal the new share price of $1 per share, and the previous investors' equity after the current round would have been 67 percent (i.e., their $2 million prior investment divided by the current round post-money valuation of $3 million). Thus, in the case of a full-ratchet, the old investors would own 67 percent equity and the new investors own 33 percent equity. In this case, the founders' 50 percent equity would have been totally wiped out. The full ratchet protection is thus unfair to the entrepreneur. In practice, the weighted average anti-dilution protection is often used to protect the investor from value loss.

The weighted average anti-dilution protection is a more equitable approach to adjust for the value loss of the equity of previous investors in the event that the valuation of the current round is below that of the previous round. A full ratchet anti-dilution protection places the full burden of the value loss on the founders. Note that with the full-ratchet anti-dilution, it is also difficult to attract new investors, as the new investors may feel that the founders would not have sufficient incentives left to stay motivated. The weighted average anti-dilution protection is thus commonly employed in practice.

Investors protect their interests and limit their investment loss by serving on the board of directors of the startup. The deal structure specifies the number of board seats to be occupied by the investors or their representatives. Typically, a startup has five members on the board, two representing the investors, two from management, and one independent director. When investing in an early stage venture, however, the investor may ask for a majority position on the board of directors. Investors, by being on the board, monitor management performance and shape the business strategy. Investors, through the board of directors, control the appointment of key executives, and may replace the CEO and the members of the management team in adverse performance conditions. Investors exercise de facto control over the business by holding a majority position on the board of directors, even though they may hold less than a majority equity percentage in the venture.

Investors protect their investment in adverse situations by including certain protective provisions in the investment agreement. Protective provisions require a simple majority or often a supermajority of votes of the preferred stockholders (i.e., the investors) before the management can take certain actions. These actions include any changes to the company's assets, liabilities, business strategy, or the legal structure, such as asset sales, consolidations, liquidation, issuance of dividends, issuance of new shares or debt, change in the management compensation, or change in the composition of the board of directors. Entrepreneurs prefer a simple majority of votes of the preferred stockholders to override the protective provisions; however, the investors may insist for a supermajority of votes of the preferred stockholders, such that even a minority investor can have a de facto veto right to prevent the management from taking certain actions that might harm the investor's interests. With the supermajority voting requirement, without the support of a minority investor, the management may not obtain a supermajority of investor votes to override a protective provision.

Investors also reduce the likelihood of investment loss by staging the investment, such that when the venture is not performing well, the investors may choose not to invest in the subsequent rounds. Mishra and Zachary (2014) showed that when the external risks (such as customer demand and competitive risks) are high, the investors would seek a tighter staging when investing in a venture. The staging of an investment may be ex-ante or ex-post (Kaplan and Stromberg, 2004). In ex-ante staging, the investor commits the total investment amount at the outset but provides the funding in installments subject to the venture achieving certain conditions such as performance milestones. Ex-ante staging is not common in practice as it is often difficult to fix the milestones in advance for a startup. Market conditions may change and the startup needs flexibility in rearranging and reprioritizing certain milestones. In the ex-post staging, the investors commit a smaller amount of financing in each round or sufficient for a few months of operating expenses, which forces the entrepreneur to come back to the investors to raise another round of financing. Investors provide financing to the startup in several rounds (see chapter 6).

When the external risks are high, the investor may require a tighter staging, such that a smaller amount of investment is available at each stage, and the entrepreneur needs to come back more frequently to the investor to receive additional financing. In each stage, sufficient funding is provided to mitigate the stage risks; and if the stage performance is favorable, then another round of financing may be provided to the entrepreneur. Otherwise, the investor may not make additional investments in the venture and would attempt to recoup her investment by liquidating the venture. Stage financing also enables the investors to renegotiate the investment terms and conditions as the entrepreneur comes back to raise new rounds of financing. When the external uncertainties are high and the entrepreneurial competence is low, the investor requires a majority position on the board of directors as well. With a majority position on the board, the investor has the ability to replace the founders and management team when the venture performance proves unsatisfactory.

Does the Deal Structure Provide Sufficient Incentives to the Entrepreneur?

Investors want to grow the company to a point where the venture valuation is high enough for them to exit. Investors expect a high rate of return on their investment. The venture valuation increases as the risks are mitigated and the venture becomes cash flow positive. The investors want the entrepreneur to work hard and provide a sustained effort in building and growing the business. However, the entrepreneur will work less hard when they own less than 100 percent equity in the venture, as they have to share the gain in wealth with the investor. The lower the percentage of equity the entrepreneur owns, the greater is the incentive-alignment risk that they may work less hard in the absence of further incentives (see chapter 1). Furthermore, the entrepreneur may be unsupportive of the investor's exit plan when the exit is considered through an acquisition route. As discussed earlier, most investor exits are through acquisitions.

Investors have several mechanisms to incentivize the entrepreneur and management. The possible incentive mechanisms include implementing time vesting and performance vesting of the entrepreneur's equity, stock option plan, milestone-based installment financing, contingency control option, and stock buyback rights for the entrepreneur, among others. The employment contracts with the founders and the investment agreement would include the incentive structure. The employment contracts with the company executives also include the executive's salary, bonus, benefits, and the conditions under which the board of directors can fire the executive. The ability of the investor by being on the board of directors to replace the management is a credible threat to align the management interests with those of the investors. The employment contracts also include the terms such as the share buyback rights and the non-compete conditions.

In adverse performance situations, investors may want to replace the management team and redirect the business strategy. The investment agreement, which obviously cannot cover all contingencies, may provide the investors with contingent board control rights (upon adverse performance conditions) to seek a majority position on the board of directors. With the majority control of the board, the investors can replace the CEO (and if necessary the entire management team), and bring in an outside professional CEO or management team. Even without adverse conditions, when the venture matures, the investors may feel that the founders may not have the ability to lead a complex organization and should step aside to make room for an outside professional management team.

The contingent board control provision specifies that in the event the venture fails to meet certain milestones or breaches any of the covenants specified in the investment agreement, the investors obtain the majority control on the board. The investors often seek a majority on the board or a contingent board control right when investing in an early stage startup. Mishra and Zachary (2014) showed that when the entrepreneurial competence is low and the external uncertainties (such as customer demand and competitive risks) are high, the investors might seek a majority membership on the board. However, when the entrepreneurial competence is low but the external uncertainties are low, the investors will seek a contingent board control right to be able to secure a future majority on the board in the event the management fails to achieve certain milestones. Thus, when the entrepreneurial ability is low, the investors will seek either an outright majority position on the board of directors or a contingent board control right.

The replacement of the members of the management team, if necessary, can be achieved either by a majority position on the board of directors or by a financing contingency at the time when the venture is raising new money. In a new financing round, the investors may require a contingency that outside professionals may be brought in to replace the management team, especially when the venture is not performing well. The investors may also provide the funds in installments, such that only a part of the total investment committed is disbursed and the rest of the amount is to be disbursed after the management meets certain performance conditions. However, setting the venture milestones in advance is difficult as the venture strategy might change, as it needs to respond to new information related to the market and competition. Thus, the use of installment financing in a startup based on predetermined milestones is not common. Only when the entrepreneurial ability is high and the external uncertainties are low, a scenario highly uncommon with startup investments, or one that cannot be ascertained at the time of investment (known as the adverse selection problem), might the investors use the milestone-based installment financing.

Another problem the investor may face is that a key member of the management team may quit when there is a disagreement among the members of the team or with the investor. To ensure that a key founder does not leave the organization, the investors vest the equity of the founder over a period of time. The founder's equity is typically vested over a four or five year period (consistent with the investor's exit time frame), with a one-year cliff. That is, the first 25 percent of the equity is vested after the first year and the remaining 75 percent is vested according to a predetermined vesting schedule. The vesting of the founder's equity also can be subject to the venture achieving certain performance milestones. However, as discussed earlier, the milestones of a startup may change with its business strategy; thus, milestone-based performance vesting schedules are not commonly used in practice. Furthermore, the investor may have other control rights to be able to replace the management and buy back their shares if necessary.

However, as the investors have relied on the management's strategy and their forecasts of the revenues and cash flows at the time of investment, the investors want to retrieve the unvested equity shares from the existing management when they leave the organization, so the equity can be offered to the members of the incoming management team. In the early stages of a venture development, when the entrepreneurial ability is weak, the investors may use performance and time vesting of the equity of the founders. However, a provision can be made to remove the performance-based vesting conditions at a later stage when the business model is stabilized and there is less uncertainty about the forecasts of revenues and cash flows.

The investment agreement may include a share buyback provision for the founders, in that the investor's equity percentage is reduced and the founders' equity increased when the founders have achieved their projected revenues and cash flows within a certain time period. Entrepreneurs are generally overconfident and their revenue projections are overly optimistic. If the investors feel that the financial projections are too optimistic but the entrepreneurial competence is high and the external uncertainties are low, a share buyback right may be granted to the entrepreneur. Under a share buyback arrangement, the entrepreneur can later buy back shares from the investors at a predetermined cost, not at the prevailing higher valuation, according to a buyback schedule based on achieving certain performance milestones. A share buyback arrangement can thus provide the founders right incentives to provide a sustained effort to achieve the projected revenues and cash flows, thus earning the equity back from the investors. The share buyback is used to incentivize the entrepreneur when the investor seeks a higher percentage of equity initially. However, the investor also understands that a high-ability entrepreneur may not work as hard with a low equity ownership; a share buyback arrangement may thus be appropriate for a high-ability entrepreneur.

The investment agreement almost always includes a percentage of the equity reserved for a stock option plan to incentivize the management and key executives. The percentage of the equity reserved for the stock option plan varies between 15 and 25 percent, and comes from the founders' equity share. By reserving a percentage of equity for the stock option plan at the time of financing, the investors do not have to dilute their equity when issuing stock options and restricted stock to attract key talents and employees to the venture. In a startup, as the cash flow is negative or limited, often, a major portion of the compensation given to the key executives is in stock options and restricted stock grants. The value of the stock options and restricted stock increases with the value of the company, and thus stock option plans align the interests of the management with those of the investors.

Most company founders do not set up a stock option plan until they are required to by the investors. Stock options and stock grants to the employees and management not only align their interests with those of the investors, but these plans also create an ownership culture in the company, delivering superior performance and increased productivity. In most startups, especially in technology startups where a company may not have enough money to attract and adequately compensate the specialized expertise of their employees, the key employees often expect to receive stock options as a part of their compensation. A stock option plan helps in attracting, retaining, and motivating key employees in a startup.

A creative deal structure proposed by the entrepreneur improves the likelihood of the venture getting funded. However, in the early stages of venture development, a deal structure should be kept simple; otherwise, it could become a roadblock to receiving future financings. The entrepreneur should understand the needs and objectives of the investors at the time of receiving an investment. The entrepreneur may suggest a creative deal structure to mitigate the investment risk or cooperate with the investor in setting up a risk-mitigating deal structure. This does not mean that the investment agreement should favor the investors; rather, the agreement should be a win-win deal structure such that the interests of the founders are aligned with those of the investors in building and growing the venture to a point where the venture valuation is high enough for the investors to exit successfully. The higher the venture valuation, the greater is the wealth of the entrepreneur irrespective of the percentage of equity the entrepreneur owns. To achieve sustained venture growth and a high exit valuation, the entrepreneur and the investor should work together with a shared vision and strategy, with their economic interests aligned.

REFERENCES

Amit, R., and C. Zott (2001). Value creation in e-business. *Strategic Management Journal* (22), 493–520.

Anderson, J. C., J. A. Narus, and W. V. Rossum (2006). Customer value propositions in business markets. *Harvard Business Review* (March), 1–9.

Andrew, J. P., and H. L. Sirkin (2003). Innovating for cash. *Harvard Business Review* (September), 1–8.

Barnett, F. W. (1988). Four steps to forecast total market demand. *Harvard Business Review* (July–August), 3–9.

Bass, F. M. (1969). A new product growth model for consumer durables. *Management Science* (15.5), 215–227.

Bertolotti, N. (1995). Valuing intellectual property. *Managing Intellectual Property* (February), 28–32.

Bhide, A. (1992). Bootstrap finance: The art of startups. *Harvard Business Review* (November–December), 110–117.

Block, Z., and I. C. Macmillan (1985). Milestones for successful venture planning. *Harvard Business Review* (September–October), 2–7.

Brown, R. (2001). How we built a strong company in a weak industry. *Harvard Business Review* (February), 3–8.

Bryce, D. J., and J. H. Dyer (2007). Strategies to crack well-guarded markets. *Harvard Business Review* (May), 2–10.

Capon, N. (1985). *Product life cycle*. Harvard Business Publishing, Boston: MA.

Cespedes, F. V. (2012). *Customer visits for entrepreneurs*. Harvard Business Publishing, Boston: MA.

Cespedes, F. V., T. Eisenmann, and S. G. Blank (2012). *Customer discovery and validation for entrepreneurs*. Harvard Business Publishing, Boston: MA.

Christensen, C. M., and M. E. Raynor (2003). *The innovator's solution*. Harvard Business Press, Boston: MA.

Coase, R. E. (1937). The nature of the firm. *Economica* (4), 386–405.

Dolan, R. J. (1995). How do you know when the price is right? *Harvard Business Review* (September–October), 4–11.

Dotzler, F. (2001). What do venture capitalists really do, and where do they learn to do it. *Journal of Private Equity* (Winter), 6–12.

Douglas, E. J., and D. Shepherd (2002). Exploring investor readiness: Assessments by entrepreneurs and investors in Australia. *Venture Capital* (4.3), 219–236.

Eisenmann, T. R. (2007). *A note on racing to acquire customers*. Harvard Business Publishing, Boston: MA.

Eisenmann, T. R. (2011). *Scaling a startup: Pacing issues*. Harvard Business Publishing, Boston: MA.

Feeny, L., G. H. Haines Jr., and A. L. Riding (1999). Private investors' investment criteria. *Venture Capital* (1.2), 121–145.

Fisher, M. L. (1997). What is the right supply chain for your product? *Harvard Business Review* (March–April), 2–13.

Ghemawat, P., and J. Rivkin (1999). *Creating competitive advantage*. Harvard Business Publishing, Boston: MA.

Gilbert, C. G., and M. J. Eyring (2010). Beating the odds when you launch a new venture. *Harvard Business Review* (May), 2–10.

Golder, P. N., and G. J. Tellis (2004). Growing, growing, gone: Cascades, diffusion, and turning points in the product life cycle. *Marketing Science* (23.2), 207–218.

Gourville, J. T. (2006). Eager sellers and stony buyers. *Harvard Business Review* (June), 2–10.

Hagel III, J. (2002). Leveraging growth: Expanding sales without sacrificing profits. *Harvard Business Review* (October), 3–10.

Harrison, R. (2013). Crowdfunding and the revitalization of the early stage risk capital market: Catalyst or chimera? *Venture Capital* (15.4), 283–287.

Hertz, D. B. (1979). Risk analysis in capital investment. *Harvard Business Review* (September–October), 169–180.

Hirai, A. (2013). What kills startups? http://www.caycon.com/downloads.php (Accessed December 12).

Hirai, A. (2014). Why business plans don't get funded. http://www.caycon.com/downloads.php (Accessed October 25).

Hofer, C. W., and D. E. Schendel (1978). *Strategy formulation: Analytical concepts*. West Publishing Company, St. Paul: MN.

Hoffman, D. L., and T. P. Novak (2000). How to acquire customers on the web. *Harvard Business Review* (May-June), 3–8.

Johnson, M. W., C. M. Christensen, and H. Kagermann (2008). Reinventing your business model. *Harvard Business Review* (December), 2–10.

Kahneman, D., and A. Tversky (1979). Prospect theory: An analysis of decision under risk. *Econometrica* (47.2), 363–391.

Kaplan, R.S., and D. P. Norton (2008). *The execution premium: Linking strategy to operations for competitive advantage*. Harvard Business Press, Boston: MA.

Kaplan, S. N., and P. Stromberg (2004). Characteristics, contracts, and actions: Evidence from venture capital analyses. *Journal of Finance* (59), 2177–2210.

Kim, W. C., and R. Mauborgne (1999). Creating new marketspace. *Harvard Business Review* (January–February), 30–41.

Kim, W. C., and R. Mauborgne (2000). Knowing a winning business idea when you see one. *Harvard Business Review* (September-October), 129–137.

Kotler, P., and K. L. Keller (2012). *Marketing management*. Prentice Hall, Upper Saddle River: NJ.

Kumar, V. (2014). Making "freemium" work. *Harvard Business Review* (May), 2–4.

Leidecker, J. K., and A.V. Bruno (1984). Identifying and using critical success factors. *Long Range Planning* (17.1), 23–32.

Levitt, T. (1965). Exploiting the product life cycle. *Harvard Business Review* (November–December), 2–15.

Levitt, T. (1980). Marketing success through differentiation of anything. *Harvard Business Review* (January–February), 83–91.

Macmillan, I. C., and R. G. McGrath (1997). Discovering new points of differentiation. *Harvard Business Review* (July–August), 3–11.

Macmillan, I. C., R. Seigel, and P. N. S. Narasimha (1985). Criteria used by venture capitalists to evaluate new venture proposals. *Journal of Business Venturing* (1), 119–128.

Magretta, J. (2002). Why business models matter. *Harvard Business Review* (May), 3–8.

Mason, C. M., and R. T. Harrison (2003). Auditioning for money: What do the technology investors look for at the initial screening stage. *Journal of Private Equity* (Spring), 29–42.

McKaskill, T. (2009). *Invest to exit*. Breakthrough Publications, Melbourne: Australia.

Mishra, C. S., and R. K. Zachary (2014). The theory of entrepreneurship: Creating and sustaining entrepreneurial value. Palgrave Macmillan: NY.

Moon, Y. (2005). Break free from the product life cycle. *Harvard Business Review* (May), 2–9.

Mullins, J., and R. Komisar (2009). *Getting to plan B*. Harvard Business Press, Boston: MA.

Mullins, J. (2013). Use customer cash to finance your start-up. *Harvard Business Review* (July-August), 2–4.

Ofek, E. (2005a). *Forecasting the adoption of a new product*. Harvard Business Publishing, Boston: MA.

Ofek, E. (2005b). *Forecasting the adoption of e-books*. Harvard Business Publishing, Boston: MA.

Osterwalder, A., and Y. Pigneur (2010). *Business model generation*. John Wiley, Hoboken: NJ.

Pine II, B. J., D. Peppers, and M. Rogers (1995). Do you want to keep your customers forever? *Harvard Business Review* (March–April), 103–114.

Porter, M. E. (1985). *Competitive advantage*. Free Press, New York.

Porter, M. E. (2008). The five competitive forces that shape strategy. *Harvard Business Review* (January), 2–17.

Pratch, L. (2005). Value-added investing: a framework for early stage venture capital firms. *Journal of Private Equity* (Summer), 13–29.

Rayport, J. F., and J. J. Sviokla (1994). Managing in the marketspace. *Harvard Business Review* (November–December), 141–150.

Rayport, J. F., and J. J. Sviokla (1995). Exploiting the virtual value chain. *Harvard Business Review* (November–December), 75–85.

Raz, G. (2008). *Introduction to supply chain management*. Darden Business Publishing, Charlottesville: VA.

Rogers, E. (1962). *Diffusion of innovations*. Free Press, New York.

Ruhnka, J. C., and J. E. Young (1991). Some hypotheses about risk in venture capital investing. *Journal of Business Venturing* (6), 115–133.

Skarzynski, P., and R. Gibson (2008). *Innovation to the core: A blueprint for transforming the way your company innovates*. Harvard Business Press, Boston: MA.

Shapiro, B. P., V. K. Rangan, R. T. Moriarty, and E. B. Ross (1987). Manage customers for profits (not just sales). *Harvard Business Review* (September–October), 2–9.

Stern, L. W., and F. D. Sturdivant (1987). Customer-driven distribution systems. *Harvard Business Review* (July–August), 2–7.

Sull, D. N. (2004). Disciplined entrepreneurship. *MIT Sloan Management Review* (Fall), 71–77.

Ulwick, A. W. (2002). Turn customer input into innovation. *Harvard Business Review* (January), 2–8.

Wall, J., and J. Smith (1997). Better exits. *The Journal of Private Equity* (Winter), 31–43.

Yoon, E., and L. Deeken (2013). Why it pays to be a category creator. *Harvard Business Review* (March), 2–4.

Zheng, Y. (2011). In their eyes: How entrepreneurs evaluate venture capital firms. *Journal of Private Equity* (Winter), 31–43.

Zider, B. (1998). How venture capital works. *Harvard Business Review* (November), 131–139.

INDEX

CPSIA information can be obtained
at www.ICGtesting.com
Printed in the USA
BVHW041046011219
565300BV00004B/138/P

9 781137 384492